Structuring speech

A HOW-TO-DO-IT BOOK
ABOUT PUBLIC SPEAKING

THE BOBBS-MERRILL SERIES IN *Speech Communication*

RUSSEL R. WINDES, *Editor*
Queens College of the City University of New York

GERALD M. PHILLIPS
AND
J. JEROME ZOLTEN

Structuring speech

A HOW-TO-DO-IT BOOK
ABOUT PUBLIC SPEAKING

CARTOONS   JIM VISNOVSKY
DIAGRAMS   JULES EPSTEIN

The Bobbs-Merrill Company, Inc.
INDIANAPOLIS

The Bobbs-Merrill Company, Inc.
4300 West 62nd Street
Indianapolis, Indiana 46268

First Edition
First Printing 1976

Library of Congress Cataloging in Publication Data
Phillips, Gerald M
    Structuring speech.
    (Bobbs-Merrill series in speech communication)
    Includes index.
    1. Public speaking. I. Zolten, J. Jerome, joint au-
thor. II. Title.
PN4121.P57   808.5'1   75-35824
ISBN 0-672-61366-2 (pbk.)

Editor's Foreword

In an increasingly proliferative speech-communication curriculum, less and less time is available in the basic course for public communication. Today, many introductory courses must include such diverse subjects as interpersonal communication, psycholinguistics, group communication, nonverbal communication, argumentation, persuasion, and the nature and effects of the mass media. By the time the student arrives at the unit in the course devoted to public speaking, he is, presumably, already something of a sophisticate in his understanding of the nature of human, symbolic interaction. Therefore, at this point, what both instructor and student need is a simple and economical agency for transmitting to the student fundamental information about the public speaking purposes and processes.

In **Structuring Speech** Professors Phillips and Zolten have provided one such agency. The volume concentrates on those aspects of public speaking that can be meaningfully discussed and absorbed through the channel of a book. Hence, the authors focus on audience analysis, topic selection and analysis, and organization and support. Speech presentation is a subject left for classroom consideration through critical discussion. The authors seek to present their material by specific example and useful precept. Theirs is an attempt to de-mystify the subject of public address, telling the student what it is crucial for him to know before he engages in the everyday task of amplifying ideas and making them persuasive for effective presentation to an audience.

Structuring Speech is useful not only as a practical guide for students who will end their formal study of speech communication with just one course, but also as an entry into key topics and issues that will become the focus of advanced courses. The style is decidedly nontextbook, and is sure to be welcomed by students who have tired of the pompous, the priggish, and the pedantic. The opportunity to sit in Professor Phillip's office for a winter's afternoon "talk and brew" is a pleasure that must be counted as one of the real assets of **Structuring Speech.**

Russel R. Windes

Preface

The old Hungarian grandmother of one of us once said that you shouldn't apologize for telling somebody how to do it. Although advice-giving is the province of "Dear Abby," without apology we undertake the task of offering a step-by-step "how-to-do-it" book on speech.

We believe that it is pointless to deluge beginning student speakers with books about speech. One can learn a great deal about human speech without having the vaguest idea about how to get up on his hind legs and utter some words to an audience. We also assume that just about everyone has a normal larynx and lungs, and so we are not worried about "delivery" as such. What we are concerned with are the steps in getting it together.

The steps in this book have been tested on about 750 problem speakers at the Pennsylvania State University, as well as on 225 Equal Opportunity students. In each case the students learned. They did not learn much theory; they, very simply, could get up on their hind legs and deliver a speech to an audience. Frankly, we think that if a book can instruct in this manner, the professor can lecture away about whatever theory he finds interesting.

Thanks to the students who demonstrated that the system works. Thanks to Nancy Phillips, for once again surviving the old typewriter-in-the-living room gambit. Thanks to Barbara Reeves for sacrificing her eyes to the job of proofreading and to Ellen Phillips for a complete and accurate index. Thanks to about twenty hard-nosed young instructors for teaching the steps well: Kent Sokoloff, Peter Glaser,

Nancy Metzger, Maritzie Rudden, Kathy Kougl, Doug Pedersen and his whole workshop crew, Kay DeBoer, Tim Hopf, Dave Illig, Mike George, Sue Glaser, Molly Wertheimer, Bob Harrison, and anyone else we forgot. Thanks also to the Developmental Year crew at PSU who meticulously tested the structuring method.

Contents

4. *Research: audience and topic*   *85*

5. *Structuring: putting it together*   *116*

6. *Inserting supports*   *171*

Structuring speech

A HOW-TO-DO-IT BOOK
ABOUT PUBLIC SPEAKING

ONE

Beginning

This may not be true in some places in the world, but in our society, when you want to get something done, you communicate. Most of the time, you talk. Sometimes you write. The purpose of communication is to get things done!

Communication is orderly. There are rules to follow that can help you to be more effective. Not one hundred percent; you can never really predict the other guy. But following a simple set of rules can help you gain skill in public speaking, working in groups or committees, surviving job interviews, and even talking with your friends.

This book is full of rules and advice. It is not addressed to those who fill journals with unreadable articles. It is a practical primer for persons who need to do better in their speech and can't take the time to study the process for years.

The writers (two guys named Jerry: one a professor, one an instructor and a free-lancer) combine their experiences with audiences, their years of study of the speech process, and their understanding of what a beginning student needs to know, to provide a book of steps to follow to structure the way to effective communication.

Communicating effectively: a juggler's job.

What you need to understand about communication

Communicating effectively, a juggler's job, demands organizing yourself and what you know. The effective juggler is brain-painfully aware of the articles he juggles. He tells his audience that he can keep things in order, even things that are hard to handle.

We may not like order. Usually when we use the term we mean rules and regulations that keep us from doing what we want to do. But, whether we like it or not, we don't seem to be able to get to the top at anything unless we follow the rules. There are a lot of people who can strum the guitar, but only those who can really follow the rules of right hand and left hand can make it onto the concert stage. So whether you are a painter, actor, scientist, author, musician, or even a safe and loft artist, you need to follow the rules of your profession. Furthermore, you like to be able to count on getting up the next morning, and that too depends on whether rules get followed.

Effective communication depends on making sense out of the world you live in. You can't see yourself clearly without making some kind of orderly sense out of what you know and what you are doing. Sometimes, we might let words out of our mouths because we need to get them out or because we feel bad, but usually, when we do this, we don't accomplish very much. Most communication seeks to get something done. It has a purpose, which can only be achieved by "discipline"—skill at following the rules. Our juggler would not deliver his "skill" message if he fouled up the order and the pins fell on his head. True, the audience might laugh, but that wasn't the juggler's purpose.

We need to discover what happens when we try to get someone to do something as a result of our talk. It isn't important here whether we are talking or writing. The differences between speaking and writing are matters of style, the way words are put together, rather than structure, the way ideas are put together. Most of our lives in school have been spent learning style in writing, where to put our commas and our adjectives. What we need to know is structure, because without a solid structure, no style can succeed.

For example, if I were writing about effective speaking, I might say:

> Effective speaking is a process through which a human being can employ symbols in order to bring about some change in the behavior of the people around him. Their needs, goals and drives must be considered as he develops his message.

If I spoke the same message, it might come out:

> An effective speaker tries to change behavior. He does this by using symbols. He hopes that his symbols will change the way in which people around him are behaving. He must consider what they want as he decides what to say.

Speakers use short phrases. Writers may stylize, and deal with more complicated ideas. Speakers need to be understood immediately. Writers can allow their readers time to digest the material. Both, however, need some structure of ideas, stuff that their speaking and writing is about.

We can highlight the difference between speaking and writing by looking at how speakers and writers approach their audiences. The speaker is concerned with what happens right now. He is like cold water thrown on a sleeping face. His audience must move, jump, do it, right now. The writer is looking for something more permanent, so his pace can be more gentle and penetrating. A reader may take his time. A reader may select a time and place to read, and he may decide how long he will spend doing it. You, at present—holding this book—don't expect to finish it, simple as it is, in one sitting. You don't need to. You can dip in a toe, slide in gradually; or you can shudder, hold your nose, and plunge in. Whatever, you can still get out. You don't have to sit here and read this book unless you want to. If you were listening to a speaker, as at that last lecture, you would have to sit there until he is done; and he would have to do everything needed while you were sitting there. When it's over, for a speaker, it is **over**.

That means a writer can deal with complicated material. We have a problem writing this book. We could talk it to you much more simply. If we could talk it to you, we could watch your face and find out what you didn't understand. We could stop and go over that portion again. We could keep giving you information—up to a point, the point where you have to leave. And that's it. But we can't see you personally. And even so, we couldn't take the time to see all of you. So we write a book. That's risky. Even a book like this takes a little bit of courage, because the authors have to live with it. When we change our minds, the book doesn't. Any mistake we put in print is permanent, it follows us forever. We don't have the chance to correct any misunderstandings you might get from reading the book. And we have to depend on your interest, your commitment to the ideas in this book, in order to get our message to you. We have tried to write simply and to give information that is worth having. Now it's in your hands. If we reward you for your efforts, you keep reading. Now that you have been rewarded by all the information so far, we have to tell you that the best of our writing wouldn't hold up, if there weren't something to hold it. Like:

> Abner walked down the street. It was raining in Newark. The quick brown fox jumped over the lazy dog. You can't roller skate in a buffalo herd. And that's why Big Ben bongs.

That's kind of interesting, but you couldn't take very much of it because there is no structure. A book needs to be organized so that when you, the reader, are interrupted, you can come back to it without losing the thread. If we can't get your attention right at the start you won't get much from the book; and if we get your attention and then don't give you some ideas, you waste your time with the book. You are going to decide on the first page whether or not you want to read the book. And that's why we gave you a cartoon there. Hopefully, if you can't get interested in our first words, maybe you'll read on just to see if there are more cartoons.

Our task in writing this book is to give you a reason to read. We must be able to predict in advance what you would like to read and keep that in mind as we develop our ideas. And incidentally, we know that this is a textbook. We know what you think of textbooks. That makes the job twice as hard, because who would believe a readable textbook?

Now, if you want to understand the real difference between speaking and writing, think of the task your instructor has. When you walk into the classroom, you may not want to be there. He must get your attention right away and hold it. Whatever he wants you to know or understand, he has to get to you there, on the spot. You don't have the time to sit and think about what he is saying. If you don't understand something, you have to ask about it right away; otherwise he will never know.

Of course, you may tell him how well he is doing. You may yawn, squirm, put on makeup, read a paper, doze off, get up and leave. You may look him in the eye, take notes furiously or nod your head; he has to figure what you mean. And some listen well when they are squirming. Others can look as if they are taking notes and yet do not hear a single word. It is not so easy for the speaker as it appears.

If you write you may assume:

1. People will read it on their own time, if they read it at all.
2. If you can hold attention and give some substance, you will get some readers. The others will go to the movies.
3. You can't win them all, but you'll really never know about the ones you lose.

If you speak, you may assume:

1. People will have to sit and listen whether they want to or not.
2. You will have to get their attention and hold it during the time they are there.
3. You can't win them all, and the ones you lose will be obvious.

This book is mainly for speakers. But many of the methods given for putting ideas together can be applied to writing. The speaker has to be clear, simple, and direct; and he has to repeat himself over and over again (we call this redundancy) so that his listener will get the information. Clarity is one of the first things he has to learn.

We start by picking a goal

A speaker may not be clear, even to himself. Many times we start speaking before we know what we are really after. Something in the situation tells us that we must speak, it is our turn, everyone is looking at us. We start to speak, and nothing much happens, and so we stop, and we feel uncomfortable.

It is very hard to find goals in our social conversations. We are rarely clear, and we just kind of muddle through and hope for the best. Some of the more popular people snow us under. They always seem to get what they want. They get right to the point and direct others and somehow, most of us follow along. They evidently know what their goals are, and that gives them the opportunity to control what comes out of their mouths.

When we get into a formal speaking situation, where we have to give a report or talk in a committee meeting, we need to have definite goals. We need to have goals both about ourselves and our messages. We shall present the message goals later on. For now, let's think about goals such as:

1. I want people to listen to me while I talk.
2. I want to speak for five minutes and make sure everyone understands me.
3. I want to look "cool" while I am sitting at the conference table.

These personal goals direct our style. Really, they are the reason we speak, and most of the time, our goals are very simple. We want to appear strong, in control; we want to get other people to approve of us, to nod their heads, to shake hands with us when it is over. One of our greatest shrinks once said that all anyone is after is some control and some affection. We want to get people on our side; we want them to like us. If we can get people on our side and we can get them to like us, then we can feel strong, and we can like ourselves.

Well, this is not a book on personality building. If you want to read some material on goals, get a little paperback book called **Goal Analysis** by Robert Mager.* It tells how to set goals that can be ac-

* San Francisco: Fearon Publishers, 1972.

complished. That is important to you as a speaker, because if you set up goals that are confusing and unclear, you will never know when you've achieved them, and after a while you will start to feel lousy about yourself, and you may stop trying. So check it out. Maybe your instructor can help you. And dig in hard when we start talking later on about **residual messages.**

We need to keep in mind that we are talking to someone

A speaker's goals may not be clear, even to himself. He may not know precisely what he is after when he communicates. The real goals may be as hard to grab as frogs in a murky mind-pool. Listeners are limited by the speed with which they can listen, by their chairs, by the amount of time they have to spend, by what they are going to do after the speech. They are not especially interested in psyching out the speaker's goal. They will hear what they want to hear, if they hear

Everything the audience does tells you something.

at all, unless the speaker gives it to them in no uncertain terms. Sometimes the speaker might think there is someone standing behind him holding up prompt signs as on the television shows, because the audience will be doing things that do not seem to accord with what he says. Even if the speaker's mind is perfectly clear, he cannot be sure that the listener's mind will be equally clear. And the responsibility is on the speaker, whatever happens. Those people are listening to **you.** They have a right to think what they care to and believe what they care to, about you and about your message, **unless** you make things clear to them. So, one of the most important features of speaking is to find out all you can about the audience.

Everything the audience does tells you something: each yawn, each fidget, may set off an alarm clock inside the speaker. The chances are that the yawner had a bad night. There is also the chance that the yawn may be for you. In any case, the speaker, while he is on his feet, needs to change what he is doing. Speak louder, faster, give more examples, say something funny, command attention—whatever is needed to get the audience to respond correctly. One of the most important points about setting goals is defining what you want the audience to do when you talk to them. As a speaker, you need to be alert to the following possibilities:

> You may get a response that surprises you.
> You may get a response that you do not want.
> You may get a good response, but not to your goal.
> You may get no response at all.
> You may misinterpret any response you get.

Surprise. Speakers enter the arena with some expectations. Bullfighters feel they have something over the bull. If they didn't, they wouldn't take the chance. Speakers need the same assurance. Most of us feel confident enough that people will listen to us carefully and respond to us by showing that they are listening. However, no one has ever been so effective that he gets a universally favorable response. Sometimes listeners may object to our ideas, sometimes to the way that we present them, sometimes to both. They may seem hostile when friendship was expected. Like a bite from a "friendly" dog, a little hostility is enough to throw a beginning speaker. If he does not know in advance that some persons in the audience are likely to be hostile, he can be upset the first time someone catches his eye and frowns, or shakes his head back and forth in a vigorous "no" when "yes" was expected. But the clearer a speech is, the less mud kicked up from the bottom, and the more likely the listener will grab your idea and understand it. The easier it is for the listener to understand, the more likely it is that he will be friendly. He may not agree, but the chances are good that he will be civil.

A garbled, unclear presentation will generate corrugated foreheads, questioning or bewildered eyes, and bored jaws. After a while, persons sitting and listening to something they don't understand will get angry at the waste of their time, and they will take it out on you. Every nightclub comedian knows that sometime during his act some drunk will get hostile. Every speaker knows that even his best effort is going to draw a sour face from someone, but the speaker, like the showman, goes on anyway. Negative responses should not be a hook to drag you off the platform. It is not amateur night at the Bijou, it is speaking time in the classroom. That means you need to do the best possible job of preparing, take your lumps when a few people respond negatively, and be prepared to swing free when you get a sizable response that you didn't count on.

Please laugh. Speakers sometimes let words come tumbling out of their mouths so fast that they are not aware of what they are saying. Frequently, a perfectly serious statement may come out in a way that is funny to the audience. The speaker, ready to hit the most serious part of his speech, sees an audience breaking up in hysterical laughter. For example, Vice-President Spiro Agnew used to speak to college audiences and get those kinds of responses all the time.

Sometimes getting off the track a little may bring a response from your audience that will wipe out any chance you have to make your main point. You can't adjust to that kind of response, and it's almost impossible to get back to your main ideas. You got a response, all right, and it was positive. That may be enough. Think of the time you took a "last minute" hour to hack out a ten-page term paper in a panicky, pile-of-words way and you got an "excellent." If you took time to grovel for the professor, you'd ruin the whole effect. After a while, with a lot of practice, you might be able to learn to handle the response you didn't want; but at the beginning, understanding that it can happen will at least cushion the blow.

Tell me what you want! A weak organization pattern makes it difficult for the audience to decide what you want from them. It is like putting together a pile of bolts, screws, and wheels with no directions and no idea of what you'll end up with. Also, no blueprint can guarantee that you will get what you want from the audience.

For example, suppose a speaker is trying to persuade an audience that the Vietnam war was cruel. He says, offering some information, "More bombs fell on Khe Sanh in one attack than fell on Germany in the years 1942 to 1943." If he were addressing the VFW, the audience might simply respond to the information with lots of head-nodding, war-remembering, or note-taking, and the persuasive goal would be ignored. If you digress with a story, however funny, or get the parts of the speech mixed up, or make editorial comments in the midst of information, you do nothing more than mix up your audience. They can't figure whether they should understand something, believe something, or do something. Any way, you lose.

Audiences will tell you when you are losing in this manner. You can almost see the arms jerking at the elbow in a desire to rise up and signal a question. You can see the looks of bewilderment on faces. When you catch this kind of information from your audience, you need to follow what the parliamentarians call "the order of the day." That means: get down to business; get back to the goals and objectives of your speech, at this place. A speaker needs to have an outline of his objectives tattooed on the insides of his eyeballs, close his eyes to all diversions, and zero in directly on his objectives. There should be nothing in the speech that interferes with achieving those objectives. Everything you say should have something to do with your main idea, and it should all be part of your memory. Later on we shall show you have to prepare your speech to accomplish this.

Don't just stand there. There is no guarantee that you will get any response at all. The sermon rarely snares its victims or this would be a far better world. Even the most carefully planned presentation can fail to penetrate the ears of the audience, if they decide the message is not for them.

Uncomfortable rooms, distractions outside, lack of interest on the part of the audience, failure of the speaker to get attention, may transform a speech into a soggy lump of words. A message from a speech doesn't zip from the platform and glide into the listener's mind. The listener has to have a glove up in the air to catch it. If he does not do that, then he doesn't get the message. The speaker can try to hit the heart of the plate, he can shout that the message is coming, and he can keep trying. But the "lecturer syndrome" can hit any time. You know what you sometimes do to those who lecture to you: give zero response, limp apathy, unawareness, refusal to understand. And in spite of all this, an audience cannot be blamed. They came to hear the speaker for one reason or another, and it is his job to make it worth their while.

Tell me again. Standing on the platform looking at a sea of faces— and even when there are only two or three, they sometimes look like a sea—can be a very confusing activity. You can see a lot if you look at your audience, and it all means something. The problem is, you don't know for sure what it means and you have to make some guesses so that you can respond properly.

Any response can be misinterpreted. It is the frame of mind of the speaker that influences the meaning of audience responses. There is no way that the speaker can interview his listeners to find out how they look when they are listening intently as opposed to when they are bored. Thus, the speaker must decide. A smile, for example, could mean: "I am pleased with what the speaker is saying"; "The speaker is a jerk"; or "I just thought of something that happened at breakfast." A grim set to the lips may be interpreted as intense interest or hostility. It may also be the way in which the listener's face is constructed. A speaker with a strong image of his own ability will be able to interpret most responses optimistically and carry on. Actually, most responses will be supportive. People don't really like to shoot speakers down. But if you lack confidence in your ability you may misinterpret in such a way that you demoralize yourself. So, remember, it isn't the audience that topples you; you topple yourself.

The quality of the interaction between a speaker and his audience is a product of the people involved and their goals. It is the blending of spices to produce one flavor. In a social conversation, meanings are often unclear. People look for strange things in their social relations. They want kindness, or they want to get close to someone. Sometimes they want nothing more than a little "balling." But most of these goals are not set in advance. We do not normally "premeditate" goals with our friends, and often we get into trouble because of this.

There is no reason to believe that the rules get changed in any situation. What we can find any time communication goes on is:

A situation
with two or more people in it
with each person playing some role
and with some rules limiting the movements of people
and each person has a goal, which he might even be aware of
that he tries to seek
through communication
and when he tries and gets a response
we have a new
situation
and so on ...

A **situation** refers to a place where people can meet each other. It defines how the people behave. One situation may be you on the platform and fifty persons listening. Another may be six of you sitting around a table trying to work something out. Still another might be you and your friends entertaining yourselves. If you are at the front of the room, you may have to talk louder than if you were speaking with a friend. If there are spectators, you can expect them to be playing **roles**. A **role** is nothing more than what you expect a person to do. A doctor behaves like a doctor. A teacher behaves like a teacher. A speaker behaves like a speaker and an audience behaves like an audience. In more private situations, you may have trouble figuring out the roles. Though a friend may behave like a friend, each of us has different kinds of friends who behave differently with us than they do with others.

In any event, there are some rules (which we call **norms**) that tell everybody in the situation what is possible. In a formal situation, people normally do not interrupt a speaker by shouting or throwing things. In an informal situation one person is not normally permitted to speak for a long period of time while the others listen. It is important that as a speaker, you live up to the expectations the people in the situation have for you. They will expect you to speak in a voice loud enough to hear, to present material in a way that can be understood, and to provide enough variety so that they do not get bored. They may also expect you to take into account their goals. They will not do what you want them to, unless there is something in it for them.

When you have figured, as best you can, what you want and what the others, your audience, are likely to want, and have fitted all of this into an organized pattern of talk—taking into account the goals your audience want to achieve—you are ready to speak. You do this, and you see what happens. After it happens, you are in a new situation, and you can start all over again.

Your main job is to **analyze,** to figure out what the situation is like and how the persons in it are likely to behave. **Analysis** is the first thing you do before you speak. And your analysis includes figuring out your own goals as well as psyching out the individuals you are speaking to.

Get Ready! It's exercise time!

Putting it together: exercises

1. Go to a lecture and listen to it. Don't take notes. Find a couple of friends to listen to it also. When it is over, each of you write down about four sentences entitled "important stuff that I heard in this lecture." If you agreed on anything, you might conclude that the lecturer was doing a good job, and you may go out and try again on a bad lecturer. If you found disagreements, try to figure out why what you heard was important to you and why what your friends heard was important to them. Such as, he said, "American society is facing a crisis." I guess I am worried about my own problems in American society. Or, he said, "American society is capable of solving its problems." I guess I don't want to believe that American society is going to get any worse, because I can barely handle what I have to now.

2. Sit down and make a list of the things you need to have done for you every day: the requests you make, the invitations you issue. Things like "Pass the salt," "Go to the movies with me," and "Hey, doc, I'm sorry I missed the last class; can you fill me in on what happened?" Compare your list to lists made by others. That should give you some idea of how often we need to persuade others with our way. Now look at some TV and read the papers and check out how much others are asking you to do. "Buy my toothpaste," "Vote for my man," "Watch me next week," "Believe in what I tell you!" Try to figure how many of these persons really give you a reason for their requests. What are those reasons?

3. Here's a piece of writing from a philosopher, Søren Kierkegaard. He was a Swede and a religious revolutionary. He had this to say about communication.

> A group in its very concept is the untruth. . . . The falsehood, first of all, is the notion that the group does what in fact only the individual does, though it be every individual. For "group" is an abstraction and has no hands, but each individual ordinarily has two hands. . . . The group is untruth. Hence none has more contempt for what it is to be a man than they who make it their profession to lead the crowd. . . . The witness to the truth is to engage himself if possible, with all, but always individually, talking to everyone severally on the streets and lanes. . . . In order to disintegrate the crowd, though not with the intent of educating the crowd as such, but rather with the hope that one or another individual might return from this assemblage and become a single individual.

This is an example of some very complicated writing. Sit down with a group and try to figure out what Kierkegaard was trying to say. Then try to put it into words. How would you **say** it to someone else? What are some of the reasons to say it the way you do? And incidentally, take note of how hard it is to figure what Kierkegaard is saying. It is almost like cracking a code. You may have to go to the dictionary several times and really discuss the quote and think about it before you get an idea of what he really meant. Doing this should give you some notion of the basic differences between speaking and writing. If you want to practice some more, your instructor should be able to supply you with some tough readings that you can translate into speaking.

4. Working from your own point of view, you might be able to give some important advice to your instructors. You know by now what you like to listen to and what turns you off. Try to prepare a set of instructions to your lecturers, about what they would need to do to hold your interest. You might come up with:

> Speak slowly and when you want me to take notes, hit it hard. Tell me how what you say fits into my life.

or some such. Bounce these ideas off of your speech instructor. Let him tell you about some of the difficulties he might have in following your instructions. He will have to tell you his goals and how his goals often get in the way of meeting your goals. And that's what it's all about—getting his goals to meet your goals so that you can both get paid off.

Check out your audience.

5. Pick a day when a friendly instructor is giving a lecture. Ask if you can sit at the front of the class and watch it behave. (If you have videotape at your school, you can videotape the audience. That would be a good deal better.) As you watch, try to describe the behaviors that are going on. Don't try to decide what they mean, just describe them. Then, after the lecture, sit down with the friendly instructor and ask him how he would interpret each of the behaviors you saw. If you have a videotape of some audience responding then your whole class can work on figuring out how it would interpret the behaviors.

6. Try to pick a goal by asking yourself the following questions:

Why am I speaking in the first place?
What do I want to get out of it?
Who do I have to get it from?
What's the best thing that can happen to me?
What's the worst? And what do I do if it happens?

Check your goal-setting against Mager's little book. Make sure you get rid of all your "fuzzies." You may want to try this exercise several times to be sure you've got it.

TWO

Psyching it out

The basic unit of communication is the **dyad:** that is two persons communicating. You can't communicate without having someone else around, and if someone else is around you can't not communicate. Three persons named Watzlawick, Beavin, and Jackson, in a book called **Pragmatics of Human Communication,*** make a big point of this. Even when you don't want to communicate, just being there gives messages to the other person. Your clothes, your face, the way you stand, all give messages to the other person. Your job is to take control, make sure the other gets the message you want to send. And, incidentally, the other person doesn't even have to be alive and out there. You can communicate to another person inside your head. There are some authorities who think that thinking is precisely that: talking to someone else inside your head.

Analyzing the audience

When you are speaking to an audience, you have to make some guesses about what they know and believe. In order to do that, you have to "analyze." Such an analysis is more a feeling for the group

*New York: W. W. Norton, 1967

mood than a task in arithmetic. Usually you don't have the time to give a questionnaire to the audience and count the answers. It would be hard to tell what you could do with the answers anyway. When you analyze an audience, you try to get some feeling of what they know and what they believe, and how they are likely to respond to material they already know, to material they don't know, to material they agree with, and to material they disagree with. You need to have something on which to base a judgment of how well you are doing as you talk to them.

One way to think of your audience is through the notion of **figure and ground.** The diagram below could be interpreted in two ways. If

Figure 2.1

you look at it one way, you see a vase. If you see it from another point of view, you see faces. We refer to the specific thing you see as the "figure" and the space that surrounds it as the "ground." When you are speaking to your audience, you will not be able to focus on all the different faces before you. You will only be able to get one face "in figure" at a time. What that face is doing will guide what you do. If you happen to hit a friendly face, you win. If you hit one that is snarling, give it up. Now your problem is how to get only one face, and have it tell you sensible things about what to say next. What you need to do is to get one face inside your own head, a face made up of what most of the people in the audience are doing. That is your real audience. Robert Doolittle, of the University of Wisconsin at Milwaukee, studied this subject for his master's thesis, and he discovered that successful speakers are able to see this composite face. They can look at the audience as a "ground" and put together a figure in their head. You need a good deal of practice before you can do this well, but while you practice, it helps to understand that you don't have to try to please everyone.

Whatever or whomever you get in your head as an audience, it is going to be partly made up of all the memories you have about how others have responded to your speaking. The mind, like a drowning person, grabs on to any jutting memories in its attempt to make sense out of an incoming image. New information can be judged only by what one already knows. A speaker, picking up the responses of members of the audience may filter them through the memory of his "mama" during his bar mitzvah speech. Or he may remember his girl-friend looking at him during his commencement address. Or he may remember the disapproval of his tenth-grade English teacher when he gave a report on a dirty book. It is even possible that he has put together some kind of image made up of descriptions pulled from a speech book.

When we take in information, we need to compare it to old information, but we must do more than that. We must allow new situations and new responses to get into our minds as well. You can be haunted by ghosts of your old enemies, harassed by aunts and uncles to whom you have tried to explain your life, or even by the coolness of your old friends when you saw them during the first vacation home from college. These kinds of observations can get in your way. If you decide that people in general disapprove of you, you will tend to see your new responders as disapproving, and you will not get the encouragement you deserve. Somehow, you have to learn to distinguish between memory and reality, to take into account the flesh-and-blood, here-and-now individuals who are telling you things about what you are doing. You may not be able to react to all of them, but their responses to you are what you have to respond to in general.

There is always a chance that you will do the right thing by accident. There is a story about all the monkeys in the world pounding on all the typewriters in the world sometimes cranking out some really good literature. But the monkeys couldn't decide. They would need a literary critic to tell them how well they were doing. You need a literary critic also. Some of what gets you positive responses will be accidental, but you will have to keep your eye on these things, and remember what worked for you, so that you can have the option of doing similarly the next time. If you have convinced yourself that nothing will work, you can't even succeed by accident.

Accidental success, however, is too risky to count on. To be effective, a speaker needs more than a sunshine image of how good he is. He must have a clear picture of what "effectiveness" is, framed in a set of goals for the immediate audience—not a bunch of words from a textbook. A speaker needs to want something more specific than being "poised and self confident." He has to tell himself, "I want to see those heads nodding, at least half of them, by the time I get to point two in my outline."

Your situation is, however, that you are learning to speak in a class. You are surrounded by your friends. Or, even if they are not your friends, they know enough not to hassle you, because they know you can hassle back. So you can't really use your classroom as a guide to the kinds of responses you can expect. In a real speech situation, the audience may file nondescriptly through the hall, giving you no information at all. Only a few persons may make responses that you even think you can interpret. We have been trained not to respond very much, particularly to what we don't like. The old-time melodramas at least gave the audience the privilege of booing the villain. Most speech audiences have learned to be polite, even though at close look the attentive gleam in their eye turns out to be a vacant stare.

Speakers in life situations have learned to trust some basic, common clues that they can really count on. They know that if they stimulate a burst of applause, they are doing well. And they know if there is not much movement at all, even when they reach exciting parts of their speech, they are probably doing poorly. You learn how to size up audience response by experience. The more times you stand in front of an audience, the more "real" information you will be able to obtain and the more accurate your conclusions about the audience will be.

If you keep in mind that it is impossible to react to the audience as a collection of individuals and that you must select some kind of individual to speak to, you will not make the error of expecting unanimous approval. Only those persons in the audience that approximate the image you have in mind will respond on the terms expected. If you expect too much from your audience, you may look forward to perpetual dissatisfaction as a speaker. Seaching for unanimous approval is like looking for the "lost chord." And if you don't get what you are looking for, you might become so discouraged that you will retreat from further opportunities to communicate.

From the standpoint of the audience

A good way to size up what to expect from an audience is to think about the times you have been in an audience—about what you felt and did as you listened to the speaker. Just as the speaker can really retain only one image in his mind at a time, the audience member can concentrate on only one thing. At any time, the supposed listener may not have the speaker in his mind at all. He or she might be looking around for an attractive female (or male). He might be running some fantasy through his head. He might be thinking: "What if the speaker got sick and they asked me to come on stage. Wow! I'd show them. I'd be a dynamo, a whirlwind. I'd take this audience apart." Or, "Gee, the speaker is a world-famous person and here he is calling me up on the stage for special mention." Or, "After the speech I'm going down to Kelly's and Gert will be there and the beer will be nice and cold and. . . ." We have all been listeners and we are aware of the many devices we can use to avoid paying attention to the speaker. Those of us who have attended many lecture classes may have learned the trick of sleeping with our eyes open. Others learn how to make rhythmic nods throughout a speech in order to con the lecturer into believing that they agree with him. With this kind of response possible, the speaker has only himself to blame if he depends too strongly on his guesses about how the audience will behave. And by hanging loose, the speaker can set himself to handle anything that comes.

Interceptions in foul territory may also plague a speaker reaching out for responses he can interpret. Remember the times you had to convert your wave to a head-scratch because you responded to a wave that was intended for someone else. The speaker might mistakenly interpret any response intended for someone else as intended for him. The listener may be responding to circumstances entirely irrelevant to the speech. A restless person may not be suffering from boredom but rather from restroom pain. Anyone who has lived through a rock concert knows that not a single word or note penetrates the screaming wall of the audience, yet everyone comes out with an image of extreme pleasure derived from the performance. The pleasure image is based more on anticipation than on actual performance. In many cases, the Beatles could have stood on the stage and chanted, "Thank you for giving us the money," and received the same response they got from "Norwegian Wood."

Performers like the Beatles had a quality called "charisma." They were famous; they were the best. Their audience expected them to perform like the best, and consequently, they were prepared to pay off with a worshipful response. Ordinary mortals like you and me are not so fortunate. We may have hardly any image at all—just another student or just another professor. Our speech, hopefully, will give us body with the listeners. But usually, the initial responses we get are based on what the audience expects to hear—just another student, just another professor.

The speaker's task is to overcome this lethargy in the audience and grab a spotlight, at least part of the time. If he never comes across to his listener as a clear human being, he will have a hard time accomplishing his goals, whatever they are. Professional comedians understand this problem and try to make it work for them. They try to build an image in advance. Sometimes, a warmup comedian comes out to loosen up the audience. Often, a claque is planted in the audience, a small group who guffaw and cheer at everything that goes on, suggesting to the rest of the audience that they ought to participate too. Hopefully, when the comedian comes out, he is strong enough to retain the attention that has been generated by artificial means.

The problem with watching these kinds of professionals, however, is that they plant disturbing notions in our heads. We begin to think that if we can't be at least as funny as Henny Youngman, at least as charismatic as the Maharaj Ji, then we are failures. Not so! What we have to know is that we must move toward the development of our image with a particular audience by grabbing their attention and holding it. We need to analyze as best we can the language the audience will respond to—examples that will mean something to them, appeals that will strike home. We must talk as directly to them as possible, without modifying our own ideas, of course, but we dare not expect them to give us what we have not earned.

We sometimes need to rely on illusion. For example, real contact with individuals in the audience is rare. If the audience is large, it is virtually impossible to see every single member, even briefly, during a speech. Sometimes, however, the speaker will encounter a pair of eyes in the audience that seem to spark back at him, and the speaker will know he has met the mind of another human being. The whole process of speech-building demands the manipulation of ideas, sentences, and words so that the possibilities of such encounters can be maximized. We want as many persons as possible to feel, "Gee, he was talking directly to me." This response from a member of the audience is gratifying when felt by the speaker, who realizes, "He heard me and he believes me." But such assurance will never come from the entire audience.

In short, the term "audience" is often very confusing. It is a myth, built out of events. The way the word looks in print, we tend to think of "audience" as a thing. From what we have told you, however, it ought to be clear that we cannot afford to do this. In the first place, much of what we see when we speak to an audience is the product of our memory. We tend to see what we have seen before. Sometimes we have to work on our own minds to adjust our expectations, for if we are used to seeing an audience as threatening, even the most courteous audience will not dispel the image.

In the center of the myth of "audience," is our image of ourselves as speakers. If you have seen yourself as a success, part of that image will be built out of the way in which persons in audiences have responded to you. If you see yourself as a failure, you will have another kind of image of how people behave when you talk to them. In either case, to consider the audience you are presently speaking to the same as previous audiences is dangerous. Take them as they come. Make some sensible definition of what you can expect, and go to it. You can probably bet on simple courtesy. Accept it and don't argue with it. What gets applauded in front of one group might be met with stony silence is front of another. If you do a satisfactory job of advance analysis, this analysis, together with your goal statements will help you get a realistic idea of what to expect.

More analyzing the audience

Again, there is always the possibility of doing the right thing by accident. Many monkeys on many typewriters might be able to crank
out all of Shakespeare, or more likely write a few good short stories.
The problem with those monkeys, however, is that they wouldn't know
"good stuff" when they saw it. As a speaker, your intuition about individual responses, on any occasion, could be quite accurate. When
you make a lucky guess, you are likely to do a very good job of
speaking and get a rousing audience response for it. If your image
of yourself is very strong, you might even convince the audience to
respond to you the way you think they ought to, and block out the
possibility of failure. Your illusions might be enough to carry you to
success.

Accidental success, however, is too risky to count on. A speaker
needs more than a sunshine image of his own potential to be uniformly effective. If you are on a job that requires public speaking, you
can't afford to count on spotty successes. A teacher needs more than
one good day out of five to earn a top merit rating. A salesman had
better be able to make it with more than a few customers. An engineer, explaining designs to the board of directors, had better be able
to maintain a consistent level of performance if he expects to advance in the company.

In each case, a speaker must have a definition of effectiveness
built out of goals that he sets for the particular audience, and not in
textbook phrases or generalized terms. In the classroom, the audience is programmed to respond with "proper" cues, attentiveness,
and politeness. It takes no great skill to anticipate how your classmates will respond to you the second and third times. And part of
this will depend on how you respond to them.

If you define success simply as an "apparently courteous hearing," you may pretty well assure yourself of success in every case—
at least in the classroom. You may count on your performance to be
approved. The student who hoots at you runs the risk that you might
hoot back. So we conspire to support each other, and thus we provide
an illusion of effectiveness. Sadly enough, even in the classroom, a
speaker can only perceive surface behavior, and there is no possibility of digging into the listeners' minds to find the real feelings.
Only the individual listeners know about the "monsters" lurking

beneath the surface; and most listeners take care not to expose them. Consequently, if you take responses to you in the classroom as a gauge for expectations of responses away from the classroom, you are likely to experience a delusion that will spell failure for you, when success really counts.

A common method of looking at audiences is to classify them as "hostile," "neutral," and "friendly" to you and to your topic. Such a classification scheme assumes that audience attitudes exist on a continuum that is discernible to the speaker. All he needs to do, according to this system, is to insert the audience climate into the proper slot and then follow the instructions for appealing to that audience.

But the situation is not as simple as that. Individual members of the audience do not react exclusively to the speaker and his Ten Commandments. Rather, they are involved in a process of reacting: to the speaker, to each other, to a cosmic ray bombardment of stimuli throughout the speech. Everything that hits their minds will evoke some kind of response, including many events that have nothing to do with the speaker and his ideas. You would need some very complex mathematics and computers to predict, for sure, what an audience might do in a given case. And, of course, if you could make these kinds of predictions, you wouldn't have to prepare the speech; you would get the computer to prepare it. Until that day, you will have to be your own analyst and use the maximum persuasion you can muster. The responsibility, of course, is on you. Speakers often blame the audience for poor responses, but in reality, it is the speaker who is asking for time from the audience, and therefore, he shoulders much of the burden for what happens.

In most cases, the individuals in the audience are strangers to the speaker. You can find out only very simple things about them in advance. You can find out why they came to the gathering, what they might expect. You might be able to find out where their group stands on some issues, although these issues are often irrelevant to your speech. The audience exists almost in a state of randomness as far as you and your topic is concerned. Even if you know the majority attitudes on issues related to yours, you cannot expect to extend those beliefs automatically to your own ideas. In any event, you have to gain acceptance for yourself, then for your ideas. You have to reach some emotional level with the audience, and most of all, you have to be able to speak to the audience in ways that they will understand. It is very disheartening to hear the comment, "He spoke well, but I cannot remember a thing he said."

Much of your success as a speaker depends on what you can glean from your observation, on-the-spot, of what the audience is doing as you speak. Your interpretation of this information might be helped along by some of the information obtained in advance, but in any case, if you don't do anything about what you see, you won't improve much as a speaker. The best advice is: when you go into a situation, be **aware** of the **range of possible responses** and be prepared to handle what you get.

You need to keep in mind that any interpretations you make of audience responses will be colored by your own idea of yourself. We have already shown that your observations can be colored by your mood. Observations are only reliable when the mood is objective. There was a great physicist by the name of Werner Heisenberg who said that even in the most exact experimental science, the results of the experiment depend on the eyes looking at it. The person doing the interpreting always affects the interpretation. You try your best to interpret while speaking, but it is hard to concentrate. You can't say to the audience, "Hold still while I try to figure out what you are saying to me." And you can't use the immortal words of Dizzy Dean, "How'm I doin', Edna?"

Trying to make these on-the-spot interpretations is like trying to catch the moment when the light in the refrigerator goes off as you shut the door. You may catch a mood here and there and adapt to it, but the minute you do this, your adaptation is obsolete and a new one has to be made. All of this sounds very discouraging, of course, but what we are telling you is that avoiding misconceptions about the audience will be very helpful to you as a speaker. You will learn later that there are some events you can control, and your job is to control as many of them as you possibly can.

In a sense, you are stuck. No matter what you do, you have some idea in your head about the people to whom you are talking. Your rudimentary analysis might address itself to questions like these:

Who are these persons? Why are they here?
What, if anything, do they know about me?
What, if anything, do they know about my topic?
What do they believe about my ideas?

How do they customarily respond to speakers?
How have people customarily responded to me?
What is the worst thing I can think of that might happen here?
What is the best thing I can think of that might happen here?
What would I do, if they did . . . ?

There is no reason to fish from the pier if you can get a boat. You may use some of this information to prepare in advance. You may, for example, in the introduction to your speech, use information about why people are present:

Congratulations on your twentieth annual founder's day.
It is good to see so many of you in church this morning.
You are probably all interested in health insurance.

You can use the information about what they know of you and your topic to help you gather the kind of data that will be useful to them. If they know little about your topic, you might decide to speak on a very basic level. If they know a lot about your topic, you might try something more sophisticated. If they know a lot about you (and it is favorable), you can play a bit on your goodwill, and if you think they don't like you, you can try to get them to think of you in a different way.

You may use information about their beliefs, if you can get it, to help you make decisions about the kind of evidence you are going to use. You may use information about the best and worst things that can happen, to prepare some strategy for each case (hoping you'll never have to use it in the latter case, and that you'll use it throughout in the former—but not counting on it in either eventuality). You may use information about their customary response style to help you identify simple courtesy.

But if you stay traditional and depend only on this kind of information, you will have to believe that it is possible for the audience to stay frozen and that you will have no effect on them at all. If you have an image of the audience viewing your speech in awe, as if it were Mt. Rushmore, you might overlook those in the background who are attracted to the hot dog stand or the souvenir shop. Deviations from expected responses occur frequently enough that the speaker should not be thrown by them. It is rare that you will have to encounter a man in the fifth row having a heart attack. You will have to contend with yawning, stretching, fidgeting, looking at watches (and take care if they start listening to those watches to see if they stopped), nodding heads, spontaneous applause, or laughing in the wrong place.

Audience responses can disrupt the continuity of your speech unless you are prepared to deal with them. A speech can get chopped up like a late movie and its commercials. The ideas become mutilated, and the mass of the speech becomes meaningless. This may not be the speaker's fault, but he might come on like Kate Smith doing a Rolling Stones song. What you need is a match like Kate Smith singing "God Bless America" for the Philadelphia Flyers, and in order to get close to this, you have to move fast to pick up what the audience is telling you and alter your presentation to fit it. **That is why we tell you never to write out a speech to read, and never memorize a speech.** You need to hang loose.

You may have made a faulty decision about the language to use, and the audience may be telling you that you sound stuffy and pompous. You may misestimate how much they are agreeing with you, and instead they may be telling you that you are getting on their nerves. You need to be able to continue presenting your ideas, but adjusting them and the language in which they are phrased to what the audience is doing. On the other hand, one man's boredom need

Responding to audience response.

not be generalized to include the whole audience. The tar and nicotine can never be entirely filtered out of cigarettes, and even when you are doing your absolute best, chances are there will be someone who finds you annoying. As a speaker, you need to keep your goal in mind and be able to **adapt** to what is going on, always working toward the accomplishment of the goal you have set for yourself.

Evaluating response

We have already shown that the essential of relationship between the speaker and his audience is the reaction of that audience as interpreted by the speaker. As interpreted by the speaker. **As interpreted by the speaker.** No, the record is not broken. That phrase is important enough to keep repeating, for the speaker is somewhat like a fisherman trawling the audience for response. The equipment he uses to filter the responses are his expectations for that audience and his image of himself as a speaker. We could not expect a man with a rigid backbone to know the experience of touching his toes. He is limited and misses something by his very state of being. Sometimes speakers are equally rigid, and that is why we asked you not to write out your speech or try to memorize it.

Sometimes we have tunnel vision about our observations. We see only what we want to see. Many of us have been exposed to the commencement speaker who droned on and on even though the temperature in the hall was over ninety and graduates were passing out from heatstroke, not to speak of the limp, wet condition of the audience. You need to keep yourself open so that you can alter your moves, expand your speech, stress an idea, take something, to accommodate to what you **think** the audience is telling you.

That expectancies restrict observation and evaluation is not an untested notion. At the University of California at Los Angeles investigator Robert Rosenthal did a study of "infallible" school teachers. The study involved classroom observation and it indicated that even the most professional of the teachers could not accurately predict how much attention students were paying. The teachers were asked to look at a film of children responding to a teacher and to make predictions about how well each child would do on a test. The results were random. The teachers were not able to make accurate predictions. In another experiment, teachers were told that some of their students (selected at random and for no reason at all) would make sudden learning spurts during the year. Result: the students for whom the predictions were made, did indeed shoot ahead in their learning. It makes us wonder how much of what we see really happened or how much of what we want to happen makes us see what we see.

The same applies to listeners. A person in the audience may nod consistently throughout the speech; he might have an off-center gyroscope or he might be indicating approval. More than likely, however, he may have developed a habitual pattern of response. Although his response may indicate to the speaker that the listener is thoughtfully involved in the speech, there is a chance that not a single word is penetrating the disguise. You need more than one nodder to convince yourself that people are agreeing with you.

The person next to him, that looks as if he is taking notes, might very well be writing a letter home to mother. The person who has his head bent down and is moving his pen may be a veritable Picasso of the doodling world doing an abstract image of the total speech. The first one may hear nothing. The second may hear every word. The behavior of individuals cannot be generalized into statements about the entire audience. This idea compelled the following:

> Taking notes and waving hands,
> Do not point out who understands;
> Weird position, but mind agile
> We each have our own listening style.

The alert speaker looks for trends. While he knows that each member of the audience is different from each other member and that a single behavior is not an indicator, he also knows that there are some common responses that show approval or disapproval. A lot of nods, a lot of note-takers, a lot of persons looking directly at you: Go, man go! Or a lot of squirming, yawning, loose chairs scraping the floor: Soup it up; do something to get back their attention!

One of the authors of this book started his teaching career in North Dakota. The students there were consistently undemonstrative; they put little or no apparent energy into their speeches. The instructor wanted to see more life and vigor and gave them a furious lecture on gaining attention by doing something dramatic. At the next round of speeches, the first speaker said, "I don't want to give this speech.

I think I will jump out the window." And he did. When the instructor managed to breathe again, he ran to the window to see what had happened. The class was in a state of shock. As everyone looked for a mangled body down below, the student came in through the classroom door and declared, "That Introduces my speech on the law of gravity. What goes up must come down." He had rehearsed that introduction ten times the night before, although he refused to repeat the jump when the man from **Time** magazine asked him to. This speaker had taken advantage of a situation; he got attention and he held it from then on. Every time he stood up to speak, his audience waited for something sensational to happen.

You needn't go quite that far. After all, everyone is not a trained paratrooper. On the other hand, when you ride the midnight express of speaking, there is little time to contemplate and reflect on meanings of response. Once you get the notion that your listeners are bored, that you are losing them, you will need to make a move to get back their attention. Sometimes just moving about on the platform will help. Sometimes talking louder will do it. Sometimes it takes more: a joke, some unusual movement. That's where your prior analysis of the audience helps a bit, because if you can remember what it is you found out about that audience that turns them on, that's the time to start talking about it.

During the speech, the speaker relates to the audience as himself. He projects his image onto the individuals out there and acts as if everyone who responds means what he would mean by that response. He has very little choice; he can only interpret the meanings he understands. The speaker sees what he sees through the window of his own world, based on his own past experience. "Now, if that were I sitting and doodling, it would mean I wasn't listening." Unfortunately, when it comes to nonverbal language, we do not all speak the same tongue. As a matter of fact, sometimes we do not even speak the same verbal language.

There is one way in which a speaker can use his natural tendency to see the audience as he does. If the speaker can think of multiplying himself and all of his moods several times, and then project this on the audience, he can prepare to appeal to all the different parts of himself. That would mean that he builds repetition into the speech. But not simple repetition; he repeats with style. He appeals to himself when he is in a precise and numerical mood. He appeals to himself when he would prefer a good story. He states and restates his theme each time using a different kind of proof or a different kind of illustration. It's something like being at a Bingo game. The more cards you play, the more likely you are to hit. The speaker repeats his main idea (we'll call it "residual message" later on) several different ways in order to meet the maximum possible number of moods and mental states in which he might find the audience. We call this kind of repetition "stylized redundancy," and we will talk about it a good deal more when we look at methods of preparing the message.

That means, however, that in order to anticipate the possibles, our speaker has to be a good observer. He has to understand the potentials in human response. He can learn much about that in two ways. One is by looking at all the possible reasons persons might have to speak and others to listen. The second is by examining his social relationships and studying how persons talk to each other one at a time.

In the first instance, we suppose most of you have the same notion about public speaking, "Man, I won't ever have to do that." We've heard a lot of similar statements: "I don't want to learn this stuff; I'm going into counseling." "What does an engineer need with public speaking?" "I'm going to be a doctor. They talk to patients one at a time." "I don't have to learn to speak in public just to run a machine." Well, there are a lot of excuses but few escapes. The sad (and rather exciting) thing is that most of you will have some exceptional public speech opportunities during your careers, and all of you will have a chance to take part in politics and social action. Every teacher needs to know how to perform in front of a class. Engineers (we are told by a number of executives) put their promotions on the line, if they can't deliver a good speech. Doctors are constantly addressing medical meetings. The man in the shop has his union to contend with. About the only occupations we can think of that don't have some requirement for speaking are lighthouse keeper and hermit, but then we don't really know what goes on at the lighthouse keepers' conventions.

If occupations require that speeches be given, they must also require, for good reason, that people listen to the speeches. Students need to listen to teachers in order to learn. Executives need to listen to engineers in order to make proper decisions. Doctors need to listen to each other in order to keep posted on the latest events. Workers need to present their grievances in order that the membership can decide on the conditions of the new contract. Thinking through what the audience can possibly get from your speech will help you get a handle on how to put the speech together with the maximum appeal. Even in your speech class, there is a good deal that you can do for an audience. If they don't know anything about cliff climbing and you know how much pleasure there is in it, then your audience stands to get some real pleasure if you can talk them into trying it. If they don't know how to knot macrame, they can gain a lot when you explain it to them. Maybe they can find something else to do besides watching a Marx Brothers film for the thirty-second time. If they don't understand the issues involved in the local municipal election and you do, you might save them some money by telling them how they can exempt themselves from local taxes. Think of yourself as a "servant of the people." If those folks are going to sit out there and listen to you for five minutes (let's see, five minutes and twenty people in the class, that's one hundred minutes or one and two-thirds man hours) you can give them more than their money's worth, so long as you think in terms of what they might like, what they might need, what they might find pleasurable. **But never what they want to hear** because to do that you would have to compromise your principles.

We can get a lot of good ideas from looking at how we speak to each other in pairs. When we look at a pair of persons talking together, we can eliminate a lot of distractions and get right to the business. When you talk to your friend, you are usually trying to share some information, or make some agreement about a place to go or a thing to do, or perhaps just trying to unburden yourself. He listens to you because he has something at stake. He gives you information because he may want to get some from you. He talks about where to go and what to do because he is going to participate with you. He listens to your troubles because he may have troubles of his own. It is almost as though you have a speaking-listening contract with your friend. There are times when he takes the listener role because it is demanded by what you are saying. Other times he wants you to assume that role. But you rarely talk to him for no reason at all, and you surely don't expect him to hang around to listen to you talk nonsense or tell him something he already knows or bore him or annoy him. And so, if this is true for a friend, it is also true for an audience.

Professional pairs show this same kind of contractual arrangement. A psychiatrist talking to his client is trying to give some information and persuade the client to do something to improve himself. The client puts up with the talk because he hopes there is something in it for him. Watching such a pair operate is also useful because it shows you some of the things you can look for when you are watching an audience. When the psychiatrist talks to his client he can watch for responses: the client can talk back to him. The psychiatrist gets immediate information about how well things are going. If the patient doesn't understand, he says something. If he doesn't agree, then an argument starts. The psychiatrist is continually adjusting his persuasion to meet the needs of the moment. Even though the audience is only one person, the conflict is as dramatic as it would be with a speaker talking to an audience of one thousand. And the outcome is uncertain. There is no formula. Sometimes the speaker wins, sometimes the listener.

The process of speaking and listening does not work like a computer program because people are not computers and they cannot be programmed. There has been a whole generation of scholars trying to make a science out of the art of speaking, but they have accomplished little over all the years. The problem is still one of coping with the uncertainty of the human mind. The speaker guesses as best he can and prepares all that he can, and then he tries to meet conditions as they come. We can count minimally on the long-range weather forecast in planning the picnic, but we still look at the sky on the morning of the big day.

So, our speaker tries to do all he can in advance. He tries to find every available means to accomplish his purpose with the audience. And then he meets them where they stand and does his best. The ancient Greeks named this the art of **rhetoric.** Today, we learn it as persuasion. Every speaker is a persuader. If he is giving information he must persuade the audience that the information is worth having. If he is trying to change minds, he must persuade the audience that the change is in their best interests. If he is merely telling jokes, he must persuade the audience that he is funny.

From here on, when and if we use the word "rhetoric" we refer to the persuasive elements present in every speaking situation. Remember, if anyone knew an automatic and infallible way to get everyone to agree with him, some politician or soap company already would have bought the invention. There is no such way. When we have to give information, change minds, get action, impress people, we are in a contest, and victory is not decided by some arbitrary standard of criticism but solely by how close we come to accomplishing our goal.

The art of speech criticism is still rather primitive. Sometimes the stuff of communication seems to be smothered in the lace of high literary style. Critics, like moths, have been attracted to the brightness of certain styles. Historians, for example, will declare that the Englishman Charles James Fox is a model of a great speaker. Anyone familiar with British history, however, knows that Fox was as ineffectual as a feather when it came to pounding home his points. He spoke well, but no one agreed with him. Henry Pelham is somewhat less famous and somewhat less literary. His only claim to fame is that he won just about every time he took the platform. So we let the literary critics play their games with Fox, and we look at speakers like Pelham (or Billy Graham or Charles Percy or Henry Jackson) in order to find our models of success. In every case, the effective speaker is the man who has found something to say that strikes home with the audience; he has found some reason **in them** for them to agree. Maybe that is why Aristotle said, "The fool tells me his reasons; the wise man persuades me with my own."

Real communication is an authentic transaction between speaker and listener. The word "authentic" is hazy and hard to grab hold of. It cannot be translated into things we can see. But let's say it has something to do with intensity. It happens when a good, sensitive speaker comes together with a listener who is willing to be involved if he is given a good reason to do so. The feeling does not linger. It is a brief moment in which two persons seem to resonate on the same note; and win, lose, or draw, the speaker knows he has made an ally and the listener knows he has made a friend.

This kind of authentic feeling is not something that will happen with your first speech. It is a goal. It is a feeling that you work toward and get closer to with experience. It will originate in you. Later on, when we tell you the rules and regulations, the "how to's" of putting a speech together, we will be talking about tools and equipment available to anyone. They can be used by prophets and by dictators. They have no morals. They are methods and nothing more. But the quality of the speaker's ideas, the integrity with which he presents and defends them, the respect he accords the human beings that listen to him, the care he exerts to find their needs and to appeal to them in their terms, all add up to the real success in speaking. To win means to commit your entire personality.

Many teachers are shocked when the "lump" that sat in the back of the room comes forward to talk about the influence the teacher has had on his life. The teacher never knew how much he had reached his student. But at one time or another an intense contact had been made. As speakers, we strive for this kind of contact. As listeners we leave ourselves open enough so that it can happen. And in both cases we compromise with reality—we hope for the best and buckle in for the worst.

The speaker's personality

A person with the urge to speak is bursting with needs and concerns. He has discovered some urgency in the life around him that demands his attention. He needs to put it right. There is some information that must be delivered; there is an issue that must be resolved; someone has delivered an opinion that must be countered; there is a new idea that must be shared.

The act of speaking is a release of internal pressure. The words you utter are rooted in your personality. Your listener's most forceful picture of you comes through your words. The reaction to your words is also a reaction to you. It is easy to try to get off the hook and declare that we must separate a man from his ideas. Can't be done! What people think of you will reflect on your ideas and what they think of your ideas will reflect on you. You do not exist apart from your ideas, although you might get that notion if you approach your training in public speaking in a superficial way. If you regard public speaking with the attitude you had toward your eleventh grade themes, you will not understand the meaning of what you have just read. The late anthropologist, Ernest Becker, in a book called **Birth and Death of Meaning** said that speech is the only thing that is "specifically human." He meant that the only ability man has that animals do not have is to express himself, his inner thoughts and feelings through speech symbols.

This could be a frightening idea to those of you who believe that human beings can somehow come together in a state of bliss without effort and without trouble. The history of mankind is a history of ferment and competition and struggle. Man against man and idea against idea has been and will be our lot in life—at least until that day when we are finally reduced to the state of robots.

You already know how important are your words. If you feel the least bit concerned about standing up and speaking before your class or any group, you know that you have something to lose every time you open your mouth. What do you think of: "Better to remain silent and let them think you are a fool than to open your mouth and prove it to them"?

Do you believe that statement? Do you worry about reciting in class because it might make you look like a dummy? Are you afraid to ask questions, even when you are confused, for fear that others might think you are ignorant? Does it take real strength of will on your part to stand up and face a large group and tell them what you think? If so, you already understand how important speech is to the human being. You understand the grating anxiety felt every time you have to perform; there is something at stake.

Your stake is not a tangible—not in our society. In twenty-five years of teaching speech and performing on the public platform the senior author of this book has never seen a person injured because of his appearance on the platform—although this author once stubbed his toe when climbing to the stage at a teacher's meeting at the. . . . Well, back to the issue. What you have to lose is your image of yourself—the image conferred on you by the opinions of others. That is the secret of Ernest Becker's little statement. We become who we are partly because of the way others respond to us. A doctor that looks like a truck repair man might get a few invitations over the weekend to fix trucks, but if people do not see him as a doctor, he will not be able to act like a doctor. Mr. Popular is popular only because others have responded to him in ways that convince him this is so. And Mr. Wallflower hangs on the fringes because others have told him they don't like him around. They don't do it in so many words, but they do it and he knows they do it.

Reactions to you and your speech play a crucial role in the development of a mature personality. The word "mature" is not used loosely here. It means the ability to know yourself and what you can do. You know what you know and what you can learn, and you have a sense of what it is possible for you to do. You can distinguish a friend from an enemy. You know what you like and you know what you need to avoid. It means that you are able to cope with the business of living. Not that you will know perfect bliss, but that you can deal with the normal and ordinary in your life and rise to an emergency when you have to. Maturity means not looking for things that aren't there, being able to put up with yourself with all your assets and all your limitations. We come to maturity through the development of our ability to talk with and respond to others.

Studies of speech development in children show that oral communication is essential to their maturation. Intellectual development in children grows out of their urgency to satisfy needs. The child needs to learn how to influence persons and events around him so that he can get a little food, a little comfort and a little love when he needs them. "Da, da; goo, goo" is a very persuasive argument for attention from dad, although it might not convince the mailman.

The first things a child sees are important only to him. He is on an ego trip, a center of a small universe. Mom and dad, and all the kids revolve around his needs. If they cannot meet his needs they are irrelevant to him. But he soon learns that he must meet some minimum requirements that others have if he is to get the attention he craves. He must learn to interact and to transact. That is, he must learn to relate to others according to public rules of conduct (interaction) and how to exchange services and sentiments with another person (transaction). By interacting and transacting he builds his relationships. Communication is the process out of which those relationships are built. Language is its machinery. Communication is the essential for survival. It is both a process and a relationship. And it works through symbols, not actions. We can express approval and disapproval with words; we needn't slurp faces like a Saint Bernard or attack like a weasel.

The person who communicates in actions and not symbols is a slave to his childhood and dangerous to society. We usually judge such to be criminals or mentally ill, and we put them away in order to protect the rest of us. The mature adult is a master of symbols, a Spiderman whose word-webs establish his power over his environment. He can cope. Symbols are the bait set to attract the responses that will improve his position and ease his anxiety. To develop skill in communication is to discover that mature man is a cooperative animal who plays by the rules.

Our language, for example, is rule-bound. It is made up of agreements that this set of noises stands for this set of things, and further that noises have to be uttered in a specific sequence in order to make sense. We have dictionaries and grammars, our rules of communication, without which we could not relate to others. Much of our growing up is a process of learning the rules, discovering what pattern of utterances get what responses. We find out what we need to do to solve our problems and to cope with what goes on around us. We begin to learn about rhetoric and how to use it—that is, if we become mature. If we do not use these methods, we make demands; we grab, we become threats to the existence of others, and we suffer the consequences.

Human beings seem to delight in false security. Bottled odors, complicated clothing, and yards of rolling hair do not protect from the environment. Man's naked, pink skin is useless against heat and cold. He hasn't the speed to pass a slow-moving rabbit, or the strength to wrestle a semi-grown grizzly. He can't even stand between a hungry hog and the feeding trough. The human is just not physically equipped to protect himself from his environment. But when he learns to exchange symbols in a cooperative way, according to the rules, he can and does acquire the ability to protect himself. Communication is the substance of cooperation. It is, incidentally, also the substance of conflict, for once words become part of personality they can maim as well as support. So the mature man has to be careful about how he uses his words. He needs to fit them to his society. And at the same time, he must retain his uniqueness so that he can take his stand when things look difficult and when there is an issue to deal with.

A view of the "world-in-which-I-live" is molded of perceptions. Everything that hits your eyes, ears, nose, mouth, and skin, does something to you. Perceptions are not filed neatly and uniformly in everyone's head. We are all our own secretaries with our own personal filing system. We tend to store our words in unique ways, retaining enough common meaning so that we can communicate with others, but always preserving unique interpretations which make us interesting to others as well as to ourselves. A person can share your cake with you, but he can never know the taste of it as you do. And this is what makes our existence so perilous and so rhetorical. Perilous, because our misunderstandings rise precisely in these very personal areas, and rhetorical because the only way we can work out

of our symbolic disagreements is through the sharing of talk, persuasion, argument, reasoning, within the framework of social rules.

Examining the steps through which the child goes as he develops
his symbolic skill will provide an insight into the way in which human
speech functions to make us what we are.

A child first makes random sounds. He is responded to, and he
learns somewhere along the way that he can substitute a sound for a
thing or an action. He may get confused at first. He may call out
"daddy" and expect his bottle. He needs to go through a period of
imitation where he learns some specific associations. He is socialized into the verbal community of his family. He also has to wait
until his vocal organs mature in order to make some of the sounds
that are required of him.

As he grows, he experiences responses to his words. He stores
these responses, keeping the positive ones in one place and the
negatives in another. He learns something about what he is capable
of accomplishing with others. If he has cold and rejecting parents,
he may learn how incompetent he is, and if his parents are overly
permissive, he may get an exaggerated sense of his power. At some
point, however, he needs to go out into the world and test his skill on
strangers. He goes to school and learns the talk of a new community.
He runs into all manner of children and teachers, each unique and
each struggling to maintain the social continuity. Gradually, based
on responses made to him, he finds a role in the community of his
peers. He keeps going through these growth stages. He goes from
elementary school to high school, from playground to bed chamber.
He learns how to cash in on some of his skills to make money, to
acquire power, to get the things he wants.

At some point, he is able to extend his self-awareness to others.
Childhood is a very egocentric time. The young child thinks of the
world only in terms of how it treats him. As the child grows he discovers that other children cry, that he can bring about tears or
laughter depending on how he acts toward others. Finally, as a
mature communicator, he builds a personal world of ideas and symbols which serves as a source for his choices about the world outside. He tests what he sees against this inside world. He looks at
problems through memories of experience stored in this world. He
learns what things work for him and what things do not, and he
achieves a sort of steady state of behavior, where others come to ex-

pect him to act and speak in certain consistent ways. When this happens, he has a personality. To the extent that projection of the personality can take into account the needs of others, the child can be an effective and mature communicator. He will persuade, not demand. He will think in terms of what is valuable to the other and not only in terms of what he wants at a particular moment. He will then be an adult.

What we see of adults is the outward projection of the internal world. That is why it is so hard to predict how people will respond. We do not know what is going on inside another's head. We can only guess at it from what we see him do. "I love you," may or may not represent a strong, positive emotion. It is an easy phrase to say, but a hard phrase to interpret. Thus, much of our life with others is spent trying to figure if they really mean what they say.

If the child is successful at maturing, there will be some agreement with what goes on in his head and what goes on in reality. This is important to us in our dealing with others. Excessive suspicion can lead to paranoia. Excessive trust can lead to the "con." What we all try to do is store up experience so we can decide what is best to do in any given instance. Once again, we offer the word "rhetoric." We live our lives rhetorically, trying to find out what works best with others. And "best" is easy to define in this case. We mean whatever gets others to see us as we want to be seen.

We soon find out what we can't do. The twenty-fifth attempt to climb the rope might give you some idea of whether or not you will be an athlete. Experimenting with styles will draw a few laughs and will quickly tell you what style goes well with you. Sadly, we get far more definitive information about the "can't do's" than the "cans." Most of us have a hard time, throughout our adolescence, trying to figure out who we really are and what we are capable of doing. We have lost the glow of youth; being a fireman or a nurse doesn't look good to us any more; and we know that there are a few limitations that might keep us from being president of the United States. The problem is finding out what we are suited for. Most individuals think there is some mystery and magic in this process, and they wait for some kind of revelation to tell them who they are. But there is no secret: we **are** the roles we play well. We **are** what we can do. And most of the things we can do we can learn how to do, if we want to.

Some things are important and some are not. Countless businessmen go out on the golf course every Sunday and curse their "luck" because they can't play like a pro. What they fail to realize is that the pro puts in as much time at golfing as they do at business. The golf pro, for all they know, may be cursing his "luck" because he is not a good businessman. So what does this have to do with speech?

Remember, we told you that the ability to express yourself in symbols is really what makes you human. The ability to communicate is far too important to everyone to leave to chance. Too many decisions that are going to be made about you are based on your ability to communicate. Whether you get the job, whether he walks to the altar with you, whether you get elected, whether you have friends—all these things depend on your ability to persuade others that you are the kind of person they want to be with, trust, do things for. Thus, we become very concerned with our skills at projecting the kind of person we would enjoy being.

That is a reason children play. The whole process of learning is a process of communication. Every response to the child helps him to try new things and learn to manipulate new ideas, or to avoid some danger. To insure growth, a person must be in touch with others in order to get confirmation. Stifled interaction in the early development of a child is the substance out of which later mental illness is built.

By studying the child's development of identity, we can learn to understand how important communication skill is to our own personal growth. The child participates with others out of a need to try various roles. These roles are behavior styles which he wants to use in order to get what he needs and wants from the others around him. He discovers that one technique that works with mom and dad does not work with the kids in the alley. He becomes a mechanic, and the behavior styles are his tools. He needs to find the proper tool for the proper job.

He does his first testing in the family. He learns how to influence mother first, and if he is lucky enough to have a mother that doesn't give him confused answers, he learns a style of behavior. If he is compelled to use violence in order to influence mother, he may learn that he needs to use violence on the others around him as well. But violence is not rhetoric. The ancient Greeks used to call it "inartistic proof." They said that it is not reasonable and humane to win your point through threats and extortions, tortures and compulsions. Civilized men reason with one another. Thus, when we find a child engaging in violent activity early in life, we may subject him to treatment in order to make it possible for him to function in society later on. If he persists in his violent (acting out) behavior, it may be necessary for society to take him out of the game, either by branding him a criminal or mentally ill. In either case, he surrenders his freedom to make rhetoric and he is compelled to follow the pattern laid down for him by others.

Another possibility is the child who withdraws from participation. All of us have met quiet people. We sometimes call them "good listeners." When they finally talk, we are amazed, but we usually do not take them seriously. The old adage, "still waters run deep" really doesn't make much sense. Most still waters are stagnant and are covered with green slime. No offense, but excessively quiet people are often quiet because they have not learned technique. It is not that they are "reserved" or "thoughtful." They usually either have nothing to say, or if they do, they do not know how to say it.

In any case, it is never too late to begin to learn skill at oral communication. It is relatively easy if you understand the first premise: that it is your obligation to persuade the other person that you are the person you think yourself to be. No fraud, no sham. Just honest persuasion. I **can** be trusted. I **am** a worthy leader. I **do** have a good idea. I **should** get the promotion. Yes, by golly, you will buy a used car from me.

Teaching speech would be a waste of time if your whole personality was shaped in childhood. There are some authorities like Eric Berne in **What Do You Say After You Say Hello** that claim your life script is shaped by the time you are seven. So what! Berne made a very good living changing life scripts. That's mostly what psychiatrists get paid for.

But you don't have to wait until rigor mortis sets in with your personality before you start worrying about how to change. It is possible, without going to a shrink, to learn new styles of behavior. And it is amazing how quickly people change when they discover that a small behavioral change on their part will suddenly alter the way in which most other human beings respond to them.

Adults are very concerned with "face." It is important to us that we save "face," a capacity that we used to reserve only for inscrutable Orientals. Many of us do not risk associating very much with others because we are too concerned about "face." We need to keep a constant advertisement up that our self-esteem has escaped undamaged from the bomb blast. The tough part is that we have to convince ourselves as well. We have already learned that there is considerable risk in speaking out, in any situation, but we have already learned that there is little possibility of gain without speaking out.

One line of defense we have can be thought of as the "arrow shot into the air" technique. We close our eyes and shoot a dart, claiming innocence of the target. When we damage another person, we claim, "I didn't mean it. I didn't want to hurt **you.**" Who then? We set a defensive wall around ourselves and keep everyone out, friend and enemy alike. Most of these types of communications are meant for protection, but they show little concern for the self-esteem of other persons. As pointed out, it is only when you discover that others can be hurt, just as you can, that you begin to achieve maturity as a communicator.

The mature communicator will reserve his combative posture for real issues. He will not engage in argument unless it is worth it, and he will try to win with words about the issue not with slams about the person. People who argue threaten other people. We all tell each other: Don't rock the boat or don't make waves. But sometimes waves are necessary. In fact, there is little progress on the surfboard of life without them. The trick is in knowing what is worth arguing about.

All of this information we hold in our inner world. What we do with others out there depends on the values we have inside. In our fantasies, we can be tigers; but we also know that tigers get shot, and so we learn to approach the other with caution. Sometimes we use excessive caution; and then we get shot as a rabbit. Somehow, it is necessary for the mature adult to blend his ethics and his strategies and go after what he needs to get by taking into account that everyone he meets **is doing the very same thing.** We use our rhetoric to make bargains. Our losses are more than compensated for by our gains.

If you have $300 to spare, the Dale Carnegie course can teach you how to be a winner. It is based on the precept that it does not matter what **you** mean. What is important is what the people around you **think** you mean. The Dale Carnegie people work on voice and expression in order to get your meaning across to others. They don't bother much about what is going on inside you. They teach you skill at delivering your message so that it gets through whatever resistance the other person is putting up. It is a process of teaching the management and control of words in order to achieve your goals. We declare that this is useful, but that there is a good deal more that you need to learn in order to become an effective communicator. We think you need to know how your increasing skill at speech is going to affect you **inside.** We think you ought to know that there is a close relationship between your inner world and what happens to you "out there." We hope that your knowing this will enable you to control what you seek to become; and will help you to become it with full concern in mind about the development of the other guy.

Summary. The sociologist Erving Goffman has pointed out that the responses to a communication are never fully predictable. For example, we don't know what you think of this book, how close you are to burning it or cursing it. But with this in mind, it is advisable to try to cultivate a sensitivity to communication. Part of speech training is learning how to control the environment with words. Another part is being aware of how others are trying to control you and what methods and means they are using.

We need to be sensitive to the most basic communication breakdown that comes about when we are not concerned enough about the impact our words have on others. Communication breakdowns also occur when speakers cannot cope with responses from others. The effective speaker needs to cooperate with the welfare of the other in mind all the time, but he also has to know that he can be misunderstood. There is no way to avoid misunderstanding, and one of the goals we try to reach as speakers is learning how to cope with the situation when things get out of hand.

A speaker can avoid feeling threatened by avoiding "either-or" thinking. Responses are not one thing or another, but they fall on some kind of continuum, almost a rainbow of responses, each color blending subtly into the next. Listeners are not either hostile or friendly, but have a potential for both and to various degrees. They may like you very much and find your ideas annoying, or they might like your ideas and think you are a fool. Any and all combinations are possible. But most listeners, unless they are prodded by the speaker, remain in a state of neutrality. They are not apathetic, for if they were completely apathetic they wouldn't have come to listen. But they are not as concerned about your ideas as you are. That's why you are the speaker and they are the listeners. They will wait for you to persuade them, to convince them that they ought to move in the direction you have in mind.

No listener will get involved in a transaction with you unless you show him that there is something for him in it. A speaker cannot achieve his goals with an audience unless he can show that audience that their goals have a better chance of being realized if the speaker realizes his goals. No listener is so much an altruist that he will do something for your good alone. He will inject himself into every request you make and he will ask, "Do I want and need to know this?" "Should I believe this?" and "What will it get me if I do this?" Decisions are made in terms of potential personal gain. Once again, "The fool tells me his reasons; the wise man persuades me with my own."

Part of a speaker's training is in the realm of the unexpected. Rhetoric deals with uncertainty. A speaker geared to the unpredictability of the people around him will develop skills at adapting in order to meet changing conditions. He will not waste his time cursing the audience for not being with him; he will try to figure out what state of mind they are in and he will move to meet them. Great style is fine, but it doesn't matter at all if the message makes no sense or threatens the listener. Most of us have had experience with books with beautiful covers and fancy words that made no sense at all. We respond by ignoring the books, regardless of what the literary critic tells us. If it is not for us, it is not for us, and that's it. The literary critics can play their own game.

The more you try to stylize, the more pretentious you will appear. The more you try to be helpful to your audience, by organizing so they can understand and choosing information that will be useful to them, the more likely it is that they will follow you. You, the speaker, are gambling that you will be able to cope with the sideshow of responses the listeners will present. You need to raise the odds by preparing to meet them.

A good speaker evaluates himself constantly while he speaks. He observes and evaluates what he sees in the audience. He makes decisions about what to do based on what he knows about himself and what he thinks he knows about the audience. He makes inferences. He has no facts. He can raise the odds that he can guess correctly, but he can never find a scientific formula that will tell him what is right and wrong in every case. That is the basic uncertainty about speaking; and it doesn't matter whether it is you and your husband, you and your boss, you and your class, you and the jury, you and your congregation, you and your client, you and your friend. It doesn't matter what the situation is. It is uncertain, and that is the one certainty that we have about it. We want to play our role as best we can, try to avoid looking phony, try to make the other feel that we are on his side (and incidentally, the best way to do that is really to be on his side), avoid threats and coercions, reason the thing through like a human being, and recognize that in any case we might lose. But if we play well, our wins will compensate for our losses.

Each time we communicate, we shape, partially, our personality. We are learning constantly who we are and what we can do by being who we are and doing things. We achieve involvement, a sense of adventure, and a sense of risk. Now you are ready for the next chapter, where we will begin to learn how to put it together.

It's exercise time.

Exercises

1. Let's see if you can analyze some of your dyads. What do you talk about with your parents? What topics do you avoid at all costs?

Why do you avoid those topics? Can you talk about them with your brothers and sisters (if any), cousins, uncles and aunts? All right, so you have no relatives, you are an only child, orphaned at youth. How about your friends? What topics do you avoid with your friends? Do you have some friends that you talk with about one kind of thing and other friends that you talk with about more personal matters? How did you discover this? What mistakes did you make before you found out what you could discuss with whom?

Maybe you don't want to talk about this with the whole class. Maybe you don't want to talk about it with anyone. Why would you make this choice? What risks would you take if you discussed these matters with the entire class?

2. Let's consider some of your rotten speech experiences. Think about the worst speech experience you can remember, for instance, the time you gave a speech to the whole school and forgot half of it, or when your English teacher gave you an "F" for the book report on which you worked so hard. Maybe it was when you tried to convince Sally Anne that she ought to go steady with you and she picked your best friend. Or the time you stood up at the meeting to talk and your slip was showing. You think it up and write it down in every gory detail. Now read your papers to each other—but before you do that, make some bets about what all of those papers have in common. You might try to answer the question: What did I really lose? And then, of course, you can go on and figure out (good old hindsight) what you might have done to win.

3. How about audiences? Sit yourself down in a circle with your classmates and have a brainstorm session on "things we know about audiences." Everyone begin a sentence with, "Audiences are . . ." At what point did you start laughing so much you couldn't go on?

4. Have a daydream on me! Think what you would look like if you appeared on the public platform in a truly heroic pose? Where would you be? Who would you be talking to? About what? What would your position be? How would the audience respond to you? Get the speech together and play it out. For once, act like a senator or the world's greatest salesman. And incidentally, try to answer the question, how did your daydreamed success differ from your real failures that you talked about in question two?

5. Analyze an audience. Here are some topics. You may add to the list.

dogs	baseball	woman's lib
the president	my school	dope
airplanes	calculus	dentists
socialized medicine	the king	the female mind
men, in general	athletes	knitting
zippers	brassieres	books
professors	labor unions	maternity wards
tricot panties	deodorants	the uncola
Godzilla	King Kong	Wonder Woman

You name it. Just take one of those topics at random and match it with each of the following audiences.

this class	your parents	your minister
your boy friend	your girl friend	your coach
your music teacher	the gang on the corner	the lunchroom crowd
the Rotary Club	the church group	the P.T.A.
the alumni association	a group of professors	doctors
policemen	a woman's lib group	union members

Maybe you can add a few more. This should give you some idea of what you have to find out about audiences.

Now you match it up by answering the following questions:

What does the audience know about it? How do you know they know it?
What does the audience think about it? How do you know they think that?
What do you know about it?
What you think about it?
What would you like to say about it?
How do you think your audience would take to that?

The big question after you get the answers, is what you should do about them when you prepare your speech. Try to answer this question before reading the next chapter.

6. What do you believe about people sitting out there? What signifies people are paying attention? What do you do when you pay attention? What signifies that the audience is bored? What do you do when you are bored? What signs indicate hostility? What do you do when you are hostile? What signifies friendliness? What do you do when you are friendly? Where did you get the information you have about people? You can discuss this one in class. It would be interesting to see how much you disagree and why.

7. This is a hazardous exercise. Either do it in private or with someone you trust thoroughly. Don't let your instructor talk you into doing it in class. Answer these questions:

> Who are you? Who told you so?
> Who would you like to be? Why? Do you think you could ever be that? What would you have to do in order to be that?
> Who do your friends think you are?
> Who do your parents think you are?
> How could you go about getting your friends and parents to see you as you want to be seen? Or even as you really are?

Do you understand why this is a question that should not be done in class? One thing you may discuss in class, however, is why this question should not be discussed in class. That's enough. Go on to the next chapter and start learning how to speak out.

Getting started.

THREE

Getting started

Preparing for social conversation is difficult. Skilled conversation-alists have developed their abilities over the years. They have a file of stories and examples for all occasions, and somehow, they seem to be able to come up with just the right thing, no matter to whom they are talking. They have also learned when to shut up and give the other guy a chance. They are strategists. They have figured out how to spend time enjoyably by persuading others to be interested.

For most of us, however, conversation is a difficult chore. We claim that we don't like "small talk." When we have to present ideas, we get confused and excited. Sometimes we get into arguments with our good friends over matters that really aren't that important. Even worse, we sometimes keep talking about the same old thing, over and over again, until the listener can almost predict what we are going to say. For those who are reaching out and trying to find friends, the advice that a conversational situation is just as rhetorical as a public speaking situation might be a great help. We can look at a simple model that applies to all communication in order to get an idea of the similarities.

A basic communication diagram

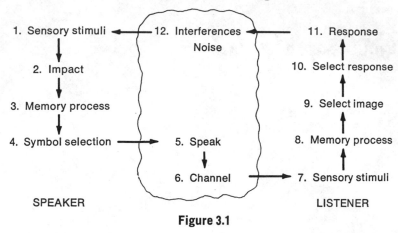

Figure 3.1

Any speaker must have a goal, whether he is in a social conversation, a committee meeting, or delivering a public speech. He must prepare in advance to achieve that goal. He must understand what needs to be known about his audience, and he must have his topic "together," if he is going to have the desired impact. Perhaps the chief difference between social conversation and public speaking is that the response in social conversation is more rapid and more immediate, and the participants take turns occupying the "platform." That's all. Believe us when we tell you there is even more at stake in socialization than in public speaking. Your friends, now and in the future, will come to you based on the image you present in social conversation.

So, as we look at the model in Figure 3.1, we shall think both of formal and informal speech settings in order to understand the basics of oral communication. We shall need to introduce some technical words, but we shall try to explain them as we go along. Just follow the numbers and arrows through the explanation.

The speaker is on the left-hand side. The listener is on the right. In formal occasions, the speaker remains the speaker throughout. In social conversation, at the time of response (11), the listener might well become the speaker. We start with stimulation (1) in the speaker. Anything the speaker sees or hears from the outside world can start stimulating him. He notices some problem. He sees a person he would like to meet. It is time to start his speech; the chairman has just introduced him. There is some critical moment that gets him started. It has an impact (2) on his mind. If he didn't notice it, it would not have an impact. In the previous chapter we talked about the figure-ground analogy. Usually what exists in the ground has little or no impact. It does not become the stimulation needed to start speaking. If it exists in figure, then it can be the stimulation for speech.

When we talk of impact we are talking about roughly the same thing that Lloyd Bitzer talked about when he introduced the term "rhetorical exigence." That is a complicated sounding term and it has all sorts of philosophical implications. For our purposes, we want it to mean noticing that there is something that needs doing that talk can help accomplish. When you have been stimulated to this point, you will start to speak.

Sometimes the impact comes well in advance of the performance. When you are to give a public speech, you know well in advance so that you can take time to prepare. Sometimes the impact comes during the normal course of conversation, or during a meeting. In either case, you go through the same process—for public speaking and social conversation, though the latter is so rapid that you may not even be aware of your planning.

Impact sets off your memory process (3). You begin a search to find out what you think and feel about what's happening, in order to make a decision regarding your response. Your memory search will bring up past experiences and personal goals. For example, you are in a social conversation and someone says, "If the Pirates keep playing as they are, they will manage to lose more games than any other team in baseball history." There is an impact. You are stimulated. You move through memory. You come from Pittsburgh and your civic pride is injured. You can't let someone talk like that about your Buckos. But you get some other bleeps as well. You once got into a fist fight during a baseball argument and the other guy broke your nose. You memory monitor tells you, "Take it easy." You are interested in maintaining a friendship with the other guy. Your practical monitor tells you, "Is it worth it to get into a fight with Louie over this issue?" But you still feel you have to say something that will salve your wounded pride. The practical monitor suggests, "Why not laugh it off." Good. A snappy retort is what is needed. You move through the symbol selection process (4) to see what you have lying around for just such a purpose. You remember that when you were in high school your math teacher bawled out Eddie Finster and told him he was the stupidest person she had ever had in class. Eddie said, "Well, if you're going to do anything at all, you might as well be best at it." There it is! There's your snappy retort, so you choose it, and put it into words and speak (5) to the other person: "Well, I always said the Pirates were the best—at whatever they do." So you now look like a quick-witted conversationalist. The women laugh, Louie smiles, the topic changes, and you come out smelling like the proverbial rose.

Suppose now you were employed by the sales department of the Pittsburgh Pirates and it was your job to sell advance season tickets, one year ahead. Here you are, confronted with the longest losing streak on record and you have to make a speech to the Metal Manu-facturers' Association dinner. They have previously bought more season passes than any other group on your list, but you are getting big competition now from the Steelers and the Penguins. No one loves a loser! The impact of the assignment is heavy, because it ap-pears to be a difficult task. The memory search is tedious and slow because you will need to look at all the difficult situations you can remember and try to figure how you pulled out of them. You might need to help your memory a bit by doing some research. Your goal is handed to you: you have to sell tickets. That's what you get paid for.

You finally hit on the theme that everyone has a little bad luck. You decide you will tell the story of the New York Mets and how they were the losingest team in baseball, but the fans stayed loyal and pulled them through until they became a winner. You decide to get emotional, to talk about how important fan support is to the team, how important it is to know that the folks at home are behind them. You decide to sound like a Knute Rockne of baseball. You also point out that while hockey and football overlap during the season, there is really no good place to take customers during the summer except to the Pirates games. You wire these ideas together into some kind of logical structure, select your symbols, and you are on your way. You give your speech!

Now, let's move to the other side of the diagram. Your listener or audience is also getting stimulated (7). He hears what you have to say. If your message falls into his ground, it won't have much impact. If he is paying attention and he gets it in figure, it may stimulate him to respond. If it doesn't stimulate a response, it will play some role in building the ground for his attention and eventually (we hope) something will come into figure for him. If it does get him to respond, he will start through his memory (8) and connect the words with some images (9). The image might be of you or of your ideas. In the social conversation, for example, Louie might get a new image of you as a smart respondent, and he may smile at you. The executive listening to the appeal to buy season tickets may think of how his son responded when no one came out to watch the Little League game and he may decide (10) to jump to his feet and declare, "I'll double my order for next season!" (11)

The process is continuous, and as the poet says, "There's many a slip twixt the cup and the lip." What you say passes through a channel before it gets to the listener's memory (6). On that channel, there are many things that can interfere with your idea (12). You will find these interferences referred to as **noise** in most books! Some of the most common interferences are:

Physical
Physiological
Meaning
Grammar
Psychological
Social

Physical noise refers to mechanical interferences like loud lawn-mowers and laughing persons. Or it may refer to the speaker's not talking loud enough, or talking too fast to be understood.

Physiological noise means the listener has a headache, his stomach is screaming for food, or he is thirsty or uncomfortable and is paying more attention to that than to what the speaker is saying.

Meaning noise refers to words that the listener doesn't understand at all or doesn't understand in the same way as does the speaker. For example, the word "rhetoric" that we have used to refer to preparation for persuasion might mean empty political talk to someone else. Or a word like "triskaidekaphobia" may mean nothing at all to the listener. (Look it up in an unabridged dictionary.)

Grammar noise refers to unclear constructions used by the speaker like, "The boy's mother saddled the mare and he jumped on her." It is not clear who did what to whom in that sentence, and when the listener hears it, it may jolt his mind while he tries to figure it out.

Psychological noise means any kind of threat that either speaker or listener feels as a result of the situation or the speech. Maybe the listener does not want to hear what you have to say because it might cost him money or he thinks it might threaten his self-esteem.

Social noise refers to different languages used by cultural groups, like the inability of the white middle-class to understand the natural language of the street, or the patient to understand the technical language of the physician.

You don't have to be a "noise analyst" to work with noise. What you have to know is that there are a lot of reasons why your listener might not get your message the first time or why it might not make an impact on him. Because of this it is best to try to repeat the main ideas in a number of ways. What doesn't get through in one way might in another.

In formal speaking, on the platform, there is a pattern to the words and ideas as they are spoken to the audience. But this pattern is not inherent in all communication. In social conversation we sometimes get an "Alice in Wonderland" sound. Everyone is talking about his own thing and paying little or no attention to what the other person is saying. It sounds like pingpong balls in a room full of kittens. It is this kind of situation that represents real meat to the good conversationalist, because he is able to make form out of the anarchy and get people interested in following some sort of conversational thread.

In formal communication, we need to be directed. There is a goal and some anticipated resistance to the goal. Both speaker and audience have something they want out of the situation. Both want to win, but it is not quite like a basketball game. Communication is the only game in which both parties can win, provided that the rhetoric operates well and the speaker persuades the audience that it was worth their while, and the audience persuades the speaker that he made an impact.

The flow of the process

There is a standard pattern or flow from the **speaker's** point of view. We are concerned with you as speaker in this section. Later on we will examine the process from the standpoint of the listener. For now, you need to understand that whether you are in a social conversation or giving a formal speech, there are a series of steps that you must go through. Some of them occur very rapidly and some of them take a great deal of time. Social conversation demands immediate processing of information and quick decisions. Public speaking demands careful, detailed planning and conversation. Participating in problem-solving discussion is somewhere between the two, involving careful preparation and rapid-fire exchange. But in any speech situation, you can find the steps.

Procedural steps for any communication

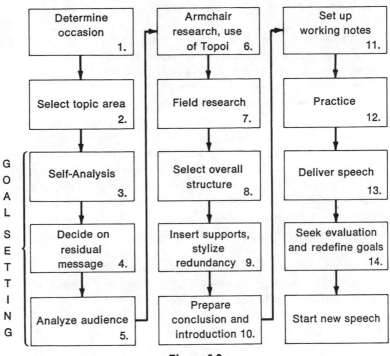

Figure 3.2

Determining the occasion

There is a motive or goal underlying any formal communication. The man who plans to deliver a speech wants to accomplish something.

He has an objective. He aims to accomplish it. He has been given a chunk of time by some group which represents the occasion for the speech. The occasion, in part, determines the approach he will take to his topic. The occasion tells the speaker something about the nature of the audience. He understands that he will not praise the women's lib movement at a meeting of brassiere manufacturers, or talk about good manners for women at a meeting of NOW. The occasion gives the speaker his first information about the kind of person he will speak to and under what circumstances, and provides the outside limits of what can be talked about. Usually, the discovery of the occasion also provides the speech topic, for in most formal situations a speaker is invited to address the group on a particular topic.

In social conversation, of course, topics are not assigned. They are also not assigned in college speech classes, so you will have to give some concern to possibilities. The nature of your audience and occasion will help you here. The college speech class, in order to operate, needs to depend on the students to generate their own topics. It is up to you to examine the occasion and yourself in order to discover what might be suitable for the particular set of circumstances. You may object to the assignment as being unrealistic, but you can make it realistic by thinking about a speech situation that you will be likely to encounter on your job. For example, if you are going to be an engineer, the occasion in the classroom might suggest that you talk about some engineering concept in order to help the non-engineers understand it better. But more of this in the next section.

A salesman cannot always select the time and place for his presentation. He needs to be ready with his persuasive speech so that he can seize the most appropriate occasion to deliver it. He is one speaker that is at the mercy of his client. Your situation in the speech classroom is something like that of the salesman. You will be required to present your speech on demand. The difference between you and the salesman is that for him, his profession provides him with something to say. You will either have to find a profession or be prepared to adapt to **your** occasion, i.e., the time you are called on to convince the instructor that you are worth an "A."

We could simplify this whole problem if your instructor were to assign you both time and topic. But your instructor doesn't know enough about you to decide on your topic. Giving the choice to you provides the opportunity to make your own judgments and build the image you want to build. Perhaps the best compromise is to start the course picking your own topic until your area of expertise is made clear, then permitting the instructor to make assignments for you.

There is another kind of speech occasion, the one dominated by a man who feels a strong need to speak. His personal need becomes a self-contained occasion. He is motivated by his drive to be heard, and he goes out to seek an audience for his ideas. Examples are the advocates that take command on social occasions, the "true believers" who take class-time to sound off, or those who organize protest meetings. You might be an advocate of women's lib or black power and get a reasonable hearing when you sound off, or you may believe in vegetarianism or cosmic dingdong or whatever. The more you sound off on your pet idea, the more you become identified with it, and the more people get bored with you. Because **you** want to speak doesn't mean that they want to listen. Thus, no matter what the urgency, customarily you wait for some kind of invitation before taking over the platform. The saddest sight of all is the man who stands on the street corner hammering out words of salvation through a tinny public address system as people silently rush past him, never noticing, and never "profiting" from his message.

Real and responsible advocates carefully develop an idea and offer others a chance to hear it. They may get an agent and go on a speaking tour. Because they have achieved celebrity status for their ideas, audiences customarily come to hear them; many will pay a considerable sum for a ticket to hear Dick Gregory, William F. Buckley, Betty Friedan, or Ralph Nader. Formal speaking tours are rewarding both spiritually and financially. In addition to getting paid, the celebrity image is enhanced. An invitation to appear before a legislative committee to present your ideas, or other opportunities to influence the society around you may result. But you must start in legitimate ways. The salesman with a great idea will try it out at the sales meeting. The teacher with a learning innovation will clear it through her superiors. Speaking prematurely, or on the wrong occasion, at best can mean an invitation to do it all over again at the right time and place, and at worst it can mean that your hearers will brand you as a fool or a bore and make you surrender your capability to be heard.

Thus giving attention to the occasion becomes the starter for the whole preparation process. Why the audience is there is as important as what the speaker is going to say.

Selection of the topic area

Persons with recognized capabilities and qualities are invited to address audiences. Most colleges, for example, arrange for some well-known public figure to address their commencements. The topic is usually an inspirational one, selected by the college and the speaker so that it is appropriate to the occasion. Mostly, the speaker will have the problem of tailoring his area of speciality to fit the occasion for the speech, taking into account the special needs of the audience. It is questionable who is the actual audience for a commencement speech. The graduates are much too concerned with impending celebrations to be very occupied with inspiration. The

**The occasion and topic area can be important factors
in the making of a good speech.**

show is directed to the parents, the alumni, and the brass, and it is the smart commencement speaker who knows this and plays to it in order to keep collecting those fat fees.

Those of you who are laboring through this book are not seeking a berth on the United States Olympic Speaking Team. When you do reach a point where you are qualified in some area, you will do the bulk of your speaking from topics from that area. When you are firmly committed to some idea or cause, you will find opportunities to speak on behalf of your cause. If you are qualified professionally or by commitment to speak on something, there is no reason why you cannot speak on it in class. If you know what your profession is to be, have some hobby to which you are dedicated, or if you belong to organizations or groups that advocate some particular cause, the speech classroom is an ideal place for you to sound off.

If you are not so committed, you may use the free choice of topic to select issues and ideas in your major area of specialization or your future vocation, with the class as a sounding board. You must, whatever you do, keep the audience in mind, for if they get bored or restless while you speak, you will probably lose in the contest for the high evaluation.

Any topic will do, really, if you can suit it to your audience. Simple curiosity has held many a classroom audience through speeches on rock climbing, the New England coastline, or the virtues of the two-cycle engine.

Here are some topics that might interest you. They have been delivered within the last two years in the authors' classrooms:

Problems in Treatment for Mental Illness on Campus
How Four Different Kinds of Levers Work
A Transportation Plan for Your County
Why We Need Jerry Rubin Back
The Work of a Lapidary
Raising Homing Pigeons
Hunting Game Animals With Bow and Arrow
History Will Know Nixon As Our Greatest President
History Will Know Nixon As Our Biggest Clown
Oil Geology of Israel
What Happens in an Encounter Group
How to Do Body Massage
The Basic Movements in Modern Dance

The Salary Differentials for Professional Women
Revise the State Anti-Abortion Laws
On the Wonders and Glories of Pot
Bring Back Prohibition
Cross-Country Jogging
Will There Ever Be Another Judy Garland
The Real Story of Gunga Din
Why Faculty Members Need a Labor Union
Learn How to Work With Your Hands, or You'll Go Mad

Time out: exercises

It is customary in these books to place all the exercises at the end of the chapter, as was our pattern for the first two chapters. But we will take a break and toss you some exercises when needed. You need some now.

1. Think about your future job. If you don't have a future job in mind, think of yourself as a civil service employee in the office of procurement of the United States Navy. After you declare your job, write down at least ten occasions when you might be called upon to speak about something related to the job. Think about audiences from one to one million. Talking to the boss, your wife, your husband, your kids, your colleagues, your friends, your customers, your congregation, all count. Don't stop until you have listed at least ten speaking occasions. Then share your list with classmates (this is a good assignment for small groups of three or four) and let them suggest opportunities you have missed.

2. Now take your list and add to it all the different topics you might be qualified to speak on five years from now. If you should become the best at whatever you are doing, what things would people expect to hear from you? List at least ten such topics. Then, while you are at it, see if you can think of ten things that you might advocate because of your job: political, economic, and social issues.

3. Now you are ready to get down to work. Try to list at least ten topics that you think you might be able to talk on now. Pick them from classes you have taken, experiences you have had, books you have read. In fact, if you want to make the assignment into a real doozy, list ten for:

Courses you have taken
Experiences you have had

Books you have read
Movies and plays you have seen

Then add ten more for each of the following categories:

Things that need changing on this campus
Things that need changing in my home town
Things that need changing at my home
Things that need changing in the country
Things that need changing in the state
Things that need changing in the world
Things that need changing about people in general

Then maybe five each for the following:

Good books I've read and you ought to read also
My great experiences in eating
My favorite recreation places

Finally, add perhaps ten wild-card topics that don't fit any of the categories. If you have trouble rounding out your list, get your group-mates to help you, and be sure the instructor has a copy of your list. One final job: After you get your list, pick out ten topics in any category that you like best, and think up three or four occasions where such a topic might be appropriate. Also start thinking about why people should be interested. Hang on to your list. You'll need it for some later exercises in this chapter.

Self analysis

OK, we've got some topics and occasions wired. Once you have a topic and you know when and where you are going to talk about it, you need to take a look at yourself and what you believe or feel or know about the topic. In social conversation, we all make fools of ourselves sometimes because we don't slow down enough to get the issue worked out. We find ourselves arguing the virtues of snake oil with some renowned physician or talking about our trip to Nova Scotia with a native of the province.

In social conversation we may have to put up with our own foolishness, but there is no excuse for it when we have to deliver a formal speech. The analysis of personal beliefs and commitments is the start of the goal-setting process, and it is absolutely crucial to success in platform speaking.

If you want to give information to an audience, you need to estimate how competent you are in the topic area, so you can decide
what you can and cannot do. Competency does not mean knowledge
you already have; in this case, it means what you have and what you
can get. In grade school, when you had to prepare a theme, you ran to
the encyclopedia and abstracted some dull passages and read them
to the class. The teacher graded them on spelling and punctuation,
and your classmates tried hard to stifle their yarns and guffaws lest
you do the same to them. The information you presented was irrelevant and uninteresting. In fact, nobody really gave a damn. So that
was not an exercise in public speaking.

Anybody can say, "Its rozzers to slip a cracker dropsy on snide."
But utterance alone is not enough. What kind of cracker? Why should
I care? How rozzer and when dropsy? Why should any person of sound
mind and body be interested in that? Why the hell are you talking
about it, if it makes no sense to you? The problem of getting something you can be committed to is crucial in developing skill. You
can't do the work needed unless you care about what you are doing.
Frankly, as a teacher, I get bored with and contemptuous of students
who stand in front of me and mumble lackadaisically on some topic
about which neither he nor I could care less. It is a real relief when
someone gets up and puts some spin on the ball and sounds off as
though something is important to him. It really doesn't matter how
simple the topic. You can do a great job with very simple topics, if it
matters to **you** whether you succeed or not. There is nothing to be
gained in a speech class with simply getting by. Anyone can do that.
The idea is to take the simplest of ideas and make them important,
and only if they are important to you can you do that effectively.

If your goal is to sell an idea based on personal beliefs, you must
give some thought to the current status of that idea. You might start
by discovering if your view is popular, or in the minority. Although
your audience might not reflect a cross-section of society, knowing
something about where the idea stands will help you decide on an
approach. If your idea is incredibly popular (control of pollution is
needed now!), you may go a good distance toward pushing the audience to action. If your idea is held by a minority (marijuana should
be legalized today!), the best you might be able to do is develop a
degree of tolerance in your audience. You might get them to accept
you as a believable person and finally to accept the notion that your

idea is not immoral. When the audience is likely to be evenly split on your idea (abortion should be the responsibility of the individual!), your goal is to shift the balance to your side by weighing the idea against alternatives and showing its advantages. Developing your goal will be the topic of the next section.

You are evaluated every time you speak to anyone. In your classroom, your instructor will probably give you a grade. So will your fellow students, though they won't write theirs in a roll book. Your speaking will give them an impression of the kind of person you are. In socialization, the decision the other person makes about whether you are worth seeing again is based on how effectively you present yourself and your ideas.

Everyone has a reputation which tends to distort what others think of him. In the classroom, your instructor can hardly avoid remembering your previous performances. He will know you as interesting, uninteresting, or somewhere in between. He will be looking forward to hearing you again or he will groan inwardly. Sometimes it gets so sticky that a person with a high reputation can do a bad job and get away with it, as the evaluator says, "He must be having a bad day." The person with a low reputation is not so fortunate. When he does a good job, the evaluator is likely to say, "Hmm, someone must have been helping him."

Another part of your reputation will be based on the contact you have had outside of class. Contact with your fellow students will have developed an image of you for them. Anytime you spoke to the instructor, greeted him in the hall, went to his office, will enter into his consideration of you. And it won't all be positive either. Many students handicap themselves severely by being too visible to the brass, while others handicap themselves equally badly by being invisible. Some kind of balance needs to be struck, so that when you do become visible, it is clearly on business and not on the con. Teachers are very sensitive about the con, although some folks get away with it all the time.

What people have heard about you will also play a role. The three elements: your previous performance, previous experience with others, and what is said about you, add up to your "image" at the time you mount the platform. As your image gets better and better, you are more likely to be believed and encouraged. When your image is not quite what it should be, people will tend to reserve judgment and play it cool. When your image is very bad, you may be greeted by either a hostile audience or rows of empty chairs. When President Nixon's popularity was at a low ebb, during the Watergate Affair of 1974, his managers were very careful about where he appeared in public. Either he went to "safe" territory like an agricultural college in Texas, or to places where even if audiences disliked him, they would not be able to do anything about it, like the United States Naval Academy. Near the latter days of his presidency, Harry Truman's stock was so high that he could appear anywhere and people would flock to listen to him.

This business of image is very important to effectiveness in speaking. Aristotle once said that there were three sources in persuasion: personal image, logic, and emotion, but image was the most important of all. In your assessment of yourself, you need to find out where you stand with those you are addressing. You don't dare make a false estimate. It is always better to undershoot than overshoot; take it easy, play it cool. None of us are ever what we would want to be in the eyes of others; though none of us are seldom as low as we estimate ourselves either.

You can see, that as we talk of image, we are also talking of "ethics." You get a good image by doing what other people find to their best interests. If you have held the attention of the audience during previous speeches, they will look forward to the present one, and they will be in a mood to pay attention. If, on the other hand, you have lied to an audience on previous occasions, word will get out, and what you say will be taken with a grain of salt. Fly-by-night, door-to-door salesmen have to keep moving from town to town. They don't dare stay too long in one place for fear word of their shady deals will get out. That's why communities have Better Business Bureaus. In addition to that, the reputation of your product will have a lot to do with your image. If you are representing a shabby product or an unpopular cause, people will tend to look critically at both you and your words, and you will have a hard time overcoming their resistance.

Much of your worth will be estimated by your attitude toward the audience. Regard them as a threatening mass, and your fear will show, stifling your effectiveness. Generally speaking, audiences should be regarded as courteous and capable of understanding your message. If you can't view your audience in this manner, then either revise your message until it is understandable, or don't speak at all.

If it is clear to the audience that you respect them and think of them as good people, they will do a great deal to support you. In the classroom, your listeners will have paid their dues with their own experiences in front of the group. Most of them will give you a fair hearing simply because they would do unto you as they would have you do unto them. When facing strangers, it is also safe to assume that they would have the same apprehensions about public speaking that you have. They will identify with your position even if they are stone cold to your point of view. Even if they reject your ideas, they will do it internally. They will not hiss and shout and they will leave alone those that agree with you.

Of course, in any audience, it is possible that there will be someone who will not give you a courteous hearing. These persons are a genuine threat to the speaker. They may heckle and show other audible and visible signs of disapproval. Sometimes it may take the police to move them from the audience. Nobel Prize winner William Shockley, in his attempts to speak at Ivy League colleges, was constantly confronted with hooting and jeering students who would not give him a chance to speak. They were so vituperative and vigorous in their hostility that his freedom of speech was jeopardized. Most of us, however, are not that provocative and controversial. Thus, when someone hassles us, the rest of the audience will take him to task and keep him quiet. Often an offensive person in the audience can do you a great deal of good. As he treats you unfairly, he pushes the audience into greater sympathy with you. If you do not let yourself get demoralized but continue to address your audience with respect, they will help you along to a successful conclusion. The rule of thumb is, speak to the friendly ones.

Your personal analysis must give you some information about how you see the human beings you are going to address. If you find yourself calling them "dumb jerks" or (expletive deleted), then perhaps you should forget about the whole thing.

Another area you will want to explore is your identity in relation to the listener. You may be speaking to an audience of those who know you. Certainly in this class, you have a reputation. When you address your family over the dinner table, they have a fairly accurate idea of who you are. It is very valuable to know where you fit into the group. If you are a leader, you can expect support from the bulk of the group, but you have the obligation to give them definitive leadership in the form of new ideas and organization to implement the old ones. If you have a reputation as a joker, you'd better crack a few in the speech, just so people won't get carried away with anticipation—but don't let them take over the speech, because you may want your audience to see you as a more serious person than they have previously. If you are "one of the troops," you can count on courtesy. And so long as you don't threaten the leaders too much, they will probably mobilize support for you. If you have a reputation as a guerilla fighter, even when you represent the most popular cause, people are likely to be suspicious. If you have been seen as a "nerd," you will have to take time to develop yourself as credible before you can really get to the meat of the speech.

Your personal appearance also communicates, and part of your self-analysis will be focused on selection of the proper garb for the occasion. Back in the 1940s, a very competent senator once lost the votes of the United Mine Workers because he wore a blue serge suit and patent leather shoes into the mines. The essayist, Tom Wolfe, in his piece called "Mau-mauing the Flak Catchers," told how members of the black community in a large city tried in vain to get the attention of the welfare people focused on some of their problems. When the protesting blacks put on dashiki shirts and went into the office cursing and yelling, the civil servants snapped to and did the job they were supposed to do.

A great many beginning teachers make the mistake of trying to dress like "one of the boys." The girls in their cute little mini-skirts suggest to their female students that they are competitors and to their male students that they are targets. The boys in their blue-jeans and muscle shirts suggest to the girl students that they are available and to the males that they are not to be respected. Propriety says that you dress: (1) like the person you are, (2) like your role suggests, and (3) like the occasion demands. One would not mount a pulpit for a formal religious ceremony in blue-jeans, but one would not go to a folk mass in a tuxedo. No one expects a doctor to be a slob, and no one expects a sportsman to be a fashion plate. All of this should be taken into account.

Your appearance has the power to shape audience attitude. Based on the way in which they see you, individuals make mental associations. This activity is hard to control. However, if you understand that your audience can be put into a position where they may irrationally oppose both you and your ideas, you are better prepared to plan ahead and make sure this does not happen. Stop for a moment and consider how you size up another person. There may have been times when you met someone and gave him a low evaluation for no good or obvious reason. His appearance led you to a decision. Often, our initial attitudes turn out to be wrong, and we have an opportunity to correct them, but in a speaking situation, this opportunity never comes. However the specific audience sees you will influence it for this speech, and you do not get a second chance. (In instant replay, it still comes out the same.)

Finally, your manner of speaking will contribute to audience response. The probability of achieving your goal is increased if the audience can hear you and understand what you say. Persons with annoying voices or who pronounce words in ways that are unfamiliar to the audience usually have to fight against considerable confusion in order to make their point. This does not mean that you must conform to some arbitrary standard of good diction. If you speak a dialect, Brooklynese, southern, or whatever, you probably can be understood perfectly well in your own home area. The only problems you will confront is when you meet an audience to whom your speech is unfamiliar. They may well begin to concentrate on how you sound rather than on what you say. If there is any doubt in your mind about the effectiveness of your manner of speaking, a professional can equip you with some simple exercises to improve your intelligibility in short order. Your instructor may need to call your attention to problems like this, and he should be able to recommend some remedies to you.

Time out.

Time out: exercise

It's time to continue the exercise we started in the last section. Take one of your lists of topics, one that you would bet has ideas that you can use. Do a **private** analysis of who you are in relation to this idea by answering the following questions:

1. What do I know about the idea? Where can I get more information?
2. What do I believe about the idea? Where can I get support for my idea?
3. How do I stand with my audience? Who am I to them? Who do I want to be? What does this mean for my speech? How must I handle the ideas and the presentation in order to reach the audience?
4. What reservations and misgivings do I feel about myself? Why do I feel them? Will they show? Has anyone ever told me about them? What do I need to do to overcome them?
5. What should be my "image" for this speech? How will I have to slant the speech? How will I have to dress?

Naturally, you can see why this should be private business and not shared with the class. If you have a trusted friend, you might seek some confirmation or denial from him. Maybe you have a distorted view of yourself. You might also check with your instructor who can tell you rather objectively how you come across to the class and to him.

Your goal: the residual message

Now we come to the critical step in speech preparation—figuring out exactly what you want to communicate to your audience. Whether spoken or written, formal or informal, the fate of a message depends on two things: the ability of the communicator to isolate his purpose clearly, and the ability to coordinate personal resources to achieve his purpose. Planning must take place before the speech is given. In social conversation, we must equip ourselves with decision points which guide us to the kind of impression we want to make on our conversation partners. In a formal speech, we must make the decision well in advance.

The standard way of looking at speech purposes is to divide speeches into three types. A speaker might want to inform or instruct. He might want to persuade—to change minds, to move to action. Finally, he might want to speak simply to stimulate some emotional response, to entertain in some way. Modern critics have left this list of possibilities as impractical.

In any case, what you finally decide must be made explicit. Once you try to do this, you will understand that no message can be communicated successfully without some emotional involvement and without some information. The listener must be emotionally involved, committed to listening to you. You know yourself that when something turns you on, there is pleasure in pursuing it. The whole process of getting and holding the listener's attention depends on the emotional involvement. So, even if the goal is simply to give some information, to show the audience how to do something, you will need to work on the audience's emotions by putting some emotional energy into the speech. The object of this is to **persuade** others that the information you are presenting is worth having.

If your decision is to persuade the audience to change their attitude or to do something, you will of course need to involve them emotionally, but you must also present them with information. You will need to make it worth their while to listen to you by giving them information they do not have. By combining information and emotion you can get the audience to have a stake in what they are to hear. In this sense, then, there is no subject that you can speak on that is **not** primarily persuasive. Initially, your task is: persuade the audience to commit themselves, to share psychological space with you, to get your remarks in figure and everything else pushed into ground.

Conveying information can sometimes be as stimulating as eating paper for lunch. All of us have sat through dull lectures, where we know our survival on the exam depends on how carefully we listen; yet the drone of the voice, and the utterance of fact after fact is more than we can handle. We nod, we doze, we snap to attention, write down a line or two, and later on panic because we do not have the message. Even when the stakes are very high, it is exceedingly difficult to listen to a purely informational speech. Stock market reports are always dull to the person who doesn't own stock. Lectures are always dull if the lecturer does not try to involve the students by showing how the material relates to them and their needs.

A show of personal involvement draws in and involves your listeners. That show, of course, moves the speaker toward the role of entertainer, but there is nothing wrong with this because it works. Information can be thought of as merchandise in a store. Merchandise has to be displayed well, otherwise shoppers will ignore it. Information must be put into a showcase of emotion, so that the audience will be attracted to it, and buy it, if it makes sense.

Thus, it is impractical to separate different kinds of speaker purposes. They do not function as isolated units. In practice, we are always informing, persuading, and entertaining. We are always giving some information, involving the emotions, and calling for action—even if the action is nothing more than sitting still and listening. A lecture on nuclear physics may not contain as much emotional material as a diatribe on the rights of some minority group. A speech supporting a political candidate will not be as informative as a speech predicting trends in the American economy. We may need to divide the purposes sometimes for the classroom, and we think in terms of "primarily." My speech is **primarily** informational, but I will have to entertain the audience to hold their attention and persuade them to listen to me. My speech is **primarily** persuasive, but I will have to entertain the audience to hold their attention and I will have to give them some information as a basis for my persuasion. My speech is **primarily** entertaining, but it will have to have some information in it, and I will have to persuade the audience that I am funny and that they should laugh.

The communication diagram in Figure 3.1 offers a format on which to base your speech purpose. One of the things we pointed out is that interference (noise) gets in the way of your message, and your job as a speaker is to develop some kind of method of getting through all that interference into the head of your listener. When this model was first presented, it was based on a diagram invented to help solve some of the problems encountered on telephone circuits. Now we certainly don't declare that human beings are mechanical instruments, and we don't even think it is a particularly good idea to draw diagrams that suggest that they are. But sometimes we can learn from problems that others have solved, and in this instance our telephone engineers, using their diagram, discovered that to break through the mechanical noise encountered in their work, they needed to amplify their message, to make it stronger. They used the word "redundant" to describe this process.

You are confronted with the same problem when speaking. There may be outside noises; you have to make your voice louder. You may have to speak more slowly or pronounce your words more carefully.

More than likely, however, the way you talk is OK, but what you say is not clearly understood by the other person because of the words you use, because of the way in which you have them put together, because of some social difference, or because your listener is day-dreaming or concentrating on some personal problem. You try one method to get through the noise and you are blocked, so you try another. When you are talking to one person, the problem is easy to handle.

> Give a quarter-turn on the bmmnnftz with the ratchet!
> **Huh?**
> Give a quarter-turn on the spindle with the ratchet.
> **How do I turn the ratchet on?**
> Hold it in your hand.
> **Oh. What's a spindle?**
> The round thing there.
> **Give me a quarter.**
> Why?
> **So I can make a quarter-turn.**
> No. See when you turn it all the way around, that's a whole-turn. Half-
> way around is a half-turn. A quarter of the way . . .
> **I get it.**

Or,

> I think your candidate is a consummate and contumelious, calculating
> conniver.
> **Thanks, I think you are backing a good man too.**
> But I insulted your man.
> **You did?**
> Yes.
> **Oh, well, yours is one, too.**

There was one authority who once said that there is no human utterance that cannot be misunderstood if the hearer tries hard enough. What goes on in a typical person's mind is enough to confuse the issue anyway, and when you put it together with a spoken message from somewhere else . . .

All kinds of noise have a damaging effect on spoken messages. Only a small portion of what you say will get through the barrier and be remembered by your listener. The estimates vary from as low as 5 percent to as high as 16 percent remembered. Whatever, the figure is still painfully low. Listeners just simply will not hear words. They will lose a whole sentence responding to a twinge from the seat to their seat. It is difficult to get what the other person is saying when your head is exclaiming, "This room is like a furnace, and how the hell do they get chairs so long?" Some ideas will get lost in a volley of words: "And so, let me recapitulate by saying that we must eradicate the endoclature of the sizemodic endolophine." Asks the listener, "Whadd'e say?" "Hey Louie," he taps his friend, "whadd'e say?" And Louie misses the next two or three paragraphs.

Your listener may also get caught up in:

> How can he wear a tie like that with that suit?
> Who does he think he's talking to, some little kid?
> Guys like him are all alike, always putting us down.
> I want to go home in time to catch Kojak on the tube.
> Holy mackerel, look at the legs on that blond in the aisle seat.

Your listener can manufacture or find a myriad of distractions. Your job is to break through. And you might as well know that the most experienced speakers understand fully that the bulk of what they say will get lost somewhere between their mouths and their listeners' heads.

Stop: exercise

Here's another quickie exercise to get you acquainted with noise and how it works. Keep a log book for one day. List in it things you have said to others and others have said to you. How often did you have to repeat? How often did you have to ask another person to repeat? How can you account for the necessity to repeat?

See if you can sit with a group of your classmates and make a list of things that you think about during lectures. Make your list as long and as specific as you can, and when you are done share it with the other groups. Think of yourself, now, as a lecturer who has to talk to you with all of those distractions. That's all. Just think about it.

The problem. How can we get the listener to focus on what **we** think is really important? That is, if we know he is going to miss a great deal, how can we increase the odds that he will not miss what **we** want him to get.

If care is not taken in meeting this problem, the listener may end up remembering a lot of unrelated facts. Beginning speakers are sometimes astounded by what their audience remembers, although they are appalled when it is not what they think they should have remembered. The speaker's problem is to focus the audience on his main idea within the given listening time. He must overcome noise so that the audience will retain what the speaker thinks is important.

Now, how to handle this problem? In the first place, you will have to make some decisions. This was suggested when you were asked to write that list of topics. At this point, you'd better be ready to select one and run with it. It ought to be one you know something about, care about, and think might be interesting to your audience. You ought to know where to get more information about it and have some idea why it ought to be important to your listeners. (This is like a card trick: pick a topic, any topic, and keep it in mind as we go through the next bit of stuff!)

So far we have subjected you to a lot of words and complicated descriptions. Now we can tie the whole thing into a recognizable bundle that can be used in the speaking situation. To solve this problem, take your topic and ask: "What about this topic do I want to make redundant?" What is there about this topic of yours that you think is worth repeating several different times in order to overcome the barriers that your audience can raise against you?

Later on we will give you tools such as structural formats and supports. You need something on which to use these tools. Giving a speech is a task that requires tools. The listeners will be sitting in front of you, each one with his own way of listening; each person operates in his own unique manner. The tools of redundancy are designed to fit the different kinds of persons in the audience: they are different ways in which the speaker may accomplish a single goal. One tool might be statistics and another time-structure. Combining the two would offer the accountants in the audience an idea of how important conserving maple trees is over a period of years. Another tool is metaphor, which can be employed to help the poets in the audience understand the importance of conserving maple trees. Appeals to the emotions are tools: "Think of the golden, thick, sweet, sticky syrup pouring out of the jug on a cold Sunday morning, flowing down the sides of grandma's buckwheats—you can't get maple syrup out of an oak tree!" Just a little deference to the gourmets in the crowd. For those who like stories, the speaker can provide one. For those who like narratives, examples, humorous tales, they are available. Visuals can be used: photos, drawings, cartoons, graphs. And each of these tools is redundant because each tool seeks to **reinforce** the idea that maple trees are in danger and must be preserved. Whatever else is left in the listener's mind, he must remember to preserve maple trees. The accountant won't remember much about syrup, but he may remember that the number of maples in the United States has declined 40 percent in the last five years—and that's why he will work to preserve maple trees. The poet may not remember the numbers, but he will remember the metaphors that make maple trees important to him. The residual message will be left in as many minds as possible, even though it gets into each mind in a different way.

What does this mean for the speaker? In order to do a successful job of building an entire speech around a single message, he must have his own goal sharply in focus. Let's review, for a moment, what we know about setting goals:

1. You must know where and when you are speaking and for how long.
2. You must know that it is necessary to hold the attention of the audience for the duration of the speech.

And we add:

3. You must have a residual message to leave in the mind of the listener and some method of determining how well that message was left.

Yes, **residual message,** the idea that breaks through the resistance, that stays in the listener's mind when everything else is forgotten. That is the **residual message.**

The whole idea of redundancy in order to get through a residual message may seem ridiculous. If the speaker has forty-five minutes, good grief, to center it all on one idea seems idiotic. It will bore the audience to tears. But think of the times you have sat for forty-five minutes listening to a lecture. How much did you really remember? Most of the time, if someone asked you what it was about, you could reply in one sentence.

The idea is to make the complexity of the message fit the time allowed. If you are giving a simple, five-minute speech in the classroom, you probably won't be able to cover "the basic issues involved in deciding on a construction style for a bridge." But you might be able to leave the audience with the idea that "designing the bridge is a controversial topic because there are different styles in construction." This small topic might be the introduction to the forty-five-minute speech, but for the five-minute speech, it becomes the entire topic.

Traditionally (and practically), organizing a speech can be summarized by a structural model like the one in Figure 3.3.

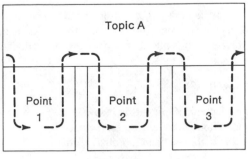

Figure 3.3

The speaker's topic rests on the supporting points. Each supporting point documents, proves, or explains the main point. Thus, you start by declaring your main point, that is, your **residual message.** Give your support number 1 and show how it supports the main message. Then move to point number 2 and show how it supports, then number 3. Close with a repetition of your main message. For example, the schools need federal aid because:

Support 1: Local communities don't have enough money.
Support 2. Local communities don't have enough technical skill.
Support 3. There is an excessive diversity in educational quality.

If you were writing the message, you would not need to be as repetitive as if you were speaking it. The reader of a message can go back to the first paragraph and check the main message. The listener cannot, and therefore, each point has to be stated and reiterated in the conclusion. The result is stylized redundancy.

Each of the supporting points could be a speech in itself. For example, local communities don't have enough money:

1. Four hundred twelve counties had to cut back on their educational offerings due to lack of funds. (Name some.)

2. More than 50 percent of the counties have reached their limit of taxa-
   tion. (Give some examples.)
3. Local communities have great demands on their limited resources.
   (Like road maintenance, welfare, police protection and fire fighting.)

If you were giving a long speech, you might be able to make all the
points. In a short speech, you would choose only one. In fact, in a
five-minute speech you might have to work like this:

> The schools need federal aid, but I don't have time to give you all the
> reasons, so, I will pick one (here comes the residual message): Four
> hundred twelve counties had to cut back on their educational offerings
> this year due to lack of funds.

(How do you know this?)

1. In the Encyclopedia of Education it says. . . .
2. Take Wombat County, for example. . . .
3. The NEA says there has been a reduction in. . . .

So, this pretty well documents the proposition that "Four hundred
twelve counties had to cut back on their educational offerings this
year because of lack of funds." We have three different kinds of
proofs to appeal to, at least three different kinds of minds.

And note that in this format, we could put the word "because" at
the end of each sentence, so that our structure of proof answers the
logical questions that would be raised by an intelligent listener.

Even if we were simply giving information: There are three main
social classes on the Island of Philoobia,

1. Shamans
2. Warriors
3. Workers

we could connect the sentences with "because" and make sense.

We shall go into detail on this kind of construction in the section
on structuring. When we get there, we shall suggest coming back to
this section in order to fit the structural ideas to your residual
message.

Now see a cartoon which illustrates the look of the speaking
situation. Picture a man-eating plant. Each jagged edge attracts
and draws the victim toward the central mouth. Your speech structure is made up of jagged edges (your supports) and the main mes-

Picture a man-eating plant.

sage, the central mouth. It is not so important that the people in the audience remember what each jagged edge is. What is important is that each jagged edge leads to that mouth **and nowhere else.** The listener must be methodically drawn to the speaker's main idea. Little should be left to his imagination, for your listener will misunderstand if he can possibly manage it.

Each of the barbs in the cartoon is a support for the residual message. Like fishing hooks, they are designed to catch and hold the listener's attention. Not all listeners; some will be caught on one hook, some on another. All of the hooks need to be interesting so that no one's attention is lost, and we need several hooks to bring in the maximum number of listeners. No part of the speech is extraneous. Beginning speakers usually have a great deal of difficulty making their points because they wander and flounder about with disconnected points. Often they have to yell at the audience, "You see, what I really mean is . . . " But if you have to do that, you are guaranteed ineffective. The whole point of organizing a message is to increase the speaker's control over the situation, to raise the chances that he will accomplish what he is after.

Do you see now why you have to be very careful in picking out a residual message?

The selection of your residual message starts inside you, but from there it is more than a matter of individual choice. The needs and capabilities of your audience must also be taken into account. You may choose to talk about the sex life of the fruit fly, but why should any audience of human beings with sound minds and bodies choose to sit and listen to you? Before you can move on to your topic, you need to analyze your possibilities with the audience by:

1. Setting a goal in which you are interested.
2. Assessing the capabilities of the audience.
3. Altering your goal so that it is practicable given the kind of audience you have.

That is why this section and the next are so closely tied together. Audience analysis is really the second step of goal-setting.

Suppose, for some reason, you were a highly contented student at a fine school and you have decided to speak on that school. In a ten-minute speech, it certainly would not be possible to cover every detail of the school. But because you know a good deal about the school you could cover at least one topic in depth. You are not sure whether you want to persuade people to like the school, or whether you want to give them information about what's going on. You'd have some choices to make, and it would be helpful to analyze your topic by taking your "school" apart. For example, your school has an administration and a budget. Would the audience be interested in these things—any audience besides a group of alumni who were paying the bills? Probably you would rule these out as topics. You might also talk about the physical plant, but you really don't care very much about the structure of the school. Your own lack of interest is a perfectly good reason for ruling out a topic. You might find the following list of topics:

1. How the students behave
2. Teaching methods in the school

3. Social activities at the school
4. How to register at the school
5. Future problems my school faces

Each of these topics can be tested against the three questions listed previously. In answer to questions one and four, you decide that you are not particularly interested in the behavior of students or registration. In answer to questions two and three, you discover that the audience might well be interested in social activities and teaching problems, but social activities are a little trivial. In answer to question five, the audience is not likely to be interested at all in future problems. But you discover that you could adjust the future problems issue to show how your school is a prototype for education, and declare that all schools face those problems. However, that would make it a persuasive speech, and you don't want to do that. You discover that there is no way you can make social activities any more than trivial, but there are some real possibilities in talking about some of the new educational techniques at your school. You have some knowledge of these techniques, but you don't really know the background. On the other hand, your reputation is good enough at the old school that people would give you information. OK, you've got it:

> Residual Message: There are some really exciting educational innovations used in my former school.

You might want to consider the possibility of advocating that they should, therefore, be adopted at this school. But that would put another kind of burden on you which you do not wish to assume. So you leave it where it is.

You may brainstorm your topic and come up with subtopics. You pick the most unusual and dramatic, because you have to document the point that the innovations are really exciting. You may be interested in what is going on in English composition, but really, that is not so exciting as what is going on in the science labs. You may not know enough yet about the science labs, but you know you can get the information. On the other hand, composition is your major interest, and you think it is a matter of concern for students around here. You've heard most of them complaining at one time or another about how bad the composition courses are, and you placed out of composition courses because you had been so well trained at your old school. Maybe you have a hook for the audience, but it appears that you have to rephrase your residual message. It comes out something like this.

There are ways to improve composition instruction at our school, and **they are...**

And when you examine what you know and can find out, you discover four main things that go on at your former school that do not happen here. You now have a residual message which says:

There are ways to improve composition instruction at our school because
1. At my former school, we...
2. At my former school, they...
3. At my former school, I...
4. At my former school, it...

And you want the audience to remember the names of the techniques:

Free topics
Criticism of ideas
Drill in style
Contract method

We now have a full residual message:

My former school provides a model for improvement of instruction in composition through free topics, criticism of ideas, style drill, and contract method.

Now, write this down in big, black letters on a card, and keep that card in front of you during the preparation of the rest of your speech. Anything that does not help you make that point is **out.** No matter how interesting it is, **out.** If it is really interesting, stow it away for another speech. You have a residual message now. You have your goal pinned down.

1. I will speak for ten minutes.
2. I will speak to my class.
3. I will speak about ... (state your message).
4. I will call myself successful if I get at least three questions at the end of the speech and no more than three yawns during it.

That last item, number 4, is arbitrary. You'll learn more about how to do that later on, and real skill comes only through experience.

Time out: exercise

Time for another exercise. Back to that list of tcpics you have been working on. This is simple. Check your list and pick five topics to which you are really committed, topics you might say that you are really "into." Translate each of those topics into a residual message. Analyze that residual message and see how it comes out after the three questions and then stipulate:

1. Whom you will talk to
2. For how long
3. What your final residual message will be

Stop! Get it all together before moving on.

You might want to go on one step and try to figure what would constitute success. There are some speech instructors who provide a chance for you to do this by giving a short quiz at the conclusion of your speech and having you predict what the scores will be. A simpler method might be to ask your audience to write down what they think your residual message was **after** you have given the speech. If you come out from 50 to 75 percent right, you probably did a good job. If you were higher, you were probably too repetitive. If lower, you probably were scrambled. You can work more on this later, but another thing you will want to do is describe what you see the audience doing when you are doing a good job.

FOUR

Research: audience and topic

You have now made a decision about your residual message, and you are almost ready to start putting a speech together. During the process of constructing your speech, you will come into contact with a great deal of information, all of which **might** be included in your speech. But, if you included it all, you would be speaking from starting time well into Labor Day. You need a method to decide what goes in and what goes out. You know that part of the method is your residual message, for we have told you: Anything that does not support the residual message is out! One of the reasons for analyzing the audience is to discover which of the "in" materials should be used, how you can select ideas and proofs so that they meet the needs of your listener.

Examining the audience

We have already told you a great deal about audience. If you think back on what you already know, it is clear that you, as a speaker, are on shaky ground. We have, for example, pointed out that the audience does not respond as a single unit. As a speaker, you face a collection of individual responses and you must sort them out and interpret them as you speak. You know that many of your interpretations will not be completely accurate because they will be distorted by your frame of mind, your expectations, your desires. We have suggested that you can get into trouble both by noticing only unfriendly responses and by noticing only friendly responses. So what then? There must be some way to approach this problem of audience in order to improve your chances of success.

The audience is number one in your mind throughout the speech process, but it is never more important than during the preparation stage. During the preparation phase, the speaker must find out all he can about his audience. He will use his knowledge about people in general in order to develop some of his standards of judgment. He must draw on his ability to understand the needs and wants of others. In an earlier book, **Communication in Education,** by Gerald Phillips, David Butt, and Nancy Metzger*, one of the authors referred to the dual perspective. We have talked about it earlier in this book. By dual perspective, we refer to the ability that a mature adult has to "psych out" the other, to discover the possibilities of feelings and desires and fears in the other person, so that he can adapt to them.

Your dual perspective will be helpful to you in the preparation of any speech, for it will provide you with a fictitious audience to whom you can address your preparation. If you think, for a moment, about social conversation, you know that the man who does an effective job has some general topics that he can use that are interesting to everyone. The good conversationalist, for example, knows that the more he can center the other person on thinking about things that matter in his own world, the more effective the conversationalist. Some authorities say, get the other person to talk about himself because there is no topic an individual is more interested in than himself. Barring this, then we need to talk about how ideas are important to the other. The other person needs a stake in what is going on or he will not be a listener. He may be physically present but psychologically inert. Thus our first effort needs to be some thought about what is necessary to get the attention of the other person. The question is, "Why would the other guy find this topic interesting/important?" If you can't get a good answer, you may have to select a new topic.

Some people are as effective in talk as firing BBs into a mountain of marshmallows. They utter this line and that, and most of the lines

* New York: Holt, Rinehart & Winston, 1974.

Hunting elephants with a pea shooter.

miss the target because no thought has been given to the needs of the listener. The man who goes hunting elephants with an elephant gun will likely be more effective than the man who tries with a pea shooter. In the same way, the proper choice of materials to fit the audience will increase your chances of success.

Maintain attention! Did you notice how those **words** caught your eye? And the cartoons and diagrams in this book—don't they jump out at you, surprise you on the various pages? They are put there to catch and hold your attention. The speaker's job is to capture and maintain the attention of the audience. A bright personality is part of it and can aid the task materially, but wit and charm don't go very far alone. As a matter of fact, very few effective speakers could make it to the quarter finals in a charm contest. Even if you lack those winning qualities, you can compensate for them by building a speech composed of materials designed to hit the audience, and thus get the attention you need in order to accomplish your objective.

Sometimes it will be necessary for you to face a roomful of strangers. The first speech you give in class will be sort of like that. Even so, you can get some information ahead of time. A good classroom lecturer is tuned in to the student body. He tries to understand trends in students in general. He keeps himself posted on what is going on through the student newspaper. He has a good idea of what in general turns students on. He also knows that his first lecture, the first day, will set the tone for the entire term of instruction, so he tries very hard to adapt his material to what he knows about students in general. He does not pull a con. He does not try to be "one of the guys." But he does take issues that are important to his listeners into account as he prepares his own material.

Grab the audience's attention and hold it.

Political speakers have a careful analysis made of the communities and organizations that they will address. Most audiences are established organizations. They have office addresses and published records and a good deal of material is usually available about their policies and what they stand for. Of course, the speaker does not dare assume that what is true of the group is true of every individual in it, but he can presume relatively safely that membership in a given organization is likely to indicate some commitment to the goals and objectives of that organization. Understanding what the group stands for will help him to a general understanding of the individual members.

Certainly this kind of understanding will help him avoid accidental insults or slurs. He can eliminate any material that might offend his listeners. It requires no great stretch of the imagination to understand that the topic of birth control must be handled differently for an audience of Catholics than for an audience of Protestants. Metaphors and images that work well for city people might slide right off the backs of small town people like wet mud on a wall. Women will probably have somewhat different interests than men, liberation notwithstanding. Football jokes that went well at the Rotary Club might only freeze the faces at a meeting of the League of Women Voters.

Every speech experience you have will help you to develop a feel for what works and what fails in a speech. You will get what the professionals know as a "sense of audience." But, let's not assume that you plan to become a professional speaker. To replace the experience that you do not have, we will offer you some main headings to consider. We know that at about this time you are yearning for another list, and of course, your instructor needs these lists so that he will have something to put on the exam. For your information the boldface sentences in the rest of this section represent main headings, and the material that follows each of them is supportive. The residual message is: A good speaker should take into account the basic elements of audience analysis in the preparation of his speech!

The physical circumstances of the speech are important. Although it may be difficult to gather vital statistics about the audience, certain basic information will be available. You will know in advance the size of the audience. You can find out about the physical surroundings: the size of the room, the kind of seats, the ventilation, and other components. You will know the time of day that you will speak, whether refreshments will be served and when, whether you are the only speaker or one of several, and if the latter, how many will come before you and how many after. This is not trivial information, for it helps you place the speech, determine its length, figure out what allowances you might have to make for adaptations to other speeches, and the kinds of attention-getting devices you might have to build in.

You will welcome the opportunity to try out the chairs that your audience will sit in. Don't be misled. Those soft, comfortable looking leather armchairs can defeat you as a speaker. When your audience begins to sink down in comfort and doze off, you will rue the day you ever saw those chairs. Or on a hot summer day when the air conditioning fails, those leather chairs can be a sweat-trap, and your audience will melt away from you out of concern for their own physical comfort. In the classroom, the position of the chairs is important. You will operate differently if the chairs are in a circle, or in rows, for example.

One of the more advanced techniques of public speaking is to develop a response pattern through the use of small groups in the audience. After a short delivery of the message, groups can be set up to do something in response to the speech. This gives the audience a greater sense of involvement and it helps the speaker to know how well he is doing. Individuals find it hard to stand up and ask questions in a large room with every eye on them, but working in a small group helps preserve anonymity and generates a broader response.

Examination of the physical circumstances will help you decide whether you can use this technique. In a relatively small room with movable chairs and a manageable sized audience (about 100), small group work is most effective. A scattered few in a sprawling auditorium with no sense of community will be hard to reach. They will feel no groupness and consequently would not be able to function even if they were placed in groups. With an audience like that you might be better advised to give a short persuasive speech before your speech with the residual message: Come down front and clump together. If you can get a spread-out audience congealed, you will be materially assisted in giving your speech.

Audience participation is very useful. In ceremonial types of speaking, it is not good manners to involve the audience, but in most other kinds the use of a question and discussion period helps drive home the residual message. Such a decision cannot be spontaneous, however, and one of the reasons you need to analyze the audience is to help you make a decision about what to do about audience participation. Questions and discussion are hard to inspire in a large group. You may have experienced the feeling in classes you have taken. It often seems embarrassing or awkward to project yourself in front of so many others. The questioner has not had a chance to prepare his case, and he could well make a fool of himself. In a large crowd, the only likely participant would be the dedicated fanatic who attempts to use **your** audience as a forum for his own speech. Therefore, if audience participation is your goal, you will have to give some consideration to the sensitivities of your audience in the situation in which they find themselves, and you will have to manage things so that each member of the audience would feel that he could contribute without a sense of intimidation.

The degree of comfort in the meeting room will help determine the length of the speech. It is wise to be brief on a hot summer day, and it is even more wise to prepare your speech so you can shorten it on that cold winter day, when the thermostat has gotten out of control in the meeting room. A speaker can plan some alternative endings so that the speech can be adjusted to the degree of comfort of the audience. You can earn considerable goodwill by being attentive to possibilities that no matter what you do or how good you are, you will not be able to overcome the simple discomfort of sitting in the room.

It is a good idea to stop early, also, if you are the last of many speakers, especially if refreshments are waiting. An old sage once said, "The mind can only absorb what the seat of the pants can endure." When the audience is dreaming of caffeine, your remarks about the ecology of the local swamplands will have very little effect on them. In any case, it is smart not to misinterpret restlessness. What the audience does may not be directed at you; it may only be a function of impending events.

The agenda of the meeting at which you speak is also a matter of concern. Organizations often do some business before they call on their speaker, and that bit of business can sufficiently annoy the audience that they will not be in a mood to listen to you. When this is the case, you may need to seek goodwill through your introduction. This is the time for jokes and stories designed to calm the audience and get them to pay attention to you instead of ruminating on the indignities of the treasurer's report. And if the meeting is to follow the speech, you may be even worse off, for the audience may be contemplating sitting there till well after the end of the Johnny Carson show dealing with the "nits and lice" of the organization and wondering when the droning speaker will end and let them get on with business.

Openings, in general, are of particular concern to the speaker. The person who introduces you may kill your effectiveness if he talks too long or is too laudatory in his remarks about you. The wise speaker always checks signals with the master of ceremonies in advance. What you want him to do is say those things about you that will qualify you as an expert on your topic in the eyes of the people listening. You do not want him to make you appear to be a combination of Demosthenes and Winston Churchill, because then the audience will expect too much, and if you appear to be a paragon of virtue, the audience may resent you because you are too holy for them to tolerate.

Some meetings open with exercises: the Pledge of Allegiance or the national anthem. Some groups open with a prayer. This can actually help you for they will at least focus attention onto the platform where the speaking will take place. It is sometimes embarrassing and difficult for the speaker to get attention from a group that is involved in many little conversations. Opening exercises thus make the speaker's job a bit easier. If there are to be no opening exercises, you will have to think up something for your introduction that will help "polarize" the audience. By "polarize" we mean gather attention so that it is focused on the speaker. This is another reason for being prepared with a joke or two. It is also a good place to talk about the organization you are addressing and pay a few compliments, hopefully to evoke some applause, for the act of applauding will distract persons from their private conversations and will help you to secure their attention.

Special factors also ought to be considered. For example, the speaker should show some respect for the sponsors of the meeting. If the meeting is in honor of some special day or event, the speaker will want to acknowledge it early in his speech. If he does not do this, the audience may feel that he does not have respect for their particular concerns. At the same time, this kind of deference can be overdone. A speaker should not distort his material simply to adjust it to a special concern in the audience. If he does, it will be noticed and resented. Organizations welcome respect, but not excessive knowledge or concern from an outsider. The speaker who is a member of the organization may use that device to build goodwill.

One of the authors addresses the seminar of Credit Unions each summer at their annual meeting. During a session last year, the author commented about how easy it was to borrow money from the credit union, and how welcome this was at the time he was buying a car. A member of the audience stood up and interrupted the speaker. He said, "You know, you are the first guy to come here to talk to us who is a member of the credit union." The comment was welcomed because it was built into the speech and did not stand out like some specially designed compliment calculated to con the group.

Thus, physical circumstances and agenda represent an important element of your audience analysis. Get all the facts you can, for it will help you materially in your planning, and particularly in the selection and placement of your material.

Gearing the speech for maximum understanding is your main job. Getting people to understand what you are talking about is a difficult job. It depends on many things: Do they care about your topic? How old are they? What do they know? What have they experienced in regard to your ideas? No matter what your purpose, you must make it possible for them to understand the essential information in your speech. You cannot persuade anyone to accept something he does not understand (although you can persuade people that they understand something they do not understand—our politicians have been doing that for years).

To the listener, it is like signing a contract without reading the fine print—to accept what you declare to be the case, if he does not understand what the case is. As a speaker, you must estimate how much information must be given in order to accomplish your goal. If your goal is mainly to give out information, and little more, then your success depends on the ability of the audience to absorb that information. It will have to be packaged for understanding and clarity. If, on the other hand, you want to change the minds of the audience or move them to action, success depends on their ability to understand just what it is you want them to do and why you want them to do it. Thus, it is important for you to gather information about what they know about your topic and how they got that information.

In the classroom, a good teacher will be concerned about what his students already know. He will have some idea of what people think about his course, and his experience will tell him what it is likely that his students already know. If it happens to be a required course, for example, he may understand that most of the students really don't care to be there. He will understand that he must prove to them that his course is worth taking. On the other hand, if he is lecturing to a group of professionally committed students, he may not need to take the time to sell them on the importance of the course. They took it voluntarily, and are even possibly eager to get the information, and the lecturer will have to plunge in to meet their eagerness.

Unlike the classroom, it is not easy in outside groups to determine the degree of knowledge about and interest in a topic. Suppose we are addressing some organization. What are they interested in? If it is the Rotary Club, you might assume that they are interested in improving the local community (unless they feel that they have to belong to some civic club in order to maintain their image). If the audience is male, you might assume they are interested in sports. If the audience is made up of mothers, you might assume they are interested in children. But these might not be the things you are talking about. How do we get more information about them that is relevant to your needs as a speaker?

We might guess that they are interested in things they have in common. If they are all members of the same organization we can assume, for starters, that they are at least mildly interested in things covered by what the organization stands for. If they are present to honor some particular event, we can start with the knowledge inherent in that event.

However, even this is not always a safe guess. Think back on your own experiences. You may have found yourself at a gathering that you really didn't want to attend. Maybe you had no great interest but felt that for various social reasons you had to attend. Or, maybe you were pushed into going by your friends or by the people who organized the meeting. The same things can happen to members of an organization. Even so, their common interests may be all you have to start with. Sometimes it is difficult to stretch the context or idea of your speech to fit the reason for the meeting. If you were making a speech about ecology to a group that has gathered to celebrate the anniversary of its founding, it would be awkward for you to try to connect that reason with your topic. Any relationships you might make would seem strained and artificial. In fact, they may even defeat your purpose. In such a situation, you might not assume anything at all, and thus be safe. A simple mention of the occasion or purpose of the meeting in the introduction would attract attention followed by the declaration that most of us (humans) are interested in preserving the world in which we live. If the rest of your information is interesting, then you have the group where you need to have them.

Information can be made interesting by taking into account the natural experiences that human beings have. Dull lectures are a good example. Even a physics lecture could be made exciting and appealing to the mass of students, if the scientific principles were explained in commonplaces that everyone was interested in or knew about.

How about referring to football when it comes time to discuss the effects of applied force and the influence of friction? This might bring the subject to life and pull audience interest right to it.

One phase of analysis would be to find out what is a "real life situation" for your audience. Here again, your dual perspective will help you, because, to the extent that you are normal (and you'd better be the sole judge of that), what would be likely to interest you could be assumed interesting at least to a great many others.

Even the dullest information can be made interesting, if you can relate it somehow to the experiences of the audience. The slowest-moving lecture you ever heard could be made exciting and appealing if the material were explained in terms of something you know about, say, a football game or some other real-life situation. Try this:

> We can think of the acid-base reaction as a war between hostile chemicals. Put them together and acid neutralizes base. They fight. Neither wins. We have salt water left. Watch this demonstration.

Or:

> There are a lot of misconceptions about the national debt. Some of you may have the picture of some Daddy Warbucks standing in the wings with a mortgage in his hand waiting to take possession of your country. But it's not like that at all. It's more like this: your right hand needs some money in order to buy something from your left hand, so it borrows money from your left hand and spends it to buy what the right hand needs. Then the right hand puts a tax on the left hand and takes the money, which it pays back to the left hand to pay off the debt. A lot of money is owed, but we owe it to us.

While this kind of speaking is not quite precise, it gives the audience a sense of relationship to the material. Once that is done, the specific facts can be stated and your audience will have some place to put them. People tend to get information by relating it to information they already have. If your ideas are too new or too complicated for the audience to appreciate, you have to discover something about which they have knowledge and make the relationship for them—or at least get them started toward making the relationship.

There are some things about which everyone has knowledge. Other types of individuals have specialized knowledge. If you were talking to a group of physicians about theory of persuasion, you might want to relate what you say to a problem that all physicians have: convincing the patient that he ought to take his pills:

> What do you do about the patient who gets confused and can't remember whether it is two pills four times a day or four pills two times a day? And what about the one who simply thinks that buying the medicine is enough? How about that diabetic that will die if he doesn't take his insulin, but he is scared to death of hypodermic needles? People don't do things automatically; they have to be talked into it. So let's take a look at how you use persuasion every day of your professional life.

Your awareness of what the audience knows and how they know it will help you pick the material you are going to use in your speech. Should you use statistics or tell a story? How would they respond to visuals, slides, diagrams? If they didn't go to college, could you reasonably expect them to understand your references to college life? If they have lived all their lives in the city, will they understand your references to farming? While these kinds of questions seem obvious, they are almost never asked, and speakers then wonder why they did not make it with their audiences.

There are some things that can be assumed about people, although nothing can be assumed for sure. A sage once remarked, "The only thing you can count on is death and taxes." As a speaker, this might be good advice for you. A wise remark about the income tax is sure to get a laugh. A reference to death is almost certain to evoke sympathy. Your references to Hank Aaron, however, might mean little to a group of women who pay slight attention to sports on TV. Your references to raising families might evoke little sympathy from the unmarrieds in the audience. Your references to political issues might draw a blank from those who pay little attention to politics. Remember, only about 60 percent of the people in this country bother to vote and there were people even in 1974 who never heard of Henry Kissinger.

A quickie exercise

Make some predictions about your classmates and friends. Whom would they be likely to recognize in public life? What do they know about the "common" ideas that are familiar to you? Give them a little quiz:

1. Who is Hugh Scott?
2. What's ex-President Nixon's wife's name?
3. What is a passed ball?
4. Who is Dustin Hoffman?
5. What is Linda Lovelace famous for?
6. Who is the editor of **Playboy?**
7. Who is Helen Gurley Brown?
8. What does a split end do? (Want to bet the girls say it makes their hair look awful?)
9. What soup is "mmm, mmm, good"?
10. Who is Johnny Cash's wife?

Make up some questions of your own. You'll find out that one man's fixation is the next guy's trivia.

In short, you can't assume too much about your audience. If there is any way you can possibly check the philosophies of some or all of your audiences, do it. If not, see what you can find out in the library or by asking around. What are Kiwanis club activities? What is the purpose of the Optimists? What is the grange? 4-H? How are Methodists different from Presbyterians? And do the Methodists and Presbyterians know it? If you can put a name on your audience, you can probably dig up some information about it.

Now, let's get to the tough stuff. Remember, we said that you probably won't have the luxury of picking your own topic when you are invited to speak. Suppose you had the assignment from your company to talk to a local audience of businessmen about some of the technical matters involved in air pollution control. You have to explain to them what equipment is used to control pollution, how it works, and how much it costs. You can assume some interest in the community. After all, pollution presents a danger to the community. All have probably read about it, heard it discussed, seen commercials about it on the tube. You will need to start with simple ideas, however, for a desire to eliminate pollution does not mean a grasp of the basic knowledge of chemical engineering needed to understand your technical concepts. Since you cannot assume that your audience has an obligation to know your material, you have to decide whether it is important to explain the details or cut them from your speech. You can do this by referring back to your residual message. If your residual message is: **Pollution control is costly,** you will need to explain how various components are essential and you will have to show what they cost. You may not have to explain how they work. If your residual message is: **This particular system is better than that particular system, even though it is more expensive,** you may have to take the time to explain the technical details.

In a case of this sort, you have to keep your eye on the time also. You won't be able to teach a whole course in pollution control in the thirty minutes at your disposal. Given this further limitation on your capabilities, you may decide to omit the technical material altogether and level with the audience:

> My task tonight is to show you why it costs so much to have pollution-free air. I shall not be able to go into the technical details (although I have specification books here for those of you that want them). What I do want to talk about are the specific steps a piece of pollution abatement equipment must perform in order to purify your air. We need, for example, a piece of equipment that can remove fly ash and other solid particles. It must also remove sulphides and other noxious gases. It must remove ozone and other ionized gases. It must remove asbestos and other inert microscopic particles. It must also remove miscellaneous substances, the consequences of their presence we do not even know. Every removal requires a separate and distinct technical process. For example. . . .

You pick out the simplest and explain it, and then declare that the other steps are even more complicated. Then, hang a dollar sign on the one step you discussed and refer to the greater expense for the other steps. And hope for the best.

You buy yourself an insurance policy in situations like this, and in many other complicated speech situations, by permitting a question period. Members of the audience will **not** besiege you. People are often very reluctant to reveal themselves in public, but if there is a real question or issue to be raised, permitting time for it will tend to soothe anyone in the audience that would be frustrated if he did not have a chance to express himself. Some speakers even go so far as to protect the members of the audience who are reluctant to ask questions in public by declaring that they will stay for awhile after the meeting to handle questions.

Another possible difficulty is that a given audience may not understand you because of its intellectual limitations. In the case we discussed above, you had difficulty because your material was very complicated. If you had had enough time, you would have been able to explain it sufficiently because you presumed your audience to be intelligent and capable of understanding. This is not always the case. There are some audiences composed of persons who simply are unable to understand. They may need to be addressed on a "See Spot Run" level. If your approach were any more complicated than that, you would be talking over their heads. On the other hand, you dare not make mistakes, for if you decide those in your audience are incapable of understanding (and they really are), they will be insulted if you talk down to them. Your best bet is to start your speech on some median level. If the audience seems to get it, then keep on. If it seems to be anticipating you, you can get more sophisticated. If it seems to be bewildered, come down a step or two. It is simply not wise to regard an audience as incapable until you have genuine proof of its incapability. Your most practical mind set is to believe that your audience is capable of learning. Let it prove to you that it is not.

The audience's general level of education as well as its specific knowledge about your topic will have some effect on how it regards your residual message. People who are very well educated pose a particular problem. While some of them will be inclined to question very carefully what you say, others will have personal commitments to their own point of view and they will be smug in their belief that they know more than the speaker. Those who are not so well educated will want to understand what kind of an authority you are before they accept your information. At no time do you dare assume that just because people have college degrees (or equivalent) they will be easier to speak to. Once again, your audience must be analyzed for the particular case, and generally, you are safest to assume intelligence and the capability to learn on the part of the audience, unless proven otherwise.

Probably most influential of all in how well you do with a given audience is what the audience thinks of you. You probably like some of your teachers better than others. Those that you like are usually successful in getting you to do some work. Those that you find unpleasant will usually convince you that you ought to resist them.

Prestige helps get you started. The star halfback will usually be more successful in getting people to listen to his philosophy of the game than the third string quarterback. But sometimes, prestige backfires. Prestige is often a very narrow asset—that is, the football star can get away with talking football on his own authority, but he has a hard time carrying his prestige over into other matters. The value of prestige is to gain listeners. When the astronaut John Glenn first decided he wanted to be a United States senator, he put his prestige on the line and was defeated by a professional politician. The second time out, however, after Glenn convinced the voters that he was **also** a politician, he succeeded in defeating that same opponent, despite the fact that the opponent was now an incumbent.

Your personality is projected to the audience in a number of ways. They may have heard something about you. They usually know your "title," and they have some attitudes about that. The more respect the audience has for you, the more you can rely on your personal experiences and opinions. If the audience does not have respect for you as an authority, you will have to establish that respect by referring to authorities that do mean something to them. Presenting solid and reliable information helps, provided you can give references and sources for your information. Add to the information a display of skill at delivering the speech and the projection of your own unique and warm personality, and the next time you will find it easier. People will remember **you,** and you will have more options at your disposal because of that.

We have been talking here about an ideal state of affairs. What we have to say sounds good on paper. In actual practice, it is very difficult to analyze your audience. You may go through a number of exercises with your class. For example:

Try this exercise

Analyze your class as an audience. You have the privilege of selecting questions, but first, you must make some guesses.

1. Are the greater number Democrats, Republicans, Independents, or "apathetics"?

2. What is their modal religious belief?
3. What do they think of you as a speaker?
4. What do they know about your subject?
5. What would you predict they all understand in common? Campus politics? The life of a student? The requirements of this course? Other things?

Now get them to hand in an anonymous questionnaire in which they give their responses. Compare their answers with your predictions. Typically, there will be some real differences.

After college you will not have the privilege of sending around questionnaires to your audience. What you can do is utilize the mind of your contact person. Whoever invited you to speak can afford to give you a little time during which you can raise some important questions. Why not list what you'd ask such a person if and when he invited you? Develop your own format of questions for audience analysis purposes.

And remember: there is no substitute for your own sensitivity to people in general. Understanding the needs, wants and desires of everyman is probably the most important step in audience analysis. *General understanding of human wants, needs, and values can assist you in planning a speech.* We are not going to try to teach a cheap psychology course here. What we are about to say is oversimplified, and will not be the least bit helpful if you try to use it on a multiple choice test in your psychology class. In looking at human beings as they function in an audience, however, we can see some basic ideas or "commonplaces" that seem to operate inside all of us. There are some generalizations that we can make about "human nature." **Be advised:** Human nature is not a scientific term. We are using it here because it helps us explain, that's all!

In this category called human nature, we group these interesting ideas: that people,

1. tend to protect themselves from danger.
2. tend to want some kind of status; they want to feel that they are better than someone else.
3. do not want to be insulted. They do not want to be made to look foolish in front of others.
4. want to believe that others like them.
5. want some excitement and fun out of the things they do.
6. are curious.

7. want to have friends.
8. like to own things.
9. are interested in sex and violence although they sometimes don't like to admit it.
10. tend to put their own concerns first; next they place their concerns about family and friends; they are rarely concerned about you or any other stranger.
11. don't like other people to step on their lawns.

If you are speaking in such a way that the audience sees you as a threat, no matter what your logic, no matter how right your appeal, it will not accept what you have to say. If you were, for example, to walk in front of a group of white householders in an all-white suburb of a large city and say:

> Every man has a right to live where he chooses, and no one has a right to interfere with this choice. Therefore, you people have got to open up your neighborhood and your hearts to your black brothers from the inner city.

you might trigger a hostility which knows no bounds. An appeal like that would present danger to the white householders. They have learned, however incorrectly, that property values go down when black people move in. They have learned a number of myths about black people. We know that these myths are false, but the householders do not, and they will resist. You might overcome their resistance by appealing to law and the possible consequences that would come their way if they interfered, or you might win some quiet acquiescence by trying to gain their sympathy for just one black man (because they have also learned that some people are different), but you will not be able to get away with clubbing them over the head with frightening statements. You also can't get away with statements that imply you:

1. think they are greedy.
2. think they are stupid.
3. are a better kind of person than they are.
4. don't like or respect them.
5. are personally threatening them.

What you must understand is that most persons will give lip service to the prevailing values, so long as they are not personally involved. The white householders in question might say that "everyone has a right to decent housing," but when it comes time to offer that housing in their own neighborhood, they may well turn violent. Think of yourself and the students you know. There are many who will say they are opposed to cheating—until they have a chance to cheat.

This does not mean that you have to change your ideas. We are merely telling you that threats of coercion rarely work in public speaking. If you have an idea that is controversial for an audience, you will probably have to proceed with it in subtle fashion. You might need to take very small steps. To throw out the challenge might make you and your supporters feel better, but it would very likely mobilize more opposition against you than you thought you had.

There are few forces that bind or hold an audience together. One of these is the need to conform, to be like others. Each person in the audience will have some group that he knows is his. People tend to group themselves together around shared beliefs. Thus, when you hit at the beliefs of one man, there are usually many others who will also be threatened.

Audiences sometimes show a solidarity. They tend to support their own, so long as the individual members act in "normal" ways. Thus, when someone asks a question, he usually has the support of the audience. If his question is long and involved, or is really an argument, or if it tends to treat the speaker unfairly, then the audience tends to react negatively to the questioner. There is a tendency among audiences to give a fair hearing to speakers. We have all been trained that way. In your classroom, for example, you can count on being treated courteously. Your listeners will make every effort to support you.

Recently, however, this behavior has been challenged. There are some speakers, like William Shockley, for example, who cannot get a fair hearing on certain college campuses because students shout them off the platform. The students who participated in this kind of activity were merely conforming to the standard way of doing things in their social group. However, from the standpoint of the speaker, the results are most unpleasant. You as a speaker need not put up with rudeness from the audience. For the most part, the speaker is doing the audience a favor by being there at all. Most people will not mount the public platform, and those that do are sufficiently rare as to be considered unusual. When you develop your skill, you too will be unusual. It is not a good idea to tell the audience about this, however. They will know it. On the other hand, if the audience treats you rudely and will not let you get on with your business, you have every right to leave the platform.

The issue of courtesy cuts both ways. No one likes to be insulted. People will feel insulted by the speaker who treats them as if they were not intelligent. Audiences will react in hostile and resentful ways to this kind of regard. The speaker can sense when an audience is responding with hostility, for he will hear muttering and he will see persons exchanging looks, dropping their attention, perhaps even leaving the hall.

On the other hand, if the speaker assumes they know too much, they will tend to restrain him by offering looks of bewilderment, asking their neighbors for answers to questions, and so forth. Part of audience analysis takes place **on the platform.** The professional speaker is tuned in to the responses from his audience. He regards it almost as a dialogue, and if he is really skilled, he can "play" his audience like a fine-tuned musical instrument. He will understand that what is true of a group is not necessarily true of the individuals in the group. If he is talking to Baptists, he will not expect that they **all** respond like the residents of Pine Tree, Georgia. If he is talking to students, he knows that not all of them are streakers, or scholars, or anything. He will be very careful to define the particular unities that the persons in his audience have, and he will expect diversity in all other matters.

The phrase, "peope are people, and you can expect them to behave that way," sounds like something your great-uncle might have said while sitting at the cracker barrel. Still, there are some things that you can count on, some questions that almost everyone will raise in his head at particular times. For example, if you are making a proposal to improve anything that requires new employees or equipment or a building, there are bound to be those in the audience who will automatically ask, "How much will it cost?" "How much work will it take?" "How will it change my life?" This last question is crucial. The speaker should anticipate it, for if he can tell the audience what his ideas mean to them, he will attract them to his ideas. Any of these natural questions that can be answered in the speech will help the speaker gain the goodwill of his audience. They become very much a part of the preparation process.

If your goal is generally persuasive, it helps to be able to make a gross classification of the audience. A classification is a broad judgment about the state of mind of the audience concerning your idea. You can do this by examining the nature of the group to whom you are speaking. There are some rules of thumb such as:

1. Older people are more likely to be conservative than are younger people.
2. Younger people have more of a sense of risk than do older people.
3. Businessmen are usually interested in how much things cost.
4. Women are more likely to be interested in references to home and children than are men.
5. Minority group members are generally concerned about how an idea will improve their lot in life.
6. Persons who have meager funds will tend to be more possessive than wealthier persons.

Furthermore, organizations that have names and constitutions will have their own ideals and goals. Examination of these will assist you in anticipating what their positions will be toward your ideas.

Once you have made an assessment of the audience's position, you will be able to select material directed to this state of mind. If the audience is neutral, you will want to build your own reputation and get it to see you as an authority so you can make your proposal and get it accepted. Neutral audiences will also want more facts and proof than a favorable audience.

An audience that is favorable to your ideas doesn't want to hear the arguments all over again. They will want to know how close we are to "winning," when the great day will come about and, what they can do to bring it closer. You can make appeals to action with a favorable audience. The hostile audience is very fragile. Most of all, you want to avoid a clash or a confrontation with them. The simplest and generally the most effective way to proceed is to try to appeal to their sense of fairness, the belief that most individuals have that people should be least be able to hear all sides of a question. You will not be able to accomplish very much with a hostile audience, and if you can leave them with a residual message like, "Gee, not all of those guys have horns," you probably will have done the most you can do.

Analysis of an audience tells you as a speaker that you **must** pick a limited goal. Sometimes, after analyzing the audience, you will want to alter your residual message. Don't feel locked in. You are perfectly free to do this. In fact, it might even be sensible to add another step to the chart on page 57 and call it 5-1/2 "revising the residual message."

Another important reason for analyzing the audience is the discovery of what you need to do in order to capture and maintain interest. You can't get the customer to buy until you get him in the showroom. Even the most careful plan of procedure with an argument will not work if you have not taken some steps to gain the attention and interest of the audience. Thus, your analysis will lead you to some ideas you can include in your introduction and conclusion. More on that later. This same analysis will suggest to you the kind of "supporting material" you will need to select and use through the entire speech. This concept may mean little now, but when we discuss it on page 180 we will refer back to this section. You have a number of options for making the same point. The trick is to pick the proper method for the proper audience.

Summary exercise

Get yourselves organized into small groups. Each member of the group is to pick a topic from the following list:

Exploring our state
Why come to this school
Should women be allowed to play on varsity teams along with men
Who should be the next governor of our state
How the reaper-combine is used
Artificial insemination of cattle
The operation of a turret lathe
Is the computer replacing the human
A required reading list for all human beings
How eyeglasses are made

If you don't like these topics, brainstorm some more. Next, state a residual message for your speech on the topic. Now test that residual message against the analysis of the following audiences:

Your classmates
A group of engineering honors students
The local philosophy club
The Republican central committee of your county
The Democratic central committee of your county

The Rotary Club
A Methodist convention
A 4-H club unit
The Young Socialists league
An army reserve group

Discuss with your group how the residual message needs to be modified after the analysis of each audience.

Each of you should come out of this exercise with at least one topic and at least ten different residual messages that might grow out of it. You may continue this assignment by generating more topics and more groups. But make sure it is discussed with your group. This will help you discover some ideas that you didn't have before, and it should also convince you that speech preparation need not be a solitary process.

Armchair analysis.

Armchair research

We could call this section "digging it up." Let's start with a little scenario. It is Tuesday night at 1215 Hooper Street, Apartment 3C, and Sally is talking with her roommates.

SAL: Ed, I have to have a speech tomorrow. What'll I do?
ED: Do you know anyone in a fraternity? They have files of old speech outlines. But you have to be careful not to get one the prof has heard before.

SAL: I don't have time for that. I have to give a speech on something
that I know about and nobody else does.

GERT (another roommate): That wasn't the assignment. It was pick
a complicated topic and make it simple for everyone.

SAL: I don't know anything complicated. What'll I do?

ED: How about faking it? Talk about grass or something. I gave a
speech once on how to use a hash pipe, but my instructor was a
head, so he gave me a "B."

GERT: Won't help with this guy. I did mine over the weekend. I'm
going to try to explain Boyle's Law to the humanities majors.

ED: What's that law about? What does it tell us we can't do? Hah, hah.
(Ed is his own best audience.)

SAL: But I don't know anything complicated.
(Curtain)

The curtain was a curtain of charity. As the scene went on, Ed
went to his room and got stoned. Louise came home with another
roommate who made a suggestion—get into your own head baby. Sal
dug around a bit and discovered that she knew something about
hooking rugs. She decided to start with that and then she dashed off
to the library and looked up the manufacturing process used for
hooked rugs and took some notes. She got home from the library at
12:30 A.M. She worked till 3:00 setting up an outline and some notes.
And if she hadn't been so sleepy the next day, she might have delivered a good speech.

Most student speakers fail to look into their own heads when
speech time comes. But remember, we keep telling you that people
invite you to speak because you know something. So the speaker who
dashes off to the library and cribs some notes from an encyclopedia
really isn't doing the job. And if speech teachers were a little less
merciful (dollar-for-dollar, pound-for-pound, speech teachers are the
most merciful teachers you will find), most of those students would
flunk. As it is, they flunk in their own eyes when they see the bored
expressions on the faces of their fellow students who really gave
them every chance to get them involved.

The exercises we asked you to do on pages 13 and 47–50 were designed to help you get into your own head. If you followed the pattern
we suggested, by the time you reach this section, you ought to have
discovered a good deal about what you know, about what you are
interested in, and about where you might go to get more information.

If not, this section should be a little reminder. **You need to know what you know about a topic** before you decide to speak on it.

One of the first rules in speech preparation is "Paper Is Cheap." At this point in the preparation process, you have picked your topic, decided on a residual message, analyzed your audience and you are ready to start managing the details. The main hunk of details you will need to manage is the stuff of the speech. We need to see what that looks like before we can put it all together. Your topic is "Dogs," and your residual message is: There are _____ steps in housebreaking a dog, and they are _____. Now is the time to take out some note cards and write down what you think you know. You have decided that you are going to talk about some steps. What steps do you know already? Write them down.

> Get a dog.
> Get some paper.
> Take the dog out at regular times.
> Praise the dog when he does it right.
> Punish the dog when he does it wrong.
> Expect accidents from time to time.
> Paper-train the dog indoors first.

Sometimes the owners get housebroken, not the dog. You now have eight note cards. Take each one and see what else you can write on the card. For example:

> Praise the dog.
> > Some dogs will respond to verbal praise.
> > Some dogs need a pat.
> > Some dogs will like a piece of food.
> > You need to make an agreement with your dog about what praise consists of.

You have four ideas of things to say about praise. And this cues you to something you should have thought about earlier, so you pick up another note card and you write: "Housebreaking a dog is a conditioning process." Then you add it to the stack and try another card.

> Take the dog out at regular times.
> > After meals is best.
> > First thing in the morning and last thing at night.
> > Take the dog to the same area.
> > Give him enough rope to let him sniff.

If you see him acting peculiarly at the door, take him out.
Don't expect him to do something every time.

And so on, for each of the cards. You discover when you get to the "Housebreaking is a conditioning process," that you really can't prove it from what you know. So you go off to the library to find out just how housebreaking is a conditioning process.

You have demonstrated that you know something about the topic. You have taken inventory of what you know and you have discovered what you need to find out. That is the basic pattern you will work with for all of your speeches.

If you don't have enough in your head about the topic to produce a half dozen cards, then you had better go to another topic. The audience would not care to listen to someone who knows less about a topic than they do. It is good to learn new things, but not during speech preparation. An educated person will continue his learning long after his college days are over. He is constantly adding to his total knowledge, broadening the range of topics from which he can choose. He will use much of his knowledge as a conversationalist. In conversation, he will not have to worry about gaps. Someone else can fill them in, or he can admit that he lacks the knowledge. It really doesn't matter. But in formal speech, gaps in the organization will have to be filled in from outside sources. And the library is not the only place to which you can go for this information.

Field research

After you have produced your note cards out of your head, a glance at them will tell you that you have some holes big enough to drive a tank through. One thing you might need, for example, is an overview. The statement "Housebreaking is a conditioning process" would be an overview. It lets you see the shape of the whole thing, tells you where your topic fits in a broader scheme of things. In the next section we will introduce you to a way of getting an overview, but if you are lucky enough to discover it this early, so much the better.

You might also need some details or proofs for statements you have made. Any of your statements about housebreaking, for example, might be a little stronger-sounding, if you could find someone else that agrees with them. It is better to say,

The American Kennel Club recommends the following procedure. . . .
I have tried it and it works.

than to say,

I do the following when I. . .

You are the expert, yes, for this speech, but you become more of an expert to the extent that you can show that other experts agree with you.

The library is a good place to make contact with experts. Many beginning speakers think the library is the place to prepare a speech. Remember Sally? Well, her scenario could have gone like this:

SAL: I need to give a speech tomorrow; can you help me?

LIBRARIAN: Well, what are you interested in?

SAL: I don't know. When I was in high school and I had to give a report, I just came to the library and Miss Merple helped me find something.

LIBRARIAN: My name is Smythe, and I can't help you find something, but if you will give me a topic, I might be able to direct you to something useful.

SAL: But that's just it. There are so many topics and so many books. I just don't know what to do.

(Curtain)

At that point, feeling desperate, Sally goes back into the stacks and cuts an article out of **Fortune** magazine. She is sure her teacher never heard of that magazine. **She** never heard of it. She then makes an outline of the article and goes in and gives the speech. Her teacher says, "Hmmmm, sounds just like an article in **Fortune** magazine I was reading the other day. Sally, stop after class will you?" And once again, we pull the curtain of charity.

We do our armchair research so that we know what we are doing when we get out into the field. What we really do is equip ourselves with questions that we may take to the library for answers. Or, we may find an expert. There are experts on almost everything hanging around colleges, and one can get almost any question answered. People don't particularly like to be used to prepare someone's work for them, but if you should go to the psychology professor and say,

"Doc, housebreaking a dog is an example of conditioning, right?"

"Yep."

"Can you clue me into something to read about that?"

"Sure, try. . . ."
you'd have it made. You use a minimum of his time, a minimum of your time, no wasted motion, no grubbing around in the stacks. You go right to the book you need.

That of course adds the second rule of speech preparation:
Don't be afraid to do it the easy way.

This section is not supposed to be a lesson in use of the library. In fact, most school libraries have a staff prepared to take you on guided tours, to tell you how the library works, how to find things, what you can ask for, and so on. We will go so far as to urge you to do that. But the main point of this chapter is to show you how to make the research phase of speech preparation easy and convenient. Let's look at another topic.

Topic: The High Cost of Living

Residual Message: The high cost of living is our own fault because we want too much.

Audience: This class

The armchair analysis turns up a set of cards headed as follows:

> Americans are spending too much on cars.
>
> Americans are willing to pay for style changes.
>
> When people are willing to buy uncritically, they lose control of their money.
>
> Only when people are willing to resist buying can they force prices down.

And you look at your cards and you know that if you were a world-renowned economist, people would probably let you get away with saying these things and they would believe all of it. But you are not a world-renowned economist, and if you tried to say these things based on your own authority, you'd probably be in trouble. So, it is time for "the field." First stop, your friendly economist. An interview with a local economist convinces you that you are on the right track. He recommends some books, but he also makes some statements that he will permit you to quote, so you write those down on cards also:

> The boycott works only when the commodity is not essential.
>
> Companies tend to play to consumer's concerns about being in style.

That's a good start. You also have a book he gave you, **The Waste-makers** by Vance Packard, plus a reference to an article in a current journal, and a xerox clipping from a **Harper's** magazine article and a reference to a current market analysis text. A trip to the library is worthwhile, largely because you know what you are looking for.

An hour or two in the library produces about twenty-five more note cards. After all, you only have to speak for about seven minutes, and there are about forty cards ready for use. Now you face the big problem, how to put them together. That is the substance of Chapter Five, which will be the longest chapter in the book, for this phase of speech preparation is critical. It is relatively easy to get ideas and to get material for a speech. Where most writers and speakers go astray is in structuring the material.

This exercise is important.

Important exercise

Suppose you have decided to give a speech on the topic "Society" with a residual message: **It is important to study society.** You searched your own head and came up with a series of note cards. In each case, the **main idea** on each note card is underlined.

When there were a great number of dialects, mass communication was difficult. Mass communication cannot take place without a common language.

Today colleges are not specialized. Most of them provide vocational and liberal education and in any case more colleges are truly liberal today than ever before.

Knowledge appears chaotic and fluctuating. We can't get a grip on it sometimes, and we need some way to organize it.

Around the turn of the century, communities were isolated from one another and each had its own unique character.

There were few changes in education in the early 1900s.

Some colleges were entirely vocationally oriented in the 1900s. They trained people for their careers or jobs.

Today, mass transportation brings people closer together than ever before. The California suburbanite lives the same kind of life as the Long Island resident.

Today, the family is reduced in size to mother, father and the children. The grandparents are in a retirement village and the uncles, aunts, and cousins are scattered across the country.

In the college of the 1900s, curricula were limited. The student had little choice of what he would learn.

The extended family was a throwback to the old peasant heritage. Family was good, strangers were objects of suspicion.

In the 1900s, the social structure was stable.

Today's college is truly open to new knowledge, and fads and fallacies can flourish alongside the wisdom of the past.

Today, there is a greater demand for education than ever before. New knowledge is produced at a rapid rate.

Our life today confronts us with a constant barrage of conflicting values.

In the 1900s we understood who we were and what we were. Knowledge seemed clear and certain.

There is considerable conflict in the typical 1970s community. Communities today have difficulty being cohesive.

Today's family is highly mobile. The typical American family will make seven major moves in its lifetime.

The community of the past was centered around personal and familial values.

The extended family system was predominant in the community of the 1900s.

Today, families are really together only for a short time. Children go their own way and are not held in the home community.

In the 1900s, mass communication was poorly developed; consequently, there were no national norms or standards.

Today's social structure is dynamic. We are constantly experimenting with alternative life styles.

There is no one theory that explains how the world operates today. Our knowledge is unclear and constantly changing.

Around the turn of the century, there was little mass transportation. People mostly stayed around the community in which they were born.

Now, believe it or not, these are the note cards a professor of sociology used in order to give a speech at a recent convention of his national organization. If you read the cards in sequence, you will get a very garbled message. Keeping in mind the residual message, **It is important to study society,** see if you can get these cards shaped around so that the message makes sense. Write out the entries on cards and juggle them around. And keep your cards because you will need them for exercises in the next section, where we will try to make clear to you how to put things together.

FIVE

Structuring: putting it together

The most important thing in creating a speech is the development of a basic structure. A structure holds the speech together and makes it a solid working unit. The tighter the structure, the better the chance to get across the residual message. A structured speech presents ideas in some logical order, a progression of thoughts that help the audience to an understanding of the whole idea. If the residual message represents the total idea, then the structure is the units and pieces out of which the idea is built.

A great philosopher, Alfred Korzbyski, once said, "All knowledge is knowledge of structure." People tend to have orderly minds. They cannot take in information as fast as you can say it, so, in order to reach their minds, the information must be put together in ways that will make it acceptable to their heads. You can't make any points with an audience that does not understand what you are talking about! When you attend a lecture, you have a notebook and pen, and you write things down. Even if they don't make sense at the time, you can go back to your room and look at the notes and talk them over with someone and eventually get them to assume some kind of order. Audiences do not typically do that. In fact, even your lectures would be easier to follow if the lecturer took the time to structure his ideas so that they would appeal to your mind. With a regular audience, you simply cannot succeed until you get your material arranged in the simplest and most logically appealing way. It really doesn't help if people see you as a charming speaker but they can't remember a word you say. As a matter of fact, sometimes even very dull and dry speakers manage to win their point because their material is so well constructed.

A substantial and logical structure will help you to lead the audience through the thoughts they need in order to understand your residual message. One idea is built on another, repetitions are built in, until the whole message has been completed. Every unit in the structure has something to do with the residual message. The re- dundancy you put into your speech is stylized so that it is not boring and so that it will appeal to as many minds in the audience as possiule.

Structure building is also a way of analyzing your ideas. By draw- ing a structure for your speech, you will be able to see your strengths and weaknesses and you will be able to do something about the "holes" **before** you get on the platform. Your diagram will reveal lack of proof and lack of balance. Furthermore, structuring will guide you to the information you need for your introduction and conclusion.

In this book, we are not advocating outlining. We shall talk about why we think outlines are pointless later on in this book. We offer you instead a method through which you can put your ideas into order and test them out, so that you have the most understandable presentation it is possible for you to build.

The process of structuring is not just a gimmick designed to make you look busy. It has a purpose: to make preparation easier and to guide and streamline the work of organization and presentation. Keep that purpose in mind. We can daydream about how our stunning words overpowered the audience, or how some brilliant just-before- the-speech inspiration will bring the audience to our feet giving us a great victory. But these fantasies should not overshadow the need for organization. Even the greatest writers, speakers, and poets must plan carefully their new ideas.

The giving of a speech, however, is not a poetic experience. Aris- totle, the father of speech-making, was careful to separate his advice on speaking (in the **Rhetoric**) from his advice on literary forms (in the **Poetic**). Any idea, no matter how brilliant, must be developed in a clear and precise way. Failure to do so results in confusion for the audience, and consequently, your personal failure in reaching your goal. There is no single cause for failure in speaking more common than poor structuring.

Another reason for using structuring is to turn your energy to what is important in speech preparation. In an earlier day, speech training had to do with performance: such things as diction, gestures, posture, bodily movement, eye contact. Today, we concentrate on the form and content of the message, for we know that almost any person armed with a well-prepared message will succeed in getting it to his audience. You don't need to be a performer. Speakers are made, not born.

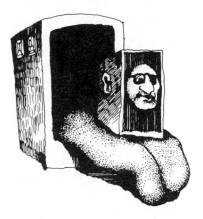

Speakers are made, not born.

There are a great many ways in which speaking is not like acting. Most important of these, is that the speaker needs to be able to change his "lines" depending on the response of the audience. For that reason, we do not normally memorize our speeches nor do we try to read them from manuscripts. We use the **extempore** methods, which means **we are well prepared** by knowing our material and having put it together well, so that we can adapt where and when needed. Adaptation can only come about when your material is logical and well structured. If it is not, all the performance skill in the world will not be able to help you do anything more than transmit brilliant confusion to your audience.

Beginning speakers often get preoccupied with "style" of speaking.

Oral, or spoken, style is very different from written style. Trying to make the speech sound like a work of fine literature can weaken the residual message. It dilutes the impact of the speech on the audience. As we have said earlier, written style assumes that the reader can go back and check out his confusions. Spoken style must be simple and clear enough so that there is no confusion in the first place. The moment a member of the audience cannot follow the thread of the speech, you have lost him entirely. There is no way he can go back or catch up. And the best way to lose audiences is to have a speech that is so incoherent that the parts do not stick together. The minute someone in the audience says, "I wonder what evidence he has for that point," or "I can't see how he came to that conclusion," you have lost him permanently.

Developing structure is a way to deal with the complexity of the human mind. The mind is like a strange creature reaching out into its surroundings with many arms, bringing in things to examine. Our senses are the "arms" of the mind. They pull in details from the outside; such as sights, sounds, and smells. The mind tries to make intelligence of them, but the mind cannot handle them one at a time. Experience has to be organized, classified.

The senses do not perceive things as they "are." The senses do not tell us that every object we see is really a whirling mass of electrons. The mind has the capability of organizing those electrons into a manageable mass. The mind takes in a thing, and even then, not a unique thing, but a thing like other things it has stored away. It takes what it sees and finds a category for it, and then pulls a label from that category, and then it understands what it sees. In short, the mind organizes, structures, the information that comes to it. If it tried to take things one at a time, we would go mad. By classification and order we maintain our sanity.

So this creature, the mind, bites off only what it can chew. Our whole communication system, our language, is structured so that it presents the maximum clarity to our minds. In addition to getting the words right, we have to get the words in the right order. A Pennsylvania Dutchman can make sense out of, "The boy his mother the cream gave," but speakers of general American English flinch at the construction and if we get too much of it, we get very confused.

Thus, our mind selects only noticeable features of what is perceived, and these are grouped into orders and structures that we can understand. We are not even aware of this process of selection. It takes place unconsciously. So, when we see a collection of features, we do not think of such things as "brown," "four legs," "motionless," "seat," and "cushion." We think "chair." The chair we see may be unique in some features. It may be unlike any other chair in the world, but before we can attend to those uniquenesses, we have to classify it, put a label on it, and then we can work with it.

We tend to put similar things in similar categories. We have learned to focus first on the samenesses between things. If we were to stand on a street corner, many metal things on wheels would pass by. No two of them look exactly alike. They are different colors, different shapes, different sizes, with different people operating them. But we see the similarities first, and we put them into a category, "cars." When something that is not a car comes by, we are often jarred by the difference. Put a horsecart on Madison Avenue and everyone pays attention. You will learn how to do this in your speeches. But the variety that comes from the unusual depends on our understanding the usual. It is so in putting together a speech. We need a main structure so that variety really looks like variety. Too much variety, too many things that do not fit together, and all we do is confuse.

We need to think of relativity, too. A simple idea like "hot" can categorize such objects as music, liquor, pavements, women, and stolen goods. In order for the word to make sense, it has to fit into a structure. We call this a "context." We can understand what the word means by looking at how the words around it are put together.

"A hot the down girl street came" makes no sense at all, but if we juggle the words, we can get the right order, so that all the words make some sense. They contribute to the message of the sentence. Man's understanding of similarities makes it possible for him to think ahead. The mind can make connections between categories and develop relationships. One thing comes along with another. One thing causes another. We can predict with reasonable accuracy what is likely to happen when this group of things is brought together with that group of things.

Our ability to predict makes it possible to control the world around us. Prediction made it possible to invent complicated things like the wheel and simple things like the computer.

Did that last sentence jar you? You have learned that computers are complicated? And wheels are simple? The use of the adjectives bothered you? Good. For that illustrates how we can gain attention by using an understanding of structure. If I go on and complete the idea, I might be able to make clear the distinction between calculus and simple algebra. But not in this book!

AT ANY EVENT, OUR ABILITY TO THINK IN STRUCTURES is the power that lets us rise above the level of other animals. Remember, ALL KNOWLEDGE IS KNOWLEDGE OF STRUCTURE. Think of why you pay attention to what is in capital letters. You have learned that most words in books are written in lower case letters. You have learned that capital letters are unusual because you have learned what is usual.

A sensitive person will be able to attend to differences because he knows how to handle similarities. He knows that differences are important, particularly when we deal with human beings. The differences between individuals determine who is worth knowing and who is not. Just "any old guy" will not do. The late Irving Lee, an expert on language and meaning, used to say, **"We tend to discriminate against, to the extent that we fail to distinguish between."**

When we are dealing with lifeless things, uniquenesses do not matter so much. We can develop general rules for chairs or footballs. But when we deal with persons, the differences between them are crucial. The people in your audience, in one sense, are members of the same group—listeners. But, if you lumped them into a featureless ball, and failed to note their individual differences, you would be bound to make mistakes in judgment. Your understanding of audience is a blend of general knowledge about humans, particular knowledge about a particular group of humans, and the ability to attend to the individual responses each member makes. You start with the general structure and work down to the particular case. If you present information in an orderly fashion, and then restyle it in various types of order, you will tend to make your audience receptive. They will receive your information and they will take it in to fit their own unique thought process, as well as their own needs. As a matter of fact, they will tend to create order out of disorder, if they have to. But the problem is, you cannot control what kind of order they will make out of the disorder, and your best bet is to impose the order initially, so that one way or another, your residual message will get through.

This is the reason why structuring is so important to the process of preparing a speech.

The main structures

In our society, there seem to be certain types of questions the mind asks about things. In fact, you can use some of these basic questions as a form of analysis to help you select a topic, and you can certainly use them to explore a residual message. They help you do a kind of brainstorming to generate information, and they tell you something about the source of the basic structures into which material can be put. We can list these questions.

1. Is it?
2. What is it? How is it classified?
3. How much is there?
4. What does it look like?
5. How is it used? What can I do with it?
6. Where is it?
7. When is it? How long does it take?
8. What is it made of?
9. How does it move?
10. How does it change?
11. How strong is it?
12. How good is it?
13. What is it like?
14. What comes along with it?
15. What is it different from?
16. How likely is it?

Some of these overlap. For example: questions 1, 2, 3, 4, 8, and 9 seem to have something to do with classifications. Questions 7 and 9 seem to have something to do with time. Questions 4 and 6 seem to relate to space. We shall show later that these are the three basic structures into which information can be fitted. For now, look at what can be done with this list of questions. Take a topic and try to generate a residual message out of the topic, using each of the questions as a source. The topic is "light bulbs."

1. Light bulbs are real. (nonsense)
2. Light bulbs are one of many ways in which to use electrical energy.
3. How large are light bulbs? (nonsense)

4. Light bulbs look like. . . .
5. Light bulbs are used in several different ways.
6. There are some places where light bulbs are not used. (nonsense)
7. Light bulbs last a long time.
8. Light bulbs are made of glass, filament and gas.
9. Light bulbs work in the following manner. . . .
10. Light bulbs burn out. (nonsense)
11. Light bulbs come in various power classifications. (nonsense)
12. Light bulbs are very helpful to mankind.
13. Light bulbs are similar to candles.
14. Light bulbs are usually hot. (nonsense)
15. Light bulbs are different from glowworms.
16. Light bulbs don't fit. (nonsense)

Not all of the questions generated possible residual messages. The ones that did not are marked "nonsense." Basically, number 9 appeals to me, as do numbers 13 and 15. I think I can show how a light bulb works by talking about the similarities between a light bulb and a candle and showing how it is different from a glowworm. I also think that a residual message like that would appeal to my audience, who I think is very familiar with light bulbs and probably won't pay much attention to me, unless I can help it to see light bulbs in a new way.

Stop for a quickie exercise

Take some of those topics you had lying around from Chapter Two and see if you can work them through the list of questions. Try some practical topics like razor blades, knitting needles, and lettuce as well as some abstract ones like prosperity, good manners, and civil liberties. See what kinds of ideas you get.

The questions are a quick aid to you as a speaker to help you look at the possible ways you could phrase your residual message. They help to **structure** the residual message because they are normal ways in which humans understand things.

Topics can be analyzed in still another way. Bess Sondel, in her book **Humanity of Words,*** lists seven basic ways in which the mind can handle information. They represent the seven structures we shall talk about here.

* Cleveland: World Publishing Company, 1960

1. **Time.** People think of things historically, developmentally, or in steps. Where did it come from? How did it get to be the way it is? How does it work? are all questions that fit into a time structure.
2. **Space.** People tend to think in locations and relationships between objects or points in space. Questions like "Where is it?" or "How does it look?" are questions that can fit into a space structure.
3. **Classification.** People tend to think in categories. How can a thing be divided? What are its parts? These are normal and natural questions.
4. **Analogy.** What is it like? When confronted with the unfamiliar, people like it tied to something they know about.
5. **Contrast.** What does it differ from? Are there things that it looks like, but which are really different? In what way?
6. **Relationship.** What caused it? What does it cause? What comes along with it? What does it fluctuate along with? What are the possible connections it has with other things or events.
7. **Problem-Solution.** If it is a problem, what might solve it? If it is a solution, to what problem does it apply?

Each of these structures carries with it a set of obligations. If you can locate your residual message in one of these structures, you have a virtual formula for procedure in the preparation of your speech. If, for example, your speech fits a time structure, then you know that your main organization pattern will be a series of time blocks, each one dealing with some historical or developmental aspect of whatever you are talking about. If your residual message is a proposal to accomplish some new thing or eliminate some difficulty, there will be the obligation to show a need for your ideas, show that they will solve the problem, that this is practical, and that your solution will not bring along a worse problem. Let's examine, now, how we can test our residual messages and classify them into structures.

Exercise time. Here are some residual messages:

A poor education spells poverty.
Making gulyas is a complicated process.
There are three main kinds of levers.
This is how the mainspring operates your watch.
The Mazda engine is superior to all the others.
We need a plan to regulate imports of foreign wines.

The first is clearly a causal relationship. It fits category number 6 of the seven basic structures. The second implies that we shall go through a procedure following some steps. It is obviously number 1. The three kinds of lever are a classification, number 3. The mainspring operates your watch could imply a causal relationship, number 6, but more obviously it will require some kind of diagram, so we put it in number 2. The discussion on the Mazda engine would contrast the rotary engine to the piston engine and would be number 5. The final one states a solution to a problem and so falls into number 7.

It is relatively easy to make this initial decision about a structure. Sometimes, however, when you begin to draw your diagrams, you find something lurking in the residual message that you were not aware of that would change your structure. Discussing the Mazda engine, for example, may represent the solution to a problem. Simply comparing it to the piston engine would not be enough to make your point. You might have to talk about some major problem confronted by all engine designers and show that the Mazda solved the problem more effectively than the other proposed solutions.

Doing a criticism of something or advocating a man for office represents another type of problem. Is John Smith the solution to a problem, or is there some more efficient way of approaching this kind of issue? Most of you have heard the word "criticism" and probably think it implies "running something down." This is not so. A criticism is a comparison of something to a set of standards to see how well it fits. Thus, when we call something a good painting or an exciting book, what we really mean is that it meets the standards that have been set for a good painting, or those for an exciting book. What we have is an **analogy,** a comparison of something with something else to spot the similarities—in this case, the similarities between the thing being examined and the standards for goodness. Thus, when we advocate John Smith for governor, we might be saying that there is a problem to which Smith represents the solution, or we might be saying that there are a set of standards for a good governor and that John Smith meets them.

Now you may continue this exercise by listing several of the residual messages you dreamed up for yourself and trying to fit them into the various structures. Get together with a group and talk it over. Remember that you are looking for a basic structure. As we will show later on, you will be structuring each heading, each subheading, maybe all the way down to the paragraph and the sentence, and you will have the privilege of using whatever structure fits what you want to say. The reason for doing this is to get your message clear enough for easy comprehension by the audience.

Time

There are various types of residual messages that span a series in time. For example, there is the message that shows the steps in the development of an idea or a thing. It looks like this:

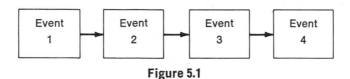

Figure 5.1

We can make substitutes in the blocks as needed. If we are dealing with the emergence of the detective story we may code:

Event 1: Edgar Allan Poe and the first English detective
Event 2: The growth of the medium on the European continent
Event 3: The emergence of the dime magazine detectives
Event 4: The detective story as an art form

We have selected four major time periods into which to divide our talk because, according to the experts, these are the major time periods. We can now "structure down" even further. We take Event 1 and declare: Edgar Allan Poe has three main stories which epitomize the detective story. See Figure 5.2.

Figure 5.2

This structure is not a time structure. It is a classification. See page 136. We could then discuss the plots of each of the stories by building another time structure, and so on. We could continue to structure right down to the sentence level. This was how this book was built, incidentally.

We also use the time structure to explain the steps in a process. The pattern is then that of Figure 5.3.

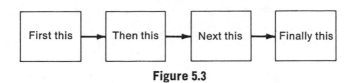

Figure 5.3

If we were presenting a recipe, each box would represent a major step in the process. If we were discussing how to start a motor, each box would be a major step in the process. If there were further directions, we would have to structure down in the boxes as necessary.

Identifying the main time periods or main steps is the problem for the speaker-expert. If you know what you are talking about, you will have no trouble mapping out the headings. For example, most of you do not know the history of the Pennsylvania State University. We do. We, as experts, present you with a time structure in which we identify the main headings. (Figure 5.4.) This structure is a way in

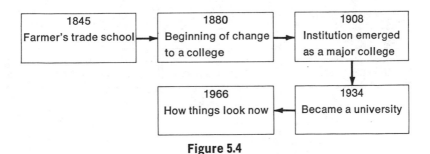

Figure 5.4

which to organize information. The note cards you have about the topic can now be classified into the appropriate boxes. Because one box comes before another, it does not mean that one event caused another. If you want to allege that one event caused another, you cannot use a time structure, because it is not logical to declare that something caused something else just because it preceded it in time. A time structure merely shows the order in which things take place.

We have a number of alternatives now in introducing you to our school. We could apply a space structure to each of our boxes and show you how the campus looked in each time period. We might want to take some consistent classifications like: students, faculty, program, service to the state, and examine them in each time period. If we wanted to show how much the campus had grown in less than one hundred years, we would need to develop a contrast structure in which we compared the space structures for 1845 and 1934. Or, if we wanted to declare that one president, more than any other, brought about the expansion of the university, we would have to build a cause-effect structure (probably within the 1934 box). But a simple time structure frees the speaker from the necessity to argue very much. He is giving only a narrative, showing the order in which things happened. It is the simplest form of narrative, but very convenient for many residual messages.

Let's take a look at the second style we can use for a time structure. Residual message: There are six major steps in baking a cake. The diagram is simple.

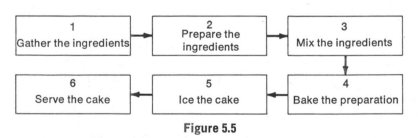

Figure 5.5

When planning to serve a cake, in box number 1, we would have to list and name the ingredients. Anything special that needs to be said about them (evaporated milk, not condensed, for example) can be inserted there. Our substructure in that box would be a simple classification. In box numbers 2 and 3 we have a series of steps in each case, so that time structures would fit most appropriately. There would be minimum commentary about box number 4; nothing more need be said than time and temperature, so there would be no sub-structure necessary. For number 5, a time structure might be neces-sary, or because of the complicated movements required, you might choose a space structure. In box number 6, you may decide on an artistic flourish for the finish and show how serving a cake is unlike serving any other dessert—a contrast structure.

Your structure acts like the harness on a horse. It **directs** the speaker's attention to the **order** of the events needed to prepare the cake. Each event is clearly named. Because of this order in the speaker's presentation, the listener can keep track of what is going on. He may miss some detail in a given box, but the chances of his missing the order of the boxes is very slim. He gets enough informa-tion so that he can ask questions about details later on, such as "Where can I get the ingredients?" "May I use my electric mixer to mix the ingredients?"

Use of this kind of structure is important in business and govern-ment. Speakers are often assigned to instruct others in simple opera-tions. Every delay in learning the operations is costly. Consequently, a well organized presentation is imperative so that employees can learn quickly. In working in such settings, the people being trained usually have a chance to ask on-the-spot questions, but even so, if you think of all the times you have been given instructions that you couldn't possibly understand, you will know how easy it is to botch this particular task.

Using this kind of preparation device, you can equip your listener (if it is appropriate) with a blank diagram to fill out as he listens. So long as you hold to the headings on your diagram, you are virtually guaranteed the attention of your listener. The names of your boxes become keys to a particular set of details. In each case, the arrows show the direction of the steps in preparation. The speaker **and** the listener know the order of things—what comes first and what comes last.

It is sometimes useful to think of these structures as storage boxes designed to hold a "clump" of information. In the first stages of structure, the speaker's job is to put labels on these boxes. Then he puts organizers into the boxes—his substructures, where they seem necessary. Finally, he puts in his "supports." Without the supports, the boxes would collapse.

In Figure 5.6, we show you one drawer of a file cabinet. It is the

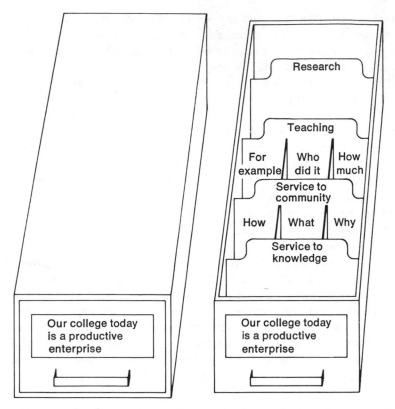

Figure 5.6

last box in Figure 5.4. When we pull out the file drawer, we find some tabs. We have substructures in the drawer. Behind those tabs we need to store information, because if we don't the tabs will fall down and the drawer will appear empty.

Stop: exercises

Practice by drawing time structures for the following topics. If you do not know the main headings, go to the library and look them up.

   1. The Battle of Waterloo
   2. The procedure of play in backgammon
   3. How to use an abacus

    4. Baking lasagna
    5. The growth of a willow tree
    6. The gestation period of the hippopotamus embryo
    7. Cultivation of winter wheat
    8. The Great American Depression
    9. The departure of Richard Nixon
  10. How to operate a fork lift

Here are rules for the use of time structure:

1. Time structure is for residual messages that cover a span of time.
2. The steps in a time structure are in **necessary** sequence. They can't be taken out of order.
3. The main attention is on sequence of events. Thus, your residual message must seek to present a series of events in order.
4. Each individual unit may have a different internal structure or sub-structure as required. Each individual unit becomes its own residual message.

Space structure

Sometimes a residual message shows a group of parts and how they make up a whole. For example, your residual message might be "A modern hospital is a complicated relationship between various components," or "The working parts of an automobile engine all function together to make the car go." You must discuss each of the parts as well as show how they fit together. The basic model looks like this.

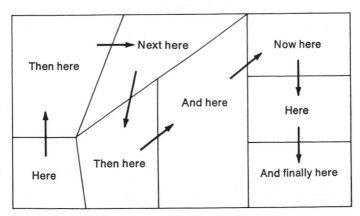

Figure 5.7

You can enter the diagram at any point, but then you have to move in some orderly sequence through the components, discussing each as you come to it. Each main part of the total thing is named in the structure. To prepare your speech, all you do is fit the information about each component into the proper box, and structure it to fit. For example, in discussing the hospital, you may have an "admitting room" in which you discuss the steps of admission in a time sequence, and a "pathology lab" in which you discuss various responsibilities in a classification structure.

In this kind of structure, balance is not so important. You need to show the relationship between parts and the relationship of all the parts to the whole. Some of the parts may be large and complicated and take a good deal of time to discuss. Other parts may be essential, but simple, and take only a little time to discuss. The importance of the part determines how much time you spend on it. In discussing the automobile engine, you would want to give more time to the carburetor than to the air filter or radiator cap. The main point is to make sure that your audience understands that each part contributes to the whole and that all the parts add up to the whole. In the hospital message, the structure would look like this:

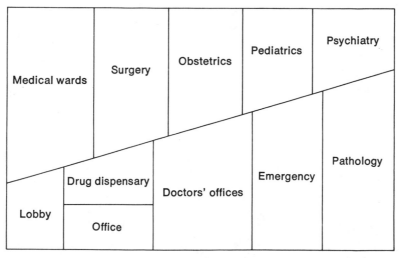

Figure 5.8

You may enter at the lobby and move down one corridor to the end, then make your turn and come back, ending at the medical wards and your exit through the lobby. Or, you may take the major components and locate and discuss them, checking them off as you go. It is your choice and depends to an extent on what kind of audience you have. The naive audience would probably follow better if you took the trip down the corridors. A sophisticated audience might respond best if you emphasized the most important components. Your concern is to do a complete job. Your speech is not over until you have talked about all the components.

You may use the space structure to show how complicated processes operate. When you do this, you are, of course, creating a kind of metaphor, but when a diagram or picture would be helpful, you are into a space structure. For example:

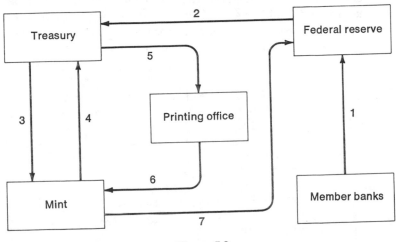

Figure 5.9

This is a combination space and time structure. The residual message is: It is a difficult process for your bank to get new dollar bills. Each of the numbers represents a step in sequence. Each of the blocks represents a location at which some process or activity goes on. The blocks do not really represent a map. They are designed to show how the elements are related to each other. This differs from a schematic like the one in Figure 5.10.

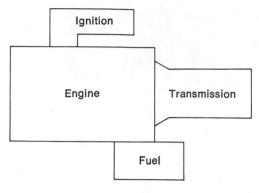

Figure 5.10

To structure the working parts of the automobile engine, the model or structure used would be a mock-up or visual representation of the real thing. You might have to draw a separate model for each component in order to develop your residual message well, showing, in each instance, a diagram of engine block, ignition system, and so forth.

In any case, you can also use this structure figuratively, as in Figure 5.11.

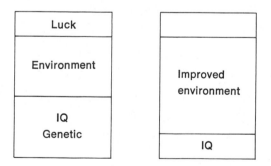

Figure 5.11

Here, you are trying to make an argument about how changes in environment can bring about changes in intelligence. You use two space structures, one showing before the change and the other, afterward. Actually by laying two space structures side by side, you have developed a contrast structure, which your residual message should reflect. In this case, the residual message is: Improvement in environment can raise IQ. You may not want to use a causal relationship structure because the actual relationship may be too difficult to argue. All you need to show, using the structure in Figure 5.11, is that in one case, the situation is this, and in another case, the situation is that. You leave the obvious conclusion for the audience to draw.

Stop: exercises

Draw diagrams for the following residual messages in a space structure. Provide a substructure in each box.

1. How the Department of Interior operates.
2. The management chart at IBM is highly complicated.
3. The operation of the Wankel engine is very simple.
4. The movements of the planet are regular and rhythmic.
5. Vacation spots in New Jersey are few and far between.
6. The federal highway system is an efficient network.
7. The flush toilet is one of man's simplest inventions.
8. The endocrine system is a complicated and delicate balance of components.
9. Eyeglasses cost a lot because manufacturing them is a difficult process.
10. A gourmet will find himself in paradise when he visits Denver.

How many times did you find it necessary to combine your space structure with a time structure?

Rules for the space structure:

1. Space structure can be used figuratively or literally.
2. Structure is not complete if one component is missing.
3. You may start at any point.
4. You may use alternative paths through the diagram, or even skip around, so long as you touch on all components.
5. Differences in importance may be emphasized by relative sizes of blocks.
6. A variety of substructures may be used in the boxes.

By this time it should be clear that the process of structuring itself is being explained through a space structure. Any time we use vis-

uals, models, diagrams, and so forth we are using the space structure, and it is necessary to deal with all aspects.

Classification structure

The classification structure may be used for any residual message
that has information-giving as its main goal. The model may be a
component in almost any kind of message. In fact, this is really the
basic model for structuring. All of the other structures are variations.
The classification structure, as we shall point out later on, is the
basic structure in any of the more complicated structures. Analogy
and contrast actually compare two classification structures. Cause-
effect or any relationship structure shows the relationship between
two or more classifications, and the problem-solution structure,
which is the basis for argumentation also shows a particular kind of
relationship between classifications.

The basic classification structure looks like this.

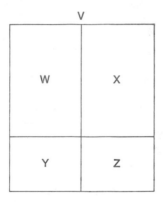

Figure 5.12

Each part of the model is meant to stand on its own, without regard
to the other parts. At the same time, each is considered relatively
equal to the others in importance, and they all total up to the residual
message. We can, if we need to, show relative size by altering the
size of each box, so that if a thing is made up of two important components and two unimportant components, we can illustrate this by

comparative size, as in Figure 5.12. In this instance, V is composed
of two important parts—W and X, and two relatively unimportant
parts—Y and Z. If our residual message is, "The university is made
up of faculty, students, maintenance personnel, and clerical staff,"
we could let W and X stand for students and faculty, while Y and Z
stand for maintenance and clerical. In giving the speech, we would,
of course, spend more time on W and X, than on Y and Z. But, we
could not discuss the whole university without reference to the minor
parts. That is what we mean when we say, in a classification, "the
parts are all-inclusive." That means that all the parts are shown; there
aren't any others.

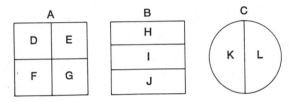

Figure 5.13

In Figure 5.13, we demonstrate how to handle a four-part, three-part
and two-part classification in which the parts are relatively equal.
C = K + L. That could refer to a residual message. We can understand how the student mind works by looking at males and females.
We could change the residual message to read: We can understand
how the student mind operates by looking at the three main levels of
students: remedial, undergraduate, and graduate. That would mean
B = H + I + J. We could state it, Undergraduates operate on four
levels each with different levels of complexity: freshman, sophomores, juniors, and seniors. That would mean A = D + E + F + G.
Note that there is no overlap among the parts. They are **mutually exclusive.** We do not talk about undergraduates, graduates, and females, because undergraduates and graduates include both males
and females. But we could introduce a more complicated two-way
classification, as in Figure 5.14.

We have now divided our material into fourteen separate compartments. We might discover that we need still another classification, by
which we could divide both males and females into "science," "hu-

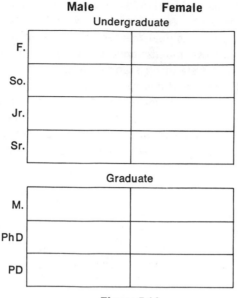

Figure 5.14

manities," "technology," "business," "agriculture," and so on. We may continue to make these classifications as long as they are relevant.

Residual messages like, "There were four main issues that divided the country before the Civil War," "There are four kinds of criminals on the FBI most wanted list," or "Dogs are generally divided into show dogs, toy dogs, work dogs, and hunting dogs" are most suitable to classification structure, although there is no topic that cannot conveniently be structured into a classification type residual message.

The squares operate like storage bins. Information can be stored within them. In practice, you may draw your structure on a large poster card and lay out your note cards on the appropriate squares. The note cards will tell you whether you need to divide a square into smaller units. Furthermore, if you have no note cards on one square and a huge pile on another, you will know what kind of research remains to be done. Or maybe, in selecting the topic, you might revise your residual message so that it refers to only the one square. For example, suppose you were talking about your university and drew a model like figure 5.15.

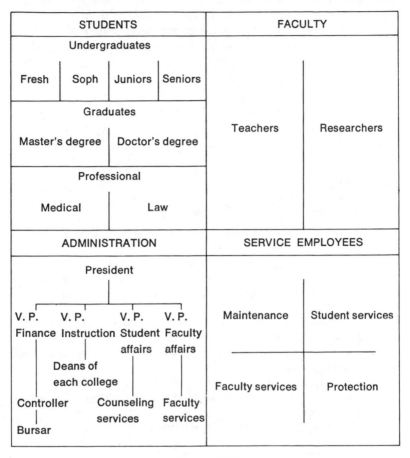

Figure 5.15

In working this out, you might have an interview with a university vice-president and take a brief excursion to the library. There you found stacks of cards mainly on the graduate student and faculty, with little on service employees or administration. You might elect to rephrase your residual message and come up with, "Graduate students at this university have three main problems; financial sur-

vival, fluctuations in programs, and an unpromising job market."
Your message is new, but you are prepared to handle it with this information. No problem. You are spared giving a speech with huge
gaps in it. And furthermore, to cover everything in the diagram in
Figure 5.15, might take a day or two longer than the time allotted.

Structuring serves as a mode of criticism for you in advance. If one
box has little information, you can collapse the box and include it
somewhere else, or you can go to the library to get more information.
In any event, the time allotted will also help you decide on the phrasing of your residual message. If your pile of cards is too large, you
know you will take too much time, and you will have to make a decision on how to cut down on the scope of your message.

Exercise time

Here are some classification topics:

1. Our school system features elementary, secondary, and vocational
   instruction.
2. My courses for this term are about equally difficult.
3. There are several things to do for fun in this town over the weekend.
4. The American government has a legislative, executive, and judicial
   branch.
5. There are seven main themes in Shakespearian drama.
6. Nuclear energy can be used for peace and war.
7. Political parties in America have a variety of platforms and complicated histories.
8. Cities are encountering a number of very costly problems.
9. There are three recommended methods for building interplanetary
   space ships.
10. The library offers a number of services to its patrons.

Substructure each down as far as you can.

Some rules to remember in using classification structure.

1. $A = B + C + D + E$, and so forth. The elements in the structure
   should be inclusive of the entire topic being discussed.
2. $B = C = D = E$. The parts should be relatively equal in emphasis,
   or if some are more important than others they should be visually
   diagrammed in relative proportion.
3. B, C, D, E. The parts should be mutually exclusive. There must be
   no overlap.

Remember that classification structure can be applied to any topic. If you discover a topic that you know something about and you are uncertain about the approach, try to build a classification first.

Analogy

An analogy is a comparison of the similarities between two things. The things can be persons, ideas, objects, events—whatever is at hand that needs comparison. It is important that the two items should be really similar. You might say, "Marriage is like a team in sports. If you play together well, you are likely to win, but if you fight each other, you are likely to lose." There are a number of ways in which marriage and team play in sports are different. There is no referee in marriage, no training camp, no official rule book, no substitute players in case one gets injured. That kind of an analogy might break down very quickly. An ideal analogy takes a form similar to Figure 5.16.

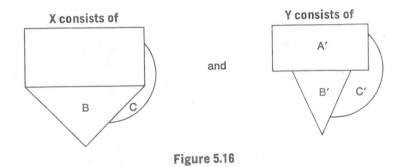

Figure 5.16

The two pictures do not claim to be exactly alike. A is a bit larger than A'. B has a wider base than B', and C is smaller than C'. But the claim is that the things being compared consist of the same elements in roughly similar proportions. Thus, for the residual message: "Many countries have modeled their governments on that of Great Britain", we might have X represent the British government, with A the executive power, B the legislature, and C the judiciary. Y would be any other country, say Canada. Now Canada has a governor-general instead of a king as the figurehead executive. Canada does not have a House of Lords, and in England the House of Lords doesn't function very much. There are some differences, but whatever is true of the **main** elements of the British government is also true of the Canadian. The analogy will hold up.

We use analogies primarily to take something familiar to our audience and explain something unfamiliar by comparison. Thus, the rules of soccer might be obscure to an American audience, but by showing the similarities to football (and of course, noting the important differences), the rules can be made clear.

Suppose you were dealing with the residual message, "Universities financed by the state are pretty much the same all over." We understand our own university. Now we need to apply a classification model to what we know. We group our university's main elements and represent them visually in Figure 5.17. Next, we select another state university. We use the same classification model for it. We then group our information, putting the cards where they belong. If our analogy holds, we shall be saying approximately the same things about one as we say about the other. Our campus may be larger, and another state university may have one or two programs that we do not have. We note this by using a variety of shapes. We can draw a blob on the other state university diagram to indicate some of these differences. But, in the main, the programs, students, and campus are pretty much the same. There are some real differences, if we look for them, but not in the areas that matter to this residual message.

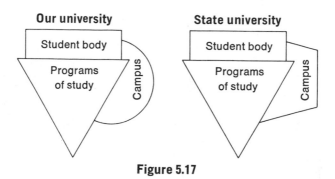

Figure 5.17

Even though the two drawings are slightly different, they are close enough to support the idea that the two universities are really similar.

Now, we may want to reason from the analogies. We may have data to indicate that activities programs depend on the nature of the student body and the programs of the university. If we can show that the student bodies of two institutions are similar, as well as the programs, we might conclude that the activities programs should be about the same. Figure 5.18 shows this diagram.

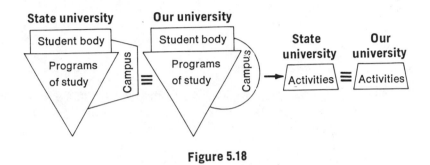

Figure 5.18

This is the kind of model that scientists use when they attempt to apply the findings of experiments with rats and pigeons to human beings, or more typically, conclusions about college sophomores to the population at large. If the basic similarities can be established, it is possible to argue for the outcomes.

Sometimes in working this way with analogies, you find yourself in a problem-solution structure. If you do, take the obligation, for the basis of the proof will be readily available to you. If you were arguing that we ought to have "socialized medicine" in the United States, and you found a working program of socialized medicine in Great Britain, you might argue that the program would work in the United States because of the similarities between the two countries. (You would then have to accept the obligation of offering a plan— take the full obligation of the problem-solution model.)

And of course, every analogy can be answered with a contrast.

Contrast

The contrast model is the opposite of analogy. To deal with a residual message like, "State University is really basically different from our university," we would use the model in Figure 5.19.

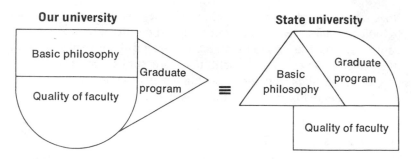

Figure 5.19

The differences in the shapes clearly illustrate the basic differences between the two universities. In Figure 5.20 we show how size and placement of boxes can carry the same message.

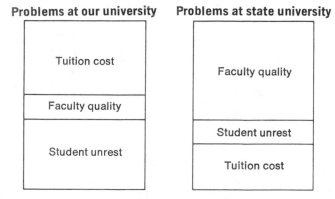

Figure 5.20

Contrast structure has the classification model as its base. It arranges the parts of the classification to reveal differences, exactly as in an analogy, and the parts are shuffled to reveal similarities. Every analogy can be answered with a contrast. The audience then would have to make up their own minds about who does the most effective job of reasoning. You will find that as you must use the more complicated structures, the possibilities increase of argument being effectively raised against you. When you are talking about the steps in a process, or the components involved, or the layout of a territory, there is little argument that can be offered, although sometimes you may omit details and someone in the audience will correct you. But every time you declare that two items are similar, someone may answer by declaring their differences. And each time you see the differences between two things as obvious, someone else will declare that they are the same.

There is no way out. We are moving into a complicated area called "argumentation." Whenever two persons are arguing, it is the audience that decides who wins. You never argue to convince your opponent, but both you and your opponent are appealing for the minds of your listeners. This means that in addition to having a good and lucid structure, you will need to select forms of support that have the maximum appeal to your audience. We shall discuss these in the next chapter. But, before we leave this chapter, we need to look at the most complicated of the structures.

Exercise time

Build the appropriate model showing analogy and contrast for each of the topics, and then state the residual message implied by each.

1. Our program should be the same as that in Louisiana.
2. See America first; it's your best vacationland.
3. Nixon was a (good, bad) president.
4. Jane Austen was a (good, bad) author.
5. Anyone who can play hockey can play lacrosse.
6. If we adopt this program, we can expect the same results as with that program. (You pick the "this" and "that.")

Think up some of your own.

And don't forget the one extremely important use of the analogy and contrast structures, their use in criticism. Any time you are making an evaluation according to some standards, you are using these two models. If your residual message is, "Melville is a typical Amercian author," you might have a structure like Figure 5.21.

You would have to prove that some valid authority agreed the four items declared to be typical of American authors were really typical. Someone else might argue with you that they were not. Then you would have to select examples to document your assertion that Melville did

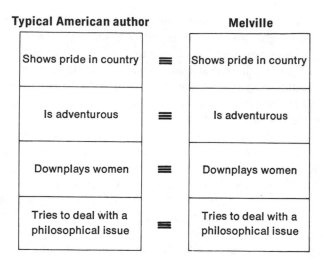

Figure 5.21

the things required of a typical American author. Someone else might argue that he did not. You can imagine the difficulty you might have in "proving" that John Smedley was the best man for the job, for you would first have to establish some criteria for "best man for the job," and then show that Smedley had these qualities. But the procedure, both constructively and in rebuttal, is the procedure of comparison and contrast. Continue the exercise by trying some of these critical comparisons.

1. Andy Warhol epitomizes pop art.
2. Skin flicks are legitimate art vehicles.
3. Dustin Hoffman is the century's best actor.
4. Acid rock music expresses the mood of youth.
5. Ballet is a virile, athletic expression.

And you can think of some more. Each of the above legitimately uses analogy and contrast as its basic structure.

Some rules to remember about analogy and contrast:

1. Critical comparisons make the most effective use of analogy and contrast.
2. Comparison (analogy and contrast) is used to explain the unfamiliar through the familiar.

3. All analogies can be refuted through contrasts.
4. It is necessary to argue that you are comparing the important elements in both analogy and contrast.
5. Contrast is used primarily for refutation.

Relationship

This is not the place for a short course in logic. You may read what you need to know about logical reasoning in a little paperback by Monroe Beardsley called **Thinking Straight.** For our purposes, we need to know how to stand up and argue about the way in which things influence each other. There are three main ways of looking at this process. One is to say that sometimes things go along with other things. They are not caused by them; they happen in conjunction with them. We do not know, for example, whether depression causes unemployment or unemployment causes depression, but we know that they are usually associated.

Thus, when we are talking about one, we had better be prepared to talk about the other. If we have things that are connected but do not know the connection, we use the model in Figure 5.22.

Another possible relationship between items and events is called

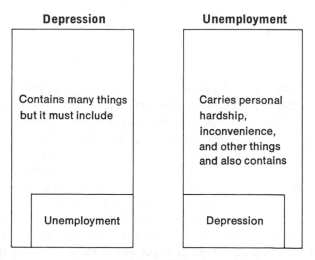

Figure 5.22

the relationship of "function." As one item increases, the other also increases. As one item decreases, the other decreases. Or, there could be a negative connection, as one increases the other decreases. Figure 5.23 illustrates the possible layout for this kind of relationship.

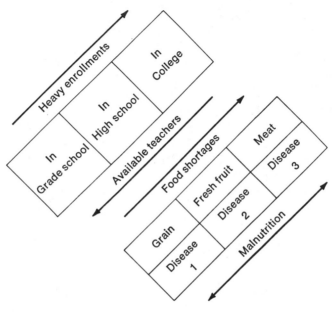

Figure 5.23

For the most part, however, in your speaking, you will most often have to deal with the **cause-effect** or **effect-cause** relationship. This kind of residual message declares that one set of events results in some other kinds of events, or that the present situation resulted from a particular set of events. The model looks like Figure 5.24.

In this kind of presentation, your goal is to convince the audience of the connection between the two events. Suppose your residual message is: "Building recreation centers in the slums will reduce delinquency." Your obligation is to build the connection between recreation and nondelinquency, and lack of recreation with delinquency. This is a hard kind of argument to make, because there are many exceptions that could be taken to the causal connection. You

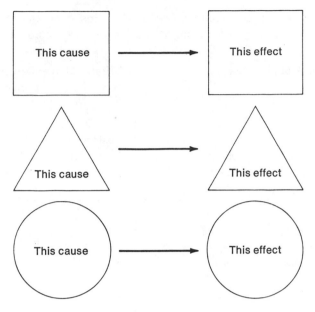

Figure 5.24

would need to rely heavily on your supports, which might include statements from various authorities, statistics about particular neighborhoods, and narratives about individual cases. You might find as you tried to put this speech together that you would want to hedge a little and maybe change your residual message to: "Recreation centers provide one way in which to combat juvenile delinquency." Then all you would have to do is argue for the efficiency of the proposal.

Also, this kind of structure seems to imply a problem-solution structure. If you are proposing recreation centers as a solution to a particular problem, you need to take on considerable obligation in proof. You will find, however, that cause-effect structures and problem-solution structures are almost always connected. You might be giving an academic speech on the residual message: "The Civil War resulted from failure of American government to take into account certain economic factors." This kind of speech does not imply a proposal and does not confront you with the necessity of defending a proposed solution.

But virtually every public proposal demands concern for causal connections. For example, look at the diagram in Figure 5.25.

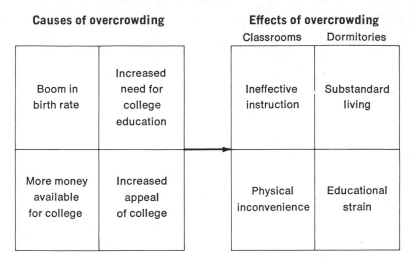

Causes of overcrowding   **Effects of overcrowding**

| Boom in birth rate | Increased need for college education | Ineffective instruction | Substandard living |
| More money available for college | Increased appeal of college | Physical inconvenience | Educational strain |

Figure 5.25

Suppose you were making a proposal to combat overcrowding in colleges. You have two alternatives: one is to work against the symptoms. You could do this merely by saying colleges should not take in any more students than they can accommodate. Your other alternative is to work on the cause, but you need to discover it first. Another way of approaching symptoms would be to set up tutorial service to compensate for ineffective instruction, and a new counseling service to handle the emotional strain. If you handled it this way, you would be in a problem-solution structure. (See next section.) If, however, your proposal involved restructuring the college scene to accommodate such things as birthrates, new money, and public appeal, you would have to handle the causal relationship first.

Doing it this way allows you maximum leeway to move. You might not want to argue for a solution with a particular audience. Your objective might be simply to have them understand the situation a little better. Another approach would be to regard your residual message as informational. For example, in Figure 5.26, we show a controversial idea handled through information-giving, in a pure cause-effect structure.

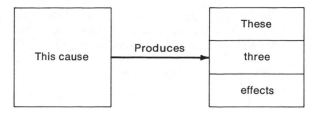

Figure 5.26

Compared to the first type of structure, this is a relatively simple speech to handle. Suppose your residual message was: "Smoking marijuana has three effects on the smoker." You needn't talk very much about the "cause." You have named it and that is enough. What you must do is document or prove that each effect is related to marijuana smoking. Thus, you may allege that marijuana smoking causes mental, physical, and social problems. You may use personal testimony, case histories, and quotes from psychiatrists to prove the first point. You may have a good quotation from a medical book for the second, and you may have to rely on your description of the counter-culture in your community for the third. But whatever you do, you have to make the effort to document the connection.

Let us remind you again, that when dealing with controversial propositions, you can never nail things down with certainty. There will almost always be some points that can be raised against you. Therefore try, as best you can, to select supports that will appeal to your audience (not your opponents), and hope that you can do the most effective job of driving these points home.

A quickie exercise

Try drawing some of the diagrams for the following residual messages, and then see if you can think up the kinds of material you would have to get to prove your points.

1. Delinquency is the result of poor social conditions.
2. Schools are doing an inferior job of teaching reading.
3. We got into the Vietnam war because of bungling in government.
4. Ways in which a new program will change the system.
   (Note that you can use cause-effect structure for futurity. Simply draw a detailed picture of the change you plan to make, and then

project into the future the results it will have. This is an important step in the problem-solution structure, as we will show later on.)
5. Vocational counseling helps people get the right kind of job.

Some things to remember about cause-effect:

1. Note that each side of the structure forms a classification structure.
2. One effect can come from many causes, and one cause can have many effects.
3. The actual relationship in any of these models **must be argued by you.**
4. This structure precedes problem-solution structure in most cases where the solution has something to do with the cause of the problem.

Problem-solution: argument

When we argue, we declare ourselves in favor of or against a position, and we give reasons—reasons that will appeal to the audience. Aristotle warned us to be careful, when he said,

"The fool tells me his reasons; the wise man persuades me with my own."

We keep in mind, all the time, that there will be persons who take an opposite position. We are not in the business of negotiating or reasoning. When we engage in argument we want to win, and winning means getting the greatest possible number of persons in the audience to agree with us. When you declare yourself in favor of some new idea or program, you have four obligations:

1. You must prove that there is a need for the program.
2. You must give the details of the program.
3. You must show that the program will remedy the problems you specified in the need.
4. You must be prepared to show that your program will not cause problems that are worse than the ones you are solving.

The problem-solution structure attempts to give a format in which you can handle this obligation, which we refer to as "burden of proof." The basic model is shown in Figure 5.27.

In this instance, the speaker would first name a problem. Next he would describe his solution, relating each step to a component of the problem. In so doing, he would take care of the three main obligations in his burden of proof.

Suppose you had a residual message: "The new zoning ordinance

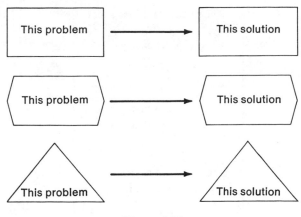

Figure 5.27

will solve the housing problem in our town." The first step would be to stipulate the components in the housing problem. By using a classification structure, you might get the model in Figure 5.28, p. 154.

In order to establish the connection between the provisions of the ordinance and predictions of what the ordinance will do, it may be necessary to insert an analogy model in your diagram, and then show on what authority you argue the analogy.

Another approach is to take a problem and attempt to meet it with separate solutions. The advantage to this is that if one of the solutions is argued down, you still salvage something. The model is pictured in Figure 5.29, p. 155.

For instance, use the residual message, "The Social Security system has effectively met the needs of the American people." The problem may have three parts, represented by A, B, and C:A, for the needs of the aged, B for the needs of widows and orphans, and C for the needs of the disabled. Solutions could be referred to as A', B', and C.' A' = old age benefits, B' = survivor's benefits, and C' = workman's compensation. But say we knew that we were going to be refuted with another proposal. We could make an analogy between proposal 1 and proposal 2, and show how each meets the basic need, arguing that whatever proposal meets more of the need should be accepted. We would then show that Social Security (Solution 2) meets more of the need than the opposition proposal.

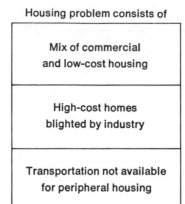

Housing problem consists of

Mix of commercial and low-cost housing
High-cost homes blighted by industry
Transportation not available for peripheral housing

The zoning ordinance contains

A provision banning mixture of commercial and residential areas	Which will	Eliminate low-cost housing in center of town
A requirement that industry install pollution devices		End pollution destruction
A provision permitting builders to run private transport systems		Encourage low-cost building in peripheral areas

Figure 5.28

Suppose the residual message actually stated the case as an analogy: "The British system for handling drug addiction is better than the American system." The components of the problem would be laid out in a classification structure. Another classification would be made of the present method of dealing with the problem, together with an assessment of how well it is working (following the obligations of the analogy structure). We would then add the third classification—the details of the British system—showing it would deal with the problem better than the American system.

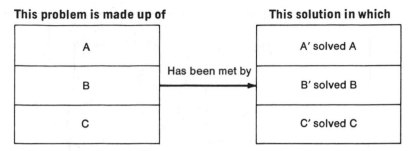

Figure 5.29

Note that as the structures get more complicated, and as you get into argument, you have to structure and substructure at the same time. Working your way through the various diagrams, you will find your own style of preparation. You may prefer to use flow charts— you may want to make your structures considerably more complicated than we have shown here. We will show you a model structured speech shortly, and you might want to work from that.

Take a time out now and go back to the propositions on those note cards about society on pages 113–115. Before you turn the page, see if you can fit the propositions together into a structure. In Figure 5.30, you can see how the speaker actually connected them. Note that even without the supports inserted, the speech seems to make sense. Note also the way in which the speaker uses arrows to direct himself through the diagram.

Sample of a structured speech

You will get a better idea of how this apparently complicated process makes things simple by examining the following set of diagrams. The structure is for a speech given by the superintendent of schools of a large educational system. The occasion was a meeting of interested citizens. The residual message was: "Our schools are in good condition and they will be ready to meet the future."

The speaker had a good reputation in the community, though schools are always a controversial topic and there are always parents whose children are not doing well and who are prepared to place the blame on the schools. The superintendent knew every detail of his system.

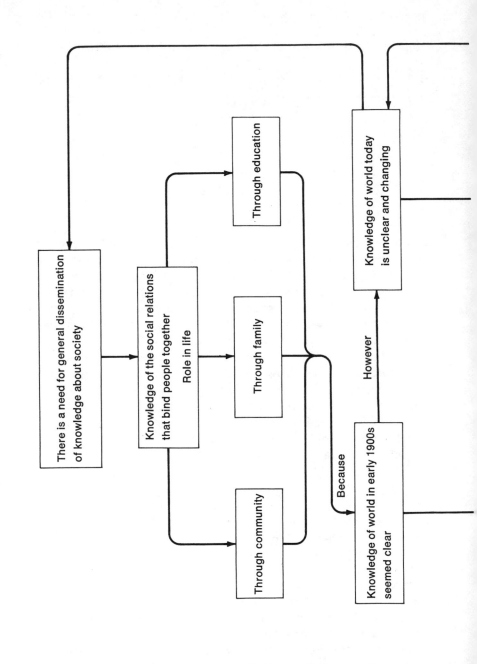

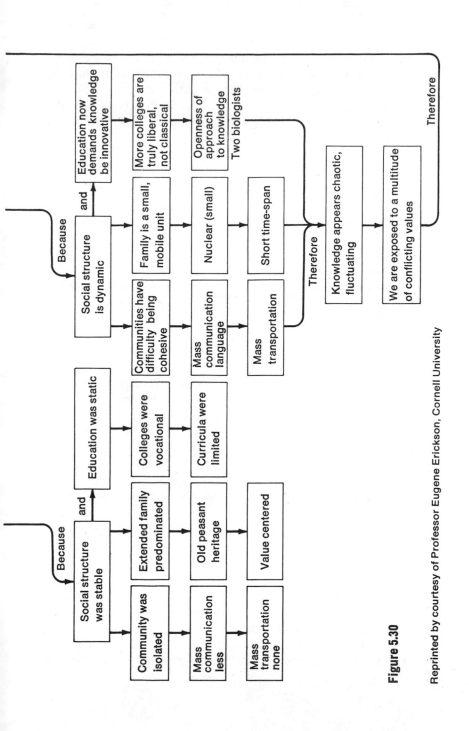

Figure 5.30

Reprinted by courtesy of Professor Eugene Erickson, Cornell University

He had a great deal of clerical help to assist him in gathering data for this speech. He needed the goodwill of the audience because he planned to propose a tax increase at a later date.

He started with a time structure around the residual message: "The area schools have shown steady growth and improvement," illustrated in Figure 5.31.

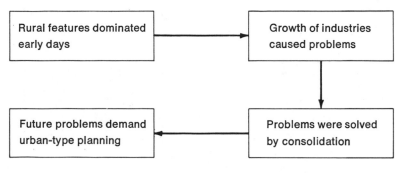

Figure 5.31

Each of these units in the time structure was expanded and detailed into a subresidual message. For instance, "rural features" started out as a classification structure. Sparse population, transportation deficiency, poorly trained teachers, and minimal demand for education were the main components of the structure (see Figure 5.32, p. 159).

He ended up with a cause-effect structure as shown in Figure 5.32, where the rural features of the community were named as the causes of the problems the schools were having. The supports he used are noted inside the boxes.

The next submessage was clearly a cause-effect structure. The residual message in Figure 5.33, p. 160, was, "The expansion of the local university and influx of industry created more problems for the schools."

The next box presented a problem-solution structure, showing how school consolidation in the area solved the basic problems. Figure 5.34, p. 161, presents this structure.

The final box developed an analogy between the local system and an urban system. The analogy was important to the superintendent

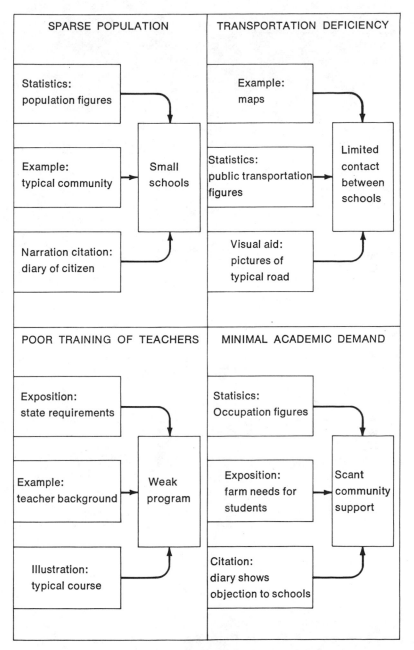

Figure 5.32

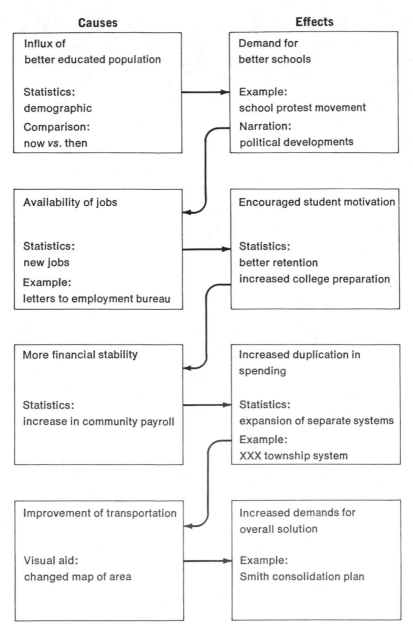

Figure 5.33

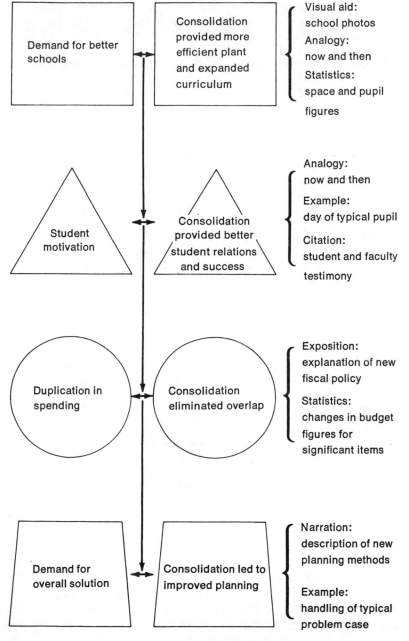

Figure 5.34

because he intended to use this analogy later on to argue for more funds. The final box is illustrated in Figure 5.35.

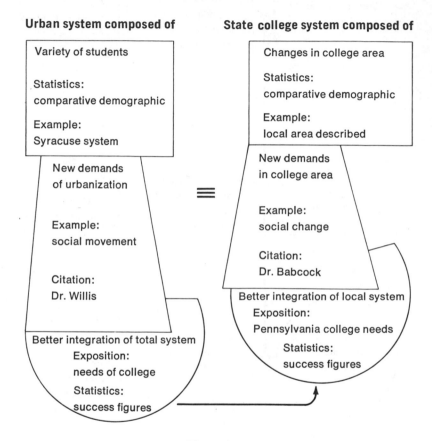

Figure 5.35

The whole structure is illustrated in Figure 5.36, next page.

When he actually gave the speech, all he had in front of him was the main structure (Figure 5.36) with references to his supports in each of the boxes. By working from the structure, the speaker was assured that everything he said would relate to his residual message. He did not to have to prepare a manuscript or commit the speech to memory. He was prepared to pay attention to his audience and respond to their

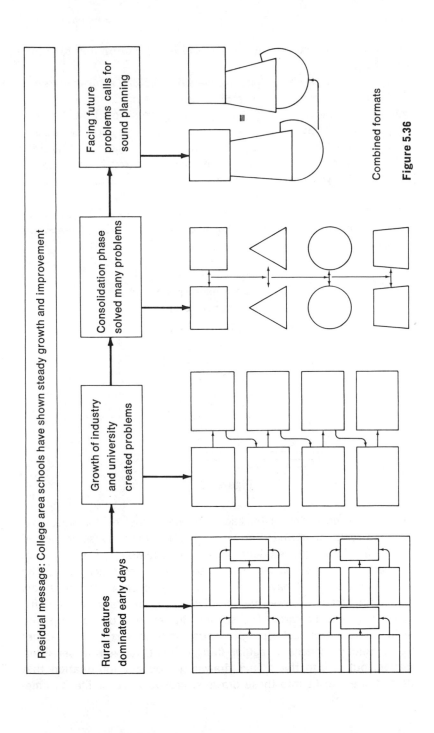

Residual message: College area schools have shown steady growth and improvement

Rural features dominated early days

Growth of industry and university created problems

Consolidation phase solved many problems

Facing future problems calls for sound planning

Combined formats

Figure 5.36

responses to him. All he needed was the visual picture that the structure gave him.

You should now know that in order to structure a message effectively, you will often have to combine the various models. The nature of
your residual message should suggest an overall model. At the same
time, once you have decided what you need to support the residual
message illustrated by the overall model, you will have identified the
subresidual messages. You can continue structuring down as far as
is needed for you own security. By holding to the structure, you are
guaranteed not to get off track.

Sometimes it helps to think of your structure as a file box. In the
next chapter we shall discuss what goes into the file box. (See Figure
5.37.)

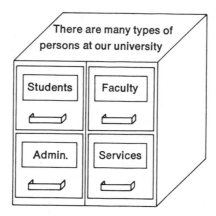

Figure 5.37

There is a special drawer for each division of the residual message.
Each drawer is for storing information. The drawers can also be divided
on the inside. In the student drawer, for example, we might have
compartments for studies, activities, social life, and other things. The
faculty drawer might have sections such as teaching and research.
The administration drawer may be divided into operations, planning,
counseling, and so forth. The service drawer may be split up into
maintenance, groundskeeping, repairs, and so forth. The cabinet
works exactly as does a regular filing cabinet. As you gather information, put it into the proper drawer. If you get information that
doesn't seem to fit into these drawers, cast it aside or file it some-

where else, for it probably will not help you to deliver the residual message.

We offer structuring as an alternative to outlining. Virtually any speech text will explain how to outline a speech. It is our view that before an outline can be made it is necessary to build a structure; and furthermore, once the structure has been built, it is not necessary to outline. Most students regard outlining as an indignity because they do not see how it helps them prepare their message. We are suggesting rather strongly that structuring **does help** in the preparation of a message, and you ought to try it. If you feel uncomfortable about this, switch to traditional outlining with the help of one of the available reference books in the library.

Loosen up! Shake it out! Get rid of those unsightly Grevitzes.

Exercise: the great grevitz problem

A nonsense exercise about the grevitz will test whether you can now shuffle material. No one ever heard of a grevitz, and all of the statements are fictitious. But there are enough clues to enable you to fill in the structure in Figure 5.38. Don't look at Figure 5.39 until you have made a try at Figure 5.38. It may help to copy each item onto a card so you can shuffle them. Or maybe your whole class will want to copy the layout sheet in Figure 5.38 on a bigger piece of paper, and you may all try to file cards on it.

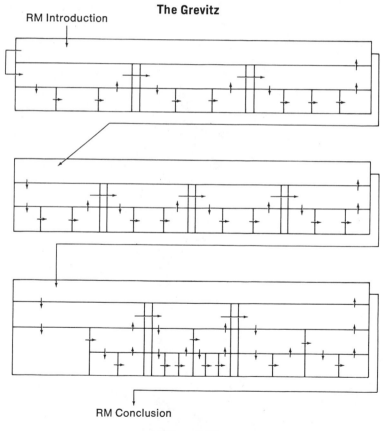

Figure 5.38

Answers to the Grevitz problem

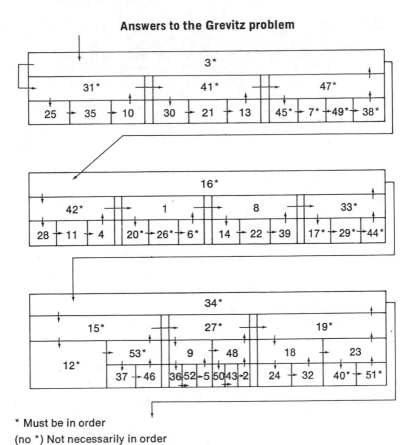

* Must be in order

(no *) Not necessarily in order

Figure 5.39

Think of each of the following entries as a separate note card. In fact, if you are working with a group on this exercise, it is a good idea to copy the items, one to a card, and be sure to number them as they are numbered here. Your job is to get every item fitted into the boxes in the blank structure in Figure 5.38. If you succeed in doing this, all that is needed is to follow the arrows to be able to give a sensible sounding speech on grevitzes. Now isn't that something worth working for?

Residual message: The grevitz has a distinguished history, illustrated by its uses and its method of operation.

Introduction: Everyone should know about grevitzes. . . .

1. Still another use for the grevitz is to put out forest fires.
2. In salting grevitz shells, drop the salt from a distance of six inches.
3. The grevitz has had a long and distinguished history.
4. The Blugars use the grevitz to induce euphoria at spring orgies.
5. If the grevitz shell begins to wiggle in the water, the water is too hot.
6. The third step in using a grevitz to stop a forest fire is to blow hard at the fire.
7. In 1955 the Wallonians contracted with the Common Market to distribute grevitzes.
8. Still another use of the grevitz is for bifurcation of the libido.
9. The water used for soaking grevitz shells should be lukewarm.
10. The first grevitz cost 3,000,046 grozziks or 14 cents American.
11. The Swiss use the grevitz to induce transluctability at chocolate euphoria ceremonies.
12. Great care should be used in removing the grevitz shell.
13. Andrejas Klorp marketed the first grevitz at Krbitzkce.
14. Grevitzes do an excellent job of bifurcation in libidinous denouement and other echdysiasms.
15. The first step in using a grevitz is to remove the shell.
16. There are four main uses for the grevitz.
17. The grevitz may be used to eliminate earwigs only in the winter.
18. While installing the grevitz, do not twist.
19. After the shell has been soaked, the grevitz should be installed in the left ear.
20. The first step in using the grevitz to put out forest fires is to throw it over your right shoulder while facing the fire.
21. Klorp associated his perfection process with the work of Denigram Geech.
22. Grevitzes do an excellent job of bifurcation in plenifors libido.
23. When inserting the grevitz, use a gentle pressure.
24. Twisting the grevitz may injure the ear.
25. Nebo Finster developed the grevitz in his laboratory at Gezornemplatz.
26. The second step in using the grevitz to put out forest fires is to stamp three times on the ground.
27. The second step in operating the grevitz is to soak the shell.
28. Greeks and other pagans used the grevitz to induce euphoria at bar mitzvahs.
29. To eliminate earwigs, use voodoo with your grevitz to seduce the male earwigs.

30. Klorp perfected the grevitz by reducing its cost to 4,005,077 grozziks or 11 cents American.
31. The first grevitz was developed by Sigwald Finster in 1801.
32. Twisting the grevitz may break off the maffle.
33. A final use for the grevitz is to eliminate earwigs.
34. To operate a grevitz takes considerable skill.
35. Finster used a distillation process to produce his first grevitz.
36. Water used to soak grevitz shells should be lukewarm (85°).
37. Shells should not be discarded because they are good to eat with lukewarm Kaltemde.
38. Today, the grevitz accounts for 60 percent of the Wallonian economy.
39. Grevitzes can bifurcate the libido in cases of delerium tremens.
40. When inserting grevitzes by the pressure method, use the left elbow to push the grevitz.
41. The grevitz was perfected in 1906 by Andrejas Klorp.
42. The first use of the grevitz is to induce euphoria.
43. Salt dropped in grevitz shell soaking water should be put in at the rate of two grains per corner.
44. After the earwig has been seduced via grevitz voodoo, stamp on it with your foot.
45. In 1951, grevitzes were mentioned in the free trade agreement with South Pludge.
46. Grevitz shells should not be discarded for they provide protection for other fleebs.
47. From 1951 to the present, grevitzes remain the mainstay of the Wallonian economy.
48. A pinch of salt should be dropped into the water used to soak grevitz shells.
49. In 1962, the Wallonians enacted the grevitz protection bill.
50. The pinch of salt dropped in the soaking waters = 8 grains/gal.
51. While pushing on the grevitz with the right elbow, the left index finger should be inserted in the right ear.
52. The temperature of water used to soak shells should be tested with the elbow.
53. After shells have been removed, they should not be discarded.

Conclusion: Now you know all about the grevitz, and the next time one is mentioned in conversation you can nod knowingly and say, "Mmm, hmmm!"

One more time. As a last word, one good way to test out the strength of your structure is to use the "because" test. You go to a main box, and then look at the subboxes, and see if you can connect them with the word **because.**

For example: The Fitch bill should be enacted (because)

1. Things are messed up.
2. The Fitch bill will remedy the mess-up.
3. Several persons say it will work.

The sentences tend to hang together with that word **because.** If you find a sentence where the because doesn't fit, you know you have something illogical and you may redo it.

Of course, it is obvious by now that you and your instructor should work out some ways in which you can start structuring some speeches along about now. And don't be afraid to use the method to get your English themes set up. It'll work.

SIX

Inserting supports

Our problem now is to collect some information to put into the boxes. What gets written on those cards that are being filed away in the cabinets?

First, what gets written on those cards comes:

1. Out of your own head
2. From interviews with experts
3. From library research

and all of it has something to do with the residual message.

Second, what gets written on those cards should be written neatly.

1. Put a reference number in the box and a reference number on the card so you will know where it belongs.
2. Note the name of the source so you will have it should you need to refer to it again.

A support is a bit of information. It is anything that clarifies, expands, dramatizes, or otherwise explains the residual message. Supports are so-called because they hold up the individual cells or cubicles in the structure. They give the message shape, just as the supports in a tent.

When we looked at the basic communication model in Figure 3.1 we saw that the main task of the communicator is to overcome the interferences (noises) that could get in the way of a clear understanding of his message. We learned then that only by "amplifying" the message, making it louder through the use of stylized redundancy, could we go very far in breaking through the interference. We use supports to introduce the stylized redundancy. Supports enable us to say the "same" thing again in different ways. For example:

> Too many marriages in the United States end up in divorce.
> According to ——, 40 percent of marriages will break up, and in California, 60 percent.
> In one community, seven of the ten neighbors in a social club ended up in divorce.
> Let me tell you the story of a typical divorce.

The speaker will appeal to those with statistical minds; he will explain the statistic to those with simpler minds; and he will tell a story for those who like illustrations. He is really repeating his main point, "Too many marriages in the United States end up in divorce," but it is not necessary for him to point this out. The redundancy through the use of supports will tell the listeners three times over what the main point is.

Every listener has a different style of listening, state of mind, and personality. Few audiences are composed of individuals who are alike in a number of respects. The effective speaker takes this into account by using as much support as he can reasonably use, with as much variety in the support as possible. He should create enough stylized redundancy to reach every style—and to provide something for every taste.

The residual message is a main frame of an idea presented to an audience. The supports are the props for that frame, the siding, the ornaments. Without the supports, there would be no reason for the audience to understand or to agree. In any case there is a pattern to presentation. You start with the frame, a statement of your proposition: Marijuana should be made legal. You offer your "proofs" (using the because test).

> 1. Present marijuana laws are based on false information.
> 2. Marijuana has been proved harmless.
> 3. Convicting marijuana users makes young people disrespectful of the law.

You have a problem-solution structure that looks like Figure 6.1. Each box needs to be structured down. We start with the residual messages of the boxes, the sentences above.

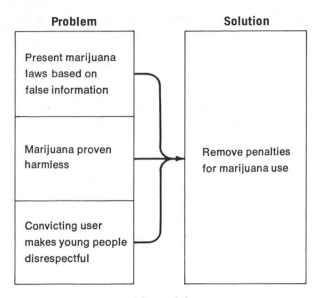

Figure 6.1

To defend the first submessage, "Present laws are based on false information," the speaker charges that since the laws were passed in the 1930s, they are based on the 1930s view of marijuana. He then proceeds to quote some myths about musicians' use of marijuana, and examines the reports of the 1930s narcotics commissioner, suggests that people have associated marijuana with poverty, and declares that marijuana laws were leftovers of morality from prohibition. The first two represent supports; they offer evidence they can be examined and evaluated. The latter two items are personal beliefs. If the speaker happens to be an authority, they might serve as supports, but if he is not, they would be questioned. To support the second point, he cites three studies from medical journals that declared marijuana harmless. These qualify as supports, but there is the danger that his opposition could cite similar reports alleging harm. The question would have to be resolved by the audience, who would probably select the point of view with the most documentation. For the final point, the supports rest on quotes from friends (hardly authorities), a book about police that offers the idea as one possible reason why young people disrespect police, plus a statement by a policeman given to a legis-

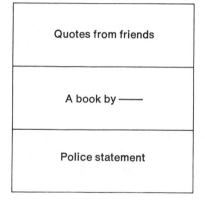

Laws based on false information

1930s view of marijuana	
Myths about musicians	Associated with poverty
Narcotics commission statements	Morality leftover from prohibition

Marijuana has been proved harmless

Study 1
Study 2
Study 3

Convictions make young people disrespectful

Quotes from friends
A book by ——
Police statement

Figure 6.2

lative committee. The last item would qualify as a support. The sentence from the book could be made to look like a support only if the speaker misrepresented it. If he honestly declared that it is only one item on a long list of items, then it is not so powerful a support. The quotes from friends, while interesting, might be from too biased a source as to be considered support. Notice, in each case, however, that the supports could be connected logically to their residual messages through the use of the "because" test.

In general, the format for using supports looks like Figure 6.3.

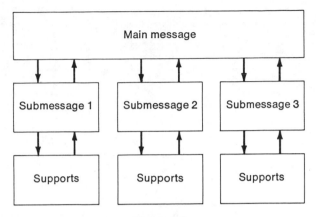

Figure 6.3

Following the arrows, the speaker would state his main residual message, offer submessage number 1 as a support, then offer the supports for message number 1. He would then restate number 1, then restate the main residual message, then proceed to submessage number 2. After that would come the supports and a restatement of number 2, then a restatement of the main residual message. Finally, a statement of number 3 would be given, then its supports and a restatement. The conclusion with the main residual message would follow. In each case, the restatement would permit the speaker to summarize and make a transition through that summary to the next point, so that the speaker is constantly pointing attention to his main residual message, using everything else in the speech—submessages and their supports —to prove or illustrate the main message.

Let's take a somewhat more informative kind of topic, a report from the city manager with the residual message: "Our town is faced with three major problems: racial unrest, finances, and pollution." This is clearly a classification structure. In each case, the three submessages would be:

> Racial unrest is a problem in our town.
> Finances are a problem in our town.
> Pollution is a problem in our town.

These are also structured as classifications, the supports for the messages representing elements of the classification. So, if we look at

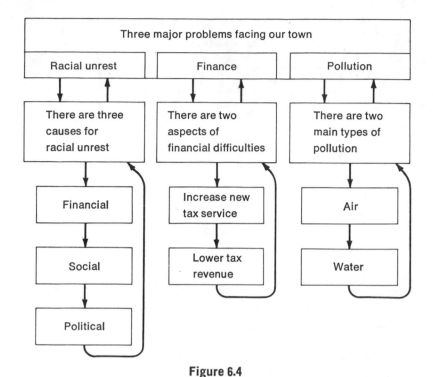

Figure 6.4

Figure 6.4 we discover that we need some data about financial problems and race. This is easy enough; a statistical comparison of black
and white income will do. For social problems, we can put up a
diagram of living areas, and make a contrast between the level of white
housing versus black housing, as well as white recreation facilities
versus black recreation facilities. To handle political problems, we
can use another statistic showing that the proportion of blacks in
government is very small in comparison to their relative numbers in
the population. To handle the financial problems we need to list the
new services authorized by the city council with a price tag on each,
and show the statistics about tax revenue, again contrasting it to income for the last fiscal year showing greater expenditures against
lower revenues. The city manager can do this on his own authority
because he is expected to have this information.

To handle the pollution issue, it is a simple matter to get quotations from the reports of the city engineer and city sanitarian. Notice how the connections are made with arrows. Using our file drawer metaphor, the supports were "inside" the three bins (the substructures). We needed to take them out to talk about them, but to make sure that they stayed where they belonged, we hooked them onto the drawer with a line. The arrows show us the direction in which to proceed. We have built our transitions into the speech by going back to each home block so that we can state a residual message, support it, then restate it. An old country preacher once offered this format as the "secret of his success" in giving sermons:

> Tell 'em what you gonna tell 'em.
> Then tell 'em.
> Then tell 'em what you told 'em.
> Siddown.

If you don't like evidence from country preachers, how about Aristotle, who argued very strongly that the speaker should state the most general proposition first and then offer its proofs? There are also some "empirical studies" that present the same conclusion. It is very difficult for a listener to handle an inductive procedure in speaking. An inductive procedure presents the evidence first and then draws the conclusion. Sadly enough, most evidence leads to a number of different conclusions and you can't always be sure your audience will select the conclusion you want them to. Thus, since it is **your obligation to organize information into a structure,** you need to make sure that the audience sees your supports actually supporting. And the best way in which to do this is to give the residual message **before** offering the supports.

Thus, supports are added to the basic format or structure of the message. They give the speech its depth and detail, and they make sure that the residual message stands up. In order to accomplish this, the supports must be strong enough to bear the weight of the main residual message and submessages. Furthermore, the supports must fit the bins. Note the drawers in Figure 6.5, next page.

You have a set of cards providing information that you think relates to "problems in our town." The headings on the cards read as follows:

1. Zoning is a process of deciding what should go where.
2. There is a regular traffic jam lasting 30 minutes each night at the corner of Main and Pincus.

RM There are three main problems in our town

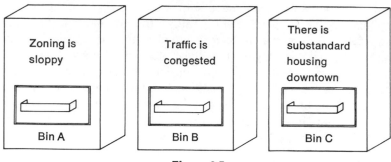

Figure 6.5

3. Motorists complain that lights are badly synchronized on Pincus Parkway and also on Gruffle Boulevard.
4. Every zoning ordinance since 1962 has related to peripheral construction.
5. Most of the family-type stores downtown have turned into cut-rate stores.

Clearly number 1 is a definition that belongs in Bin A. Numbers 2 and 3 refer to traffic (one a statistic, the other, testimony) and they fit Bin B. Number 4 refers to Bin A. Number 5 needs to be examined. Is there any relationship between the information on this card and any of the three bins you are using? Does it talk about zoning? Not directly, although it might support the statement that lack of zoning has caused the downtown area to deteriorate. It certainly makes no statement about either traffic or housing. The question is, does the statement warrant its being kept and used, or should it go on the discard pile? You need to decide whether you want to use it in Bin A. If you do, you need to reword it so that it relates directly to the contents of that bin. You might also get the idea that another bin ought to be started with the label, "The downtown area has deteriorated over recent years." If you decide this, the card can fit in that bin. If you do not make this decision, place the card in Bin S (to save for a later speech.) The one thing you don't need in setting up your speech is to permit a lot of digressions to creep in. Regarding the main boxes of your structure as bins, and testing each bit of information to see if it really fits the bin is the best possible way of making sure that everything in your speech helps to present the residual message.

If you keep coming up with a blank in Bin C, you have two choices. You may get information directly relevant to that box. Go to the city surveyor's office, to the town council records office, to the library, to the mayor, or any place where there might be information. When you go, you will have some direct questions to ask, because your purpose in going is explicit: you have to fill up Bin C. Or you may decide to put Bin C back into storage and revise your residual message to read, "There are two main problems in our town." If you have a pile of cards about deterioration in the downtown area, you may decide to replace the label on Bin C and put those cards in it. The choices are yours to make and they must be made before you go out to speak. Analyzing your information according to its suitability in specific bins, however, guarantees you the maximum clarity when you finally have things together.

Once you have all the information distributed into the proper bins, you need to make a decision about balance. A speech should be properly balanced—and you have to decide what "proper" means. Are points A, B, and C equal in importance? If so, in order to give this impression to the audience, you ought to be saying about the same amount on each point. If you have twenty-five cards in Bin A and only three in Bin C, you can bet that you will talk longer about A than C, and the audience will get the impression that A is more important (more severe or more immediate) than C. If you want to give that impression, fine! If you do not, you either have to remove some cards from A, or add some cards to C, so that you will devote about the same amount of emphasis to each.

These decisions don't just happen; they take effort on your part. You need to make decisions about each bit of evidence or support:

1. Which box does it properly fit?
2. If it does not fit any box, should it be made to fit, discarded, or should a box be made for it?
3. Does any box have too much or too little information in it?

And there will be a final decision.

4. Is there style involved in what is in each box?

If you have more than one item in each box (and it is usually wise to have more than one), you will have to deal with the issue of stylized redundancy. As we present the different kinds of supports in the following pages, you will get the idea that each will appeal to a different kind of mind. Definitions have a lot of meaning for those who believe in historical authority. Numbers are very convincing to others. Some folks like homely little narratives and stories; others want a step-by-step, blow-by-blow account. Some will need connections and associations drawn for them with a thick, black (verbal) crayon. Others will jump to the connections before you make them. Some will want diagrams and pictures; others can get the whole story in one, good illustrative yarn. Everyone will want to know where you got your material, who agrees with you, who expressed himself on the subject; and all will want to know what it means to them.

It is at this point that the audience analyses you made earlier become crucial, because you will need to make decisions about what stays in each box and what does not, based on what you know about the audience. If you get the impression that you are being advised to make sure you get far more information than you can possibly use, you are correct. The more information you start with, the more you will be able to make decisions that will adapt your material to the audience and situation. If you have just a few items, you have to use what you have, and they may not do the job. Give yourself the luxury of choice. Overload your boxes, and then sort them out neatly so that each item in a box is directed at some special type of person in that audience.

Definitions

The first, and perhaps the most basic, support you can give your ideas is to make them clear. Customarily, we do this through a device known as "definition." Most of us know definitions as complicated explanations in a dictionary, hardly helpful to an audience who really wants to know what we are talking about. But there are at least four different ways in which we can define a word:

1. Lexicographical definition—a complicated term for the history that is written in a dictionary.
2. Technical definition—explains how a thing is used and how it works.
3. Operational definition—explains how something appears to an observer.

4. Highlighting definition—emphasizes the importance of the thing being defined.

Sometimes we shall use all four in order to make a concept perfectly clear.

Lexicographical definition. The dictionary comprises a collection of meanings that have been given to words in the past. When you rely on the dictionary for the meaning of a word, you are assuming that your listener has looked at the same dictionary and chosen the same alternative that you chose. Dictionary definitions are often hard to follow. They tend to explain complicated words by using other complicated words that need explanation. Dictionaries also assume considerable knowledge of the history of language, of grammar, and of synonyms. On the other hand, a dictionary definition is often necessary to show the classes or categories into which a thing or idea fits, or to specify some identity for it.

> **Rhetoric:** The art of influencing the thought and conduct of one's hearers (in classical times).
> The art of using language effectively.

We do not have a clear image of what is meant by these definitions. We may not be clear on what is meant by "art." "Influencing" is another concept that needs to be pinned down, as does "effectively." The classical reference is a piece of history, apparently, although there are five thousand or so specialists in oral rhetoric who deal with precisely that business today.

Thus, in working with dictionary definitions, we have little with which to advise our listeners. We often confuse more than we clarify when we quote from the dictionary.

Technical definition. The technical definition enables you to specify what a thing or idea contains, or how it works. It is a more practical approach to definition, for it is not limited to a three-line entry in a dictionary. It can be as long or as short as you think it needs to be in order to make your concept clear to your listener.

A technical definition works best with persons who know something about the topic. Consequently, it may be necessary to intersperse your definition with examples and illustrations when you are dealing with a relatively unsophisticated audience.

> **Rhetoric** is both a process and a method of study. We use it as a method of study to examine how people influence others by their language. It is

the art of persuasion. When we consider it as a process, we refer to the techniques used in order to exert influence. We base our definition on Aristotle's statement, "Rhetoric is the art of finding, in any given case, the available means of persuasion." Aristotle does not specify who is doing the finding. Thus, you can be rhetorical when you try to persuade me to buy an encyclopedia, and an observer can be employing rhetoric as he studies how you try to persuade me.

When we study **Rhetoric,** we generally examine the following components...

The definition can grow very, very complicated. Your problem as a speaker is to decide when to turn off the tap. You can give an entire speech in a definitional mode. You would use the classification structure, and you would be seeking to inform the audience that:

Rhetoric is the art of persuasion and it can be studied in five parts: invention, disposition, style, memory and delivery.

or that:

Rhetoric is a process that takes place in a rhetorical situation which consists of a speaker, a situation, a goal, an exigence, and the deployment of strategy.

In either case, it is clear that the classification structure is employed, and that in each box a series of examples or illustrations would be deployed to clarify the concept that labels the box.

Definition in a speech can easily become the tail that wags the dog. It is sensible, before preparing a technical definition, to refer to your audience analysis and make a good guess about how much your audience will need to know so that you can proceed with your job. If you are talking, for example, in favor of prepaid medical plans, you might simply explain one plan and use a contrast structure to show how it is different from Blue Cross. If, however, you are presenting the same speech in a community that has never experienced Blue Cross, you might need to take more time to explain the components of the plan.

Operational definition. An operational definition explains a thing or idea by describing observable operations. It deals with the seeable only. It does not make reference to anything that goes on inside the head, nor to inferences or evaluations. We use an operational definition when we are working with science. If someone wanted to know,

"How would I identify rhetoric if it rode up to me on a camel?" You might reply with an operational definition:

> You can observe **Rhetoric** in action when you see a person speaking to another person, and in that speaking (1) make some request or specify some action for him to perform, and (2) provide reasons why that request should be honored. For example, "We really ought to go see the movie at the Bijou because it has many X-rated scenes, three Oscar winners, and the popcorn there is the best." A statement such as, "Come to the movies with me and we'll have fun" consequently could not necessarily be classified as rhetorical.

**Defining too much will make your audience feel
you are talking down to them.**

Highlighting definition. A highlighting definition is more an assertion about the value of something than it is a definition, but it fits into the definitional mode because it makes a claim about the importance of something.

> **Rhetoric:** The only method that humans have to organize the world so that it is a fit place in which they can live.
> **Rhetoric:** The substance of lawful social interaction. It is the core of the reason for having a discourse. It is the highest achievement of man's capacity to make symbols.

You might not understand all of that, but it does seem clear that we think rhetoric is extremely important.

One of the early steps in supporting a structure is to examine the words functioning as labels, as well as the words in the residual message. Using your audience analysis as a basis, figure the scope and kind of definition your hearers might need. To be effective as a speaker, you need to be careful with definitions. Failure to define when it is needed could confuse your audience. All it takes is one complicated idea undefined to throw your audience so far off balance that they stop listening to you as they try to unsnarl what you meant. On the other hand, too much definition distracts the audience from the residual message (unless the residual message is definitional). If you define too little, your audience might think they are being patronized—that you are talking over their heads. Defining too much will give the audience the sense that you are talking down to them—patronizing them by thinking them just a little stupid.

Idiosyncratic definition. Sometimes a speaker will have his own unique way of using a particular word or phrase. He will want the audience to use the word in his sense for this speech and this speech only. Words like "democracy," "justice," "love," and others, can be very confusing. The dictionary definitions do not help much. Technical definitions take all the life out of the concepts, and operational definitions are virtually impossible. Concepts like these cannot be held or seen, and you can't use visual aids to help the audience understand.

Thus, if by love, you mean:

an evaluation of the acts between a man and woman

or:

the perfect contact between two human beings

you are, perhaps, deviating from the mainstream of meaning, and you are confusing the audience just a little bit more. If it is necessary to use this kind of idiosyncratic definition, you will need to take time to explain (1) that you are defining the word somewhat differently from what your audience might expect and (2) the precise way in which you are defining the word. The result may look like a dictionary definition augmented with a description of some operations with a culmination in a highlight. And then, throughout your speech, whenever you say the word, you act as if it is in quotation marks. Some speakers even hold up the first two fingers on each hand every time they use a word that is idiosyncratically defined.

An exercise

Take the following list (alone or in groups, it really doesn't matter) and find the dictionary definitions. Then construct a technical definition, an operational definition, two or three highlights, and if you have an idiosyncratic definition, add it. When a group is done, share with another group. Read your definitions and see what questions the other groups have. Getting their questions will help you "correct" your definitions so that you get a sense of what might happen with a real audience. And, incidentally, do you know why we put "correct" in quotation marks?

Persuasion
Freedom
The law of averages
Neologism
Parapraxis
Connubial bliss
School spirit
The will to win
Sound medical practice
Effective teaching
Seduction
Loyalty
Benign neglect
Power

You may add more words if you like. The above list should provide you with enough stress, however.

Examples

An example is a statement, story, or illustration that clarifies a more general statement. Suppose a speaker makes the statement that "heavy industrial wastes have severely polluted local rivers." He might support that statement with an example:

> Think what might happen if the local paper mill stopped dumping sewage in Rock Creek. Our children would discover that water is blue, not dark brown. They would understand that water can support life, that people can swim and fish in it.

Such an example is called a **hypothetical example.** It is not actual but it accurately represents what might relate to the general statement. In this case, it is carefully selected to appeal to a local audience.

More often, speakers will use a **real example,** and refer to something that actually happened. A speaker states that "power comes to the man who can speak well." His example:

> Take Fred Smith, the mayor of our town. He had no political pull, no support from organized political parties. He was a physician who spent most of his time with his patients. But when he took the platform and talked about the problems facing our town, his eloquence drew the attention of the citizens to him, and though he had no thought of a political career, his neighbors, impressed as they were with his speaking, pushed him into the limelight and elected him to become the best mayor this town has ever known.

The speaker might want to go on and say, "When evaluating a speech, it is necessary to judge the quality of the man and his ideas, as well as his skill in speaking." For example:

> Compare Adolph Hitler and Winston Churchill. Each rose to power because of his ability to move the minds of people through speech. Yet, we regard Hitler as the very devil and Churchill as a bright model for mankind. The difference lay not in their skill at oral persuasion but in their regard for the dignity of humanity and their own personal worth.

Each part of the general statement was supported by an example.

Examples are usually short statements. But sometimes it is necessary to tell a long and detailed story in order to make a point, particularly when the story is about some local hero, or some event that has great meaning to the audience. Dwelling on the story builds the relationship between speaker and listener. Long examples of this sort are called **illustrations.** Often, they can occupy a large proportion of the speech. For example:

> I have told you how our state plans to deal with air pollution. It seems idealistic in the extreme. Many have said, "Can't be done. The citizens

won't cooperate; business won't cooperate." But if I can show you precisely how this law works, and how it does manage to clean the air in places where it is applied, then it will be clear that the state plan is worth supporting. Let us look at the Rigelsville Air Pollution Case, a classic illustration of how the law works.

The speaker had originally outlined a program of air pollution control which consisted of a classification structure using the following box labels:

Discovery of a problem by the citizens
Registering the complaint with the commission
The commission investigation
The local hearing
The state hearing
The issuance of the compliance order
The follow-up on the compliance order
The appellate procedure
The long-term monitoring program

He alleged that these were all-inclusive, but mutually exclusive, main points of air pollution control under the state act. In his illustration, he used the same box labels. In his speech he noted:

The citizens of Rigelsville discovered paint damage
They hired an attorney to carry the complaint to the capital
The commission sent professionals to inspect the area
Who testified and to what effect in the local hearing
Who testified and to what effect in the state hearing
The contents of the compliance order
What the factory did in response
The nature of the appellate case
The final developments and eventual results of compliance

It took almost five minutes to cover the general case, the state law, and it took more than ten minutes to detail the individual case. As the speaker finished with each box in the specific case, he referred back to the correlative box in the general case. He wrote the headings on the board so that the audience could see the relationship between the general statement and the illustration. He used two classification structures and compared them, which put him into an analogic structure. He demonstrated a one-to-one correspondence between the general case and the specific case, thus making the most effective use of examples.

This represents the main criterion for testing the worth of an example—hypothetical, real, or illustrative. If you can use the analogic structure, and get a one-to-one correspondence between the examples and the general statement it is supposed to clarify, you have a good example. If your example does not have that correspondence, then no matter how interesting your story, don't use it; it will only confuse the audience.

Examples are supposed to add color and provide details about general statements. A few examples are enough to make the point. If you use too many examples, your audience will begin to focus on the details of the example, rather than on the main ideas of your residual message. When it is necessary to use a great many examples, you are actually employing statistics, and you are subject to the rules of the use of statistics.

Examples are usually presented as stories. A well directed and timed story can make a point convincingly. The late Irving Lee used this story to illustrate the idea that people get into trouble by making faulty inferences:

> During World War II, a general riding in a jeep noticed a man in uniform on a telephone pole. The uniform was disarrayed. He wore no tie and generally looked a mess. "Hey, you!" yelled the general, "what's your name and outfit?" The man looked down. "Jones. Bell Telephone Company, and you can go to hell, sir!" he responded.

The story added a touch of humor to the speech. But it also corresponded one-to-one to the point Lee was trying to make and thus assisted him in carrying his residual message.

Stories don't always have to be funny. In fact, many speakers bomb when they try to be funny. The ability to make people laugh is rare, and most speakers have to rehearse carefully when they plan to use funny stories. Nothing is more embarrassing than a "no talent" story teller who wins total silence as a response to his best story. If it is done well, a funny story is a nice uplift and provides a break for the audience. You don't have to work hard to draw attention to a good story, but you need to have a realistic view of yourself. How do people respond to you at parties when you tell a joke? If they turn away, or make excuses to get to the bar, forget it, and stay with the serious stuff.

Remember, also, that a story cannot just be thrown in for its own sake. Some speakers will joke around during the introduction to the speech in order to get the attention of the audience, but if you go too far with this, the audience will see your presentation as a stand-up monolog, and they will ignore your residual message while they look for the jokes. The story must support the message. It must correspond as with any other example. Thus, you don't want to throw in a story, funny or not, just because it is one of your favorites. We could attract a lot of attention to this book if we threw in a dirty story on every other page. We wouldn't want that kind of attention though, because in picking up the stories, the ideas would be ignored. We would get laughs, but those laughs would sabotage the point of the book. Thus, we elected to refresh the reader with cartoons. The cartoons **are** related to the ideas in the text: they serve as illustrations, and they break the monotony while they reinforce the residual message.

For example, do this exercise

Below is a list of general statements. See if you can construct a hypothetical example and find a real example to clarify each of them. Where possible, provide an illustration as well (but don't spell it out because it will take too much time).

> Learning the rules of games helps a child to live in society.
> Early to bed and early to rise makes a man healthy, wealthy, and wise.
> A rolling stone gathers no moss.
> A rolling bagel gathers no cream cheese.
> To err is human, to forgive divine.
> The American system of justice is more aptly characterized by its concern for the innocent than its vengefulness on the guilty.
> Invention cannot thrive in a society that is not free.
> Science is the servant of the people; it is the handmaiden of the wealthy.
> My country, may she always be in the right, but my country right or wrong.
> Anything goes between two consenting adults.
> A man needs to do his thing.

You can think of some more. Note how many of these general statements are old "saws" and adages. These kinds of statements make very little sense to anyone unless accompanied by an example. From the standpoint of audience, your example is the way you can most closely approximate the listeners' needs. You have the privilege of selecting from all the possible examples precisely the ones that come closest to the interests, understandings, and concerns of your listeners. Thus, after clarifying through definition, the wise speaker will attempt to support the structure of his residual message with various types of examples, carefully selected in consideration of the needs of his audience.

Narration and exposition

Narration and exposition are speeches within speeches. They are extensions of illustrations, which we discussed above. A **narration** tells a series of events in the order of their occurrence. It follows a time structure and is used to clarify the connection between two main ideas in a speech. For example, if the residual message is: The fluctuations of the stock market during the first three decades of the twentieth century led to the depression of the 1930s, it may be necessary for the speaker to narrate the series of events characterizing the fluctuations of the stock market. Actually, the narration would be a series of examples (of fluctuations) arranged in sequence of time.

Exposition is a narration detailing the steps in a process. Exposition deals with process or method, not with events as in narration. Tracing the development of a community would require a narration. The process of lawmaking in that community would require an exposition. Exposition can be used to explain how something works or to show the steps in an activity, or to show the relationship between the parts of a complicated object. For example, if the speaker, talking about the stock market, decided that it was necessary to clarify the idea "fluctuations of the stock market," he might offer an exposition in which he outlined step by step the behavior of the market on a typical day. You guessed it! An exposition is often employed as part of a technical definition in order to enhance the audience's understanding of a complicated idea.

Narration and exposition are extended illustrations. Both define and clarify. They work best in informative situations. However, often it is important to offer information in order to establish a persuasive point. For example, if the speaker's residual message was: "The United States should not be militarily involved in the Near East," he would have to narrate some history showing how we might possibly become involved. To supplement his remarks, he could offer an exposition on the legal and moral justification given for involvement, showing how it ran counter to precedent. In such a case, narration and exposition work best at the beginning of the speech. If they come any later, they might be so fresh in the minds of the audience that they would distract from the main point.

The speaker should not rely too heavily on narration and exposition. For one thing, they tend to distract attention from the main point. The colorful details and excitement of following a process can easily gather the attention of the audience and keep it focused away from the point the speaker intends to amplify. Some speeches are composed entirely of exposition or narration or both. "How to make a lasagna," "The events leading to the Korean War," "The process of setting the prime interest rate," all fall into one of these categories. Most of the lecturing you hear from college professors is primarily exposition and narration. Understanding this should help you understand another peril in the use of narration and exposition, that is, they tend to bore people if overused. (No exercise for this section.)

Citation and quotation

> People love authorities, and every advertiser knows it.
> Yogi Berra uses Gillette Blades.
> Mean Mary Jean drives a Duster.
> Dr. Wald, the Nobel Prize winner, is against the war.
> **Consumer Reports** says it is a good buy.
> Norman Vincent Peale believes you can, if you think you can.
> Marlon Brando is for Indian rights.

Often an idea can be supported by associating it with the name of someone who also supports it. However, to be of any value, the audience must accept that "someone" as an authority. It doesn't help much to say:

> My mother believes I am the best man for the job.
> Cousin Moe is in favor of gun control.
> Andy Pfefferneuss told me he talked to the saucer people.
> My dad says he can lick your dad.

However, we sometimes operate in a kind of "screwball fashion" and accept Jane Fonda as an expert on politics and Bill Russell as an expert on phone books.

To make an authority stick with an audience, either he must be sufficiently famous and well qualified so that they will raise no question about his authority, or the speaker must give qualifications for the authority.

> Henry Kissinger says that things are improving with Russia.
> Dr. Alexander Reichls of the Political Science Department of Ziffschnitz University says that things are not improving with the Russians.

In any case, where there is doubt in your mind about whether your audience will recognize your authority, you will need to take a minute or two to "define" him, via a technical definition. You do this by telling who he is and why he is qualified to comment on the issue at hand.

> According to John Smedley, the curator of marsupials at the Smithsonian Institution, the opossum is a . . .

This kind of statement qualifies the authority and gives the audience something to trust. Your concern of course needs to be with the kinds of people your audience would find trustworthy. Presumably, businessmen would trust other businessmen; young people would trust popular heroes, movie stars, and so forth. Part of your audience analysis can be used to direct the kinds of authorities you select.

Interestingly enough, you can usually find competent authorities on every side of a question. Sometimes, in matters of debate, the issue is resolved in favor of the side who can dig up the most appropriate authorities for the particular audience. On the other hand, it is not sensible (because it is boring) to built a whole argument on authorities. You can string out authorities until you make the audience ill. Customarily, they will want something more than a string of names to establish a point.

Using authorities who have to be qualified is a risky process also. You have to give up valuable speech time to establish the authority. If you don't happen to hit on some kind of qualification that impresses the audience, you haven't qualified your man. You might just as well turn to some good examples. Furthermore, many people are naturally skeptical. Not everyone dashes out to buy those razor blades that the football hero is trying to sell.

A real authority has developed his options about an idea. He has read and done research, published his ideas, and has done so convincingly enough to establish himself as a genuine expert. There are some rule of thumb questions you can ask about authorities, and if you can find individuals who fit, they are usually safe to use.

1. How does he know what he knows? (Did he hear it from someone? Was he there? Did he do formal research?)
2. What is his vested interest? (Is he paid by someone who is interested in the outcome of the matter? Is he really independent from pressure?)
3. Do his ideas square with other accepted ideas about the matter? (Is he a crackpot? If he takes an unusual position, how does he go about supporting it?)
4. Is his testimony reluctant? (Would it be easier for him to say something else?)

For example:
Daniel Fobush, Ph.D., says that as a result of his studies, he would recommend that people cease from smoking since smoking is implicated in hypertension, heart trouble, and lung disorders. (Sounds good?)

1. Fobush is head of the tobacco research center of the largest state university in the tobacco-growing region. He has been head of the research project in physiological effects of smoking for the past ten years.
2. He is paid by the state, although he has taken consulting fees from tobacco companies.
3. Most other testimony agrees with what he says.
4. Since he does take money from tobacco companies, we would not expect him to speak strongly against smoking. Since he does, we can regard his testimony as "reluctant" and therefore of high value.

But Fobush and others have published so much that sometimes it is more effective to take proofs and examples and present them to the audience. You can "cite" them simply by referring to their published writing. It is not necessary to quote them directly. Their ideas do the persuading rather than their names, yet the ideas would not be acceptable if they came from the speaker. When this is the case, use a citation. If you are speaking on some topic and it is necessary for you to say something about a complicated matter on which you clearly know very little, it is sensible to **cite** the source of your information. Then, if the audience want to disagree, they can disagree with some valid authority, not you, and if they choose to accept the authority, they can examine the information and decide whether or not it proves the case. Effective use of information other than quotation raises your reputation with your audience. Information used without giving the source, however, is often not credible. We make the compromise between direct quotation and talking out of our own heads through the method of citation.

There are limits to the use of citation and quotation. These limits have to do with the qualifications of the person cited or quoted. An unqualified authority can injure your standing with the audience. Many speakers fail when they attempt to persuade because they assume that the audience will have the same heroes they do. The speaker who cites Mao Tse Tung as an authority at a John Birch Society meeting cannot expect to win a lot of persons over to his side. A listener may be following your thread of reasoning and flinch when you hit him with an authority in the person of someone he rejects. Just try quoting Richard Nixon in front of an audience at a New York City university.

Any cited or quoted authority must be qualified. As mentioned before, advertisers are enthusiastic about using public figures to sell their products. The message seems to be that if Vida Blue shaves with this razor, then it has to be good for you. A logical person would respond that, in order to find out about a razor, one should go to a razor expert; and what would Vida like to tell us about pitching? The advertisers know that their use of authority will only appeal to the uncritical in the audience. However, the advertiser doesn't really expect you to run out and buy the product. His residual message is somewhat different. He wants you to remember the name of the product. By associating the product with a famous name in sports, the chances increase that the listener will remember the product name. That is, if he is male. If it is the wife who is buying the blades on behalf of her husband, there is the virility message: look at this handsome, tough man who uses this blade. The suggestion is that your husband could look like that too, if only he would shave correctly.

A speaker, shooting for acceptance of his residual message, cannot rely on this form of name association. His goal is more immediate. Most of all, his authorities cannot alienate members of the audience. The turned-off listener may not be around at just the point in the speech that would have won him over. For that reason, you need to select authorities carefully to make sure that they support your residual message without becoming issues in themselves.

Make sure of your sources during preparation. Remember, we advised you to use note cards and put down the source of the information on the note cards. Sometimes, when you have too much material you can make the decision about which card to use by looking at the source and picking the card drawn from the strongest authority. Even in selecting your material, you need to take care that you select material from reputable sources.

Just because it is in a book doesn't mean it is so. Did you know that some of the books on your library shelf are there because the author paid personally to have them published? Anyone can get into print if he is willing to pay for it. Consequently, you need to be very critical when you select material. You can guarantee stronger acceptance from an audience if you pull from well-known sources with good reputations, and take care not to be trapped by an attractive looking book cover containing information written by an unreliable authority who paid his own way to publication.

Often reputable sources are unknown to the audience. You may have to take time, as pointed out, to qualify your man. Furthermore, long lists of names are boring. You have probably tried to hack through a book with footnote references all over the page. Those footnotes can be very distracting. As you try to read the footnote, you lose the thread of the message. Sometimes, trying in a speech to qualify your authorities has the same effect on the audience that footnotes have on a reader. Basically, if your information is defensible in itself, you needn't tell the audience where you got it, though you should be prepared to identify the source if anyone should ask.

It is only necessary to qualify your authority when you are depending on **him** as a form of support, rather than on his ideas. For purposes of preparation of your speech, understanding authority qualifications is important to you. It is obvious that citing the president of the United States as an authority on American government might go over with an audience, while citing him as an authority on classical music might sound ridiculous. We are concerned with your ability to be sufficiently critical of what you find in the library so that you select only quality material for your supports. The examples, statistics, and other supports will mostly be provided by someone else. Selecting the proper materials can make all the difference in the world in your effectiveness.

Do you know a sound authority when you see one? Take the following list of names. Each one is or has been an authority. How many do you know? How would you go about discovering in what area each man is noted.

John Cogley	Bobby Fischer
Norman Podhoretz	Will Herberg
Leslie Fiedler	Hans Morgenthau
Robert Maynard Hutchins	Joe Paterno
Robert Wald	Adlai Stevenson III
Robert Ardrey	Learned Hand
Konrad Lorenz	Daniel Boorstin
Adolph Zukor	Pierre Teilhard de Chardin

How many authorities can you name in the following fields: American history, economics, physics, astronomy, nuclear energy, coal research, ecology, consumer protection, law enforcement, local government? How many celebrities can you name in: folk rock, country-western music, pornographic movies, football, movies, comic books? If our suspicions are correct, you could name more in the second list than in the first. They are your authorities, but they would hold no weight with your audiences in life situations. And isn't it interesting that so few of us can name authorities on some of the major issues of our day?

Whenever you approach a speech composition task that will involve some library research, the best procedure is to go to whoever qualifies as a "local expert." Find the professor of . . . or the man who works in the. . . . Ask them whom they respect, whom they read. They might not qualify as authorities themselves (although they may be as close as can be found), but through their occupations, they will at least be able to identify some reliable works for you to look at or some trustworthy names for you to check out.

A reliable authority knows something more about his topic than do most persons, and this is acknowledged by his colleagues.

Sam called his mother on the phone. "Mom," he said, "come down to the waterfront and see my new boat." His mother took a cab and hurried down to Pier 69. There stood Sam, yachting cap on his head, and tied up at the dock was a huge cabin cruiser. "What are you wearing on your head, son?" asked mother. "That," said Sam, "is my captain's hat." "You're a captain?" his mother inquired. "Yep," answered Sam. "That's nice," said mama, "by you, you're a captain, and by me you're a captain. But tell me, son, by the other captains, are you a captain?"

Make sure when you select an authority that he is a captain by the other captains. (Interesting how we managed to sneak in an example of how to use a joke in a presentation. That one wasn't dragged in by the heels; it fit. And if you don't know what we are talking about, you should reread the section on Examples.)

Once you have your reputable authorities, make sure you know how to tell the audience about them. Don't name-drop. One of the writers once acted in a community theater production. The director was a young man struggling hard to make it on the Broadway stage, taking a little time off to earn some bread during the summer. When he was not putting his actors through their paces, he was trying very hard to impress them with his status on Broadway. He would stop at nothing to convince a listener of how important he was and how many stars he knew. Once, a visitor remarked, "I think Ethel Merman is just great." Said the director, "Yes, I once had lunch with the cousin of Ethel Merman's makeup man, and he agrees."

Great grief! Take it easy with your audience. Go light on the name-dropping, pass lightly over the data. Just let it be known that you have considered the qualifications of those from whom you got information. If someone wants to make an issue out of it in the question period, make sure you are prepared.

Your use of authority must be consistent with the rest of the speech. To advance a quote that disproves everything you just said, is self-defeating. The same is true of an outrageous opinion, even if the source is reputable. "And I agree with Senator——of Georgia who said, 'If we have to start over again with another Adam and Eve, I want them to be Americans, and I want them on this continent and not in Europe.' " Regardless of the fact that the man is a senator, the statement is ludicrous, and your audience might look at you either in shock or contempt, should they think this statement is representative of your thinking.

A citation alone is not proof. It has the power, at best, to make an example or some evidence stronger. If you were trying to explain Einstein's theory of relativity, a simple story from Einstein would be supportive. A quote from Irving Frump, your ninth-grade science teacher, would not. Your own explanation would be considerably stronger, and certainly far less distracting. Don't be afraid to talk on your own authority. You don't need to say, "As Arnold Palmer used to remark, 'Straight ahead,' ladies and gentleman because, in the words of Cary Grant, 'We are on our way to bigger and better things.' Yes, as Al Jolson would have put it, 'You ain't seen nothin' yet.' " The sentence, senseless as it is, would have made a good deal more sense said on your own authority.

One more caution, particularly important in the use of citation and quotation (but also important with every other bit of evidence), is the admonition to quote accurately and in context. Others can read, and there is always the possibility that someone in the audience has read the work from which you are quoting. If you do not quote accurately, or distort the meaning of a quote by lifting it out of context, you risk being proved a fool in the question period.

"Context" is the surrounding area that gives meaning to the thing within. A country boy in the city is out of context. A piston is a meaningless piece of metal outside the context of an engine. A statement outside of the context of the surrounding ideas can be just as meaningless. Plucked out of its place in a logical progression of ideas, a statement can be twisted and distorted, or denied its proper meaning. For example, if a sentence reads:

> When we have achieved nuclear parity; when we have an equivalent naval force; when we have a mobile army prepared to move anywhere in Europe and Asia—then we can have peace with the Russians.

and the speaker says, "According to Mr. X, we can have peace with the Russians," the statement is distorted. In print, it would have to appear as, ". . . we can have peace with the Russians." At least you understand that the three dots indicate something is missing, and you can be properly suspicious of the quote. But when it is spoken there is no possibility of showing that it was distorted. It becomes a deliberate lie. Mr. X cannot jump up and yell at you, "That is not what I meant."

An authority is entitled to an honest representation. When a man puts his ideas into print, he faces the situation where people can quote him and represent him against his will or without his knowledge. Many well-known authorities hate to be quoted because their ideas get bent to accord with the speaker's purpose. Often famous people have to defend themselves against damage to their reputations caused by misquotes and distortions. In extreme cases, an authority may demand to have the damage repaired, particularly when it is done in print. We have laws against libel and slander that cover such misrepresentation.

But the speaker does not escape the responsibility either. Recently, at a convocation at a large university, a speaker quoted an obscure playwright to illustrate a point. The audience was impressed until the question period, when a local professor rose up and straightened out the record. He pointed out that the playwright had never made the statement, nor even written the play, that the speaker had attributed to him. Furthermore, he was able to supply the name of the man who did make the statement and he supplied the source of it. The quotation was not important to the speaker's residual message. In fact, it was included only because the speaker felt an urgency to drop some footnotes before a scholarly article. The audience no longer trusted the speaker. Word got around. His reputation as a speaker was shot, and he was not invited to speak elsewhere.

Another problem is the issue of plagiarism. Plagiarism is piracy of ideas. It is very hard to sort out where our ideas come from. Many things kick around in our heads with our unawareness of their source. Usually harm is done when we pass them off as our own. But when quoting directly, the name of the source must be given. The young man who tries to con his beloved with "How do I love thee, let me count the ways," risks being branded as a phony, if his girl is at all literate. In short, if you are using another man's words, give his name.

Fairness is the main consideration in quoting from an authority. If that is not enough, think how being unfair can damage your message and waylay your purpose. Beginning speakers are often too anxious to discover support quickly, and they come up with quotes that, if stretched, seem to fit their ideas. The eagerness to get the job done makes them miss what is really written. They can see only the ideas that seem to back them up. The words are then paraphrased or tailored to fit the residual message, and then credited to the authority. The audience is never sure if they are hearing reshuffled words or a direct quotation. Meanwhile, the speaker hides behind the banners of impressive names. But he can go too far. If he quotes Barry Goldwater in favor of disarmament or George Wallace in favor of bussing, the audience catches on quickly.

The problem of misquoting can be controlled, first by reading the source of information **carefully;** second, by considering the context, the information, and reasoning out of which the quotation will come. Anything written down can be misrepresented. Many times an ellipsis is used by an overeager speaker. It can be abused. For example, the words in the book might say:

> To solve the problem of the black man in this country, without the full understanding of the white population, would be a waste of time and effort.

The quotation could be distorted to read:

> To solve the problem of the black man in this country . . . would be a waste of time and effort.

To be accurate, this quotation could be paraphrased as:

> The problem of the black man cannot be solved without white support.

Thus the statement is reduced in size but remains faithful to the author's meaning.

You should know that the odds on being caught in a quoting error or distortion are really very small, but the consequences are great. For one thing you have to live with your conscience. For another, if you are caught, being branded a liar in front of a large group is not pleasant. In short, be fair. Give your authorities an honest representation, and remember that an audience appreciates an honestly developed residual message more than the magic of name-dropping designed to win favor.

Exercise time

Following is a series of quotations. What kinds of residual messages could the quotations support? Practice with ellipsis, paraphrase and direct quotation. Look up the name of the authority and find his qualifications:

1. The barbarism, "communication skills," which is the contemporary jargon for reading, writing, figuring, speaking and listening, appears to have permanent relevance. These arts are important in any society at any time. They are more important in a democratic society than in any other, because the citizens of a democratic society have to understand one another. They are indispensable in a world community;

they are arts shared by people everywhere. Without them the individual is deprived and the community is too.

Robert Maynard Hutchins

2. The question has been raised whether the private enterprise system is capable of adjusting itself to meet the requirements of a clean, attractive environment. There is no doubt that it can and will do so. What will be involved are changes in patterns of production and consumption, along with the emergence of a new industry of firms producing pollution-abating goods and services. For example, the production of a pollution-free automobile will undoubtedly cost more money.

Neil Jacoby

3. As to art and literature, it is obvious from the history of tastes that these naturally belong to fashions. One does not "prove" that a novel is good; a novel is judged good by its readers, then no "demonstration" or "proof" of its goodness will be of any effect. Here again, I use the word fashion not in a derogatory but in a descriptive way.

Jean-Francois Revel

4. The Warren Court was in this sense revolutionary. It sought to direct administration. It had large notions of its own powers; and, for the sake of those powers, it developed the exasperating habit, hitherto a congressional charge, of telling other agencies of government what they should do. Local officials who did not want to do what they were told to do, and who could also point out that no means were made available for the reforms, were often as furious as they were frustrated.

Rexford G. Tugwell

See if you can track down the magazine from which these quotations were all taken. It is **The Center Magazine,** Volume VI, Number 1, January/February 1973. Read the articles containing the quotations. Find out what you can about the authorities, about the magazine and its purpose, and make some assessment of its reliability. Your instructor can give you some similar tasks based on information available to you in your local community.

Statistics

It seems as if everywhere you turn these days someone is throwing math at you. Well, if you recall, your eighth-grade math teacher told you, "You'll need all this some day." How's that for a quotation from authority?

Statistics are an essential form of support. Often, they represent the most efficient and honest way of telling your story. To prove anything at all, you will need to use some form of statistics. Most people are confused about the meaning of the word. **Statistics** can be defined in at least these ways:

1. Statistics can be a way of measuring the probability or likelihood that something will happen.

> A professor at Harvard has estimated the chance of nuclear war, provided the situation remains the same, is an increment of 2 percent a year. Anyone can do this simple calculation which shows that 2 percent a year means the chance of having a full-scale nuclear war by 1990 is about one out of three, and by 2000 it is 50/50.

2. Statistics also can be used to show the differences between two events, conditions, or effects, as in an experiment.

> Frelyngheusen showed that the group exposed to the treatment reduced their anxiety by 15 percent on the average as measured by the psychogalvanometer, while the group receiving the placebo actually increased their anxiety by 5 percent. The odds on this happening by chance are less than one in one thousand.

3. Statistics can be any number or expression of quantity. With relation to human beings, this is called demographic data.

> Six thousand American students studied abroad and received degrees from foreign institutions during the last three years.

> The population of Central Pennsylvania is mostly white of Appalachian-English and German origin. The few urban areas are cosmopolitan, showing essentially the same ethnic breakdowns as other large cities, with the exception of a black population approximately one-third that of major urban areas in Pennsylvania.

> Smith had the larger plot of land.

4. Statistics can be used as a complex example, a gathering together of evidence from which a conclusion may be drawn. One instance is an example; ten instances of the same quality cannot be discussed in detail, but they can be offered in support.

> Those communities that clean up the air show an attendant drop in emphysema and lung cancer. For example, one year after air pollution

controls were instituted in Clarsville, the two diseases dropped by 40 percent. There are at least ten other communities that show similar drops.

In 1973, George Wald, winner of the 1968 Nobel Prize for medicine, said:
"During World War II, the entire American Army numbered 268,000 men. Now we have 3½ million men under arms: about 600,000 in Vietnam, about 300,000 more in "support areas" elsewhere in the Pacific, and about 250,000 in Germany. And there are a lot more at home. So long as we keep that big an army it will always find things to do. If the Vietnam War stopped tomorrow, with that big a military establishment, the chances are that we would be in another such adventure abroad or at home before we knew it."

Wald is attempting the generalization, "any time there is a big army, it gets involved" and is citing statistical data to "prove" his point.

Actually, any statement of number or quantity can be thought of as a statistic. There are statements that take the place of numbers, although they are not very exact. When a speaker says "more than" or "a great deal" or "reaching higher levels" or "never have so many," he is using statistics. Presumably he can support his statements with exact numbers filed in his preparation materials. It is acceptable for a speaker to use these kinds of statistical statements. He may know that the audience could not handle the raw numbers, but he may need to make the point. However, he must be prepared to back himself up with specific data if challenged.

Statistics are often used to describe what is "typical" of some group of persons, things, or events. When we use such techniques we work with "distributions." A **distribution** is a list of numbers drawn from similar events. A list of scores on a test in a class can be a distribution. So can the weights of the players on a football team, the belt sizes of 35-year-old males, or the number of cigarettes smoked per day by ironmongers. The scores from your class and mine could be a distribution if both classes took the same test. We could also consider them to be two distributions if we wanted to compare the classes to see which one did best.

You will find in your reading and also as you go on in school that statistics are becoming more and more important. Statisticians predict economic trends and patterns of famine. They work out plans for the testing of beer samples and tell you what kind of fertilizer to use on Durum wheat in South Dakota. They calculate insurance premiums and develop "proofs" that one method of treatment of a disease is more effective than another. It may very well be necessary for you to get some training in statistics, at the very least, so you can understand the way in which they are used and the possible frauds that people can work on you if you are not informed. Reading this section will not be enough, but if you want a relatively simple introduction to the entire statistical method, try Moroney's little book, **Facts From Figures,** or Abraham Franzblau's, **A Primer of Statistics for Non-Statisticians.**

For now, we need to concern ourselves with how to handle statistical information in a speech.

If you want to use statistics to talk about what is typical in a group, you must first look at a distribution of numbers. You need to ask one basic question, "How representative is this distribution of the things about which you are talking?" If you have all the scores from the class, the distribution is typical, because it is the entire number. But the class itself is a sample of other classes of its kind. You need to consider how representative is the sample. If the class you are considering has more honors students than most other classes, or more women, or if the students are older, you probably would not consider it typical. In fact, if you had the scores for one class and you wanted to make some statement about one hundred classes, you would be on very thin ice. There is a complex theory dealing with what constitutes a valid sample. For your purposes, since you will probably be getting numbers from some authoritative source, it will be necessary to rely on your authority and hope that he knows enough about numbers and statistical theory not to give you distorted information.

We express typicality in one of three ways: by a **mean** which is really an average; by a **median,** the mid-point in the distribution; or by a **mode,** the number that appears most frequently in the distribution. Consider the following list of values of houses on a given street.

| $100,000 | $50,000 | $40,000 | $30,000 | $20,000 |
| $100,000 | $40,000 | $30,000 | $30,000 | $10,000 |

The arithmetic mean for this distribution is $45,000. This really doesn't seem "typical" however, since the two $100,000 houses distort the average. The median falls somewhere between $30,000 and $40,000; we might say $35,000. The mode is $30,000 but this doesn't quite represent things because there is no suggestion about the more expensive houses. It would probably be most honest to talk about the neighborhood as a $35,000 price-range neighborhood, with some houses in the $100,000 bracket.

No representation of typicality will stand on its own for your audience, although the statistician can do magic with it. You will have the obligation of making it clear to the audience what the neighborhood looks like, and thus, you need to give more than just a figure.

This gets even more complicated when we start comparing distributions. Statisticians have complicated methods of comparing distributions to see if they are significantly different from one another. The word **significant,** to the statistician, means that the odds are very slim that the result discussed could have happened by chance. Incidentally, that's what statistics is all about—odds. If you see the word **significant** nested in a group of numbers, what you know is that the chances of the result being an accident is less than five in 100. Often, statisticians don't call a result significant unless the odds are one to 100. You can check this by looking for what is called an **alpha level.** Alpha = .05 means 5/100. Alpha = .001 means 1/1000. Naturally, the smaller the alpha, the more likely it is that the difference means something. If you and I were teaching the same subject out of the same textbook, following the same curriculum, to students that were about the same in ability, and my class scored 77 on the final test with yours scoring 85, we might want to decide if you really were the better teacher. If your friendly, local statistician made his calculations and told us that the odds on differences like that occurring by chance were less than one out of 1000, that would mean we would have to look for something that happened that might account for the difference. The only thing we can see is the difference in teacher, and so we might argue that you are the better teacher and that is what accounted for the difference. Note the word **argue.** One never really proves anything with statistics; he merely gets arguments of various degrees of strength. Further investigation, for example, might discover that you slipped your students the answer key to the exam, while I purposely did not cover some of the material on the exam. That would also account for the differences without requiring a conclusion about which of us is the better teacher. So, your main hope in selecting information is the amount of trust you put in your authority.

Most of the statistical information you will use in speeches is concerned with demography. You will give raw numbers or percentages.

The complicated statistical reasoning that underlies many conclusions that you will read in your research need not be shared with the audience, unless, of course, the audience is made up of professionals and that is the purpose of the speech. But, if that was the purpose of the speech, you would very likely not be giving it.

Thus, what you need to know is how to turn numbers into words. You can, of course, write numbers down on blackboards or cards and show them to the audience. We will discuss this in a later section. By and large, you will voice the numbers. "There were 86,761 marriages performed over the last five years out of which 34,704 ended in divorce," is a dull phrasing. It can be made more interesting by saying, "Forty percent of the marriages performed in the last five years have already ended in divorce." But that is not an honest representation. If we go back to the original source, we find the following exact quotation: "There were 86,761 marriages performed in the state during the last five years, while at the same time 34,704 divorce decrees were granted by the courts within the state."

Now that is an entirely different kind of statement. It does not mean either of the things expressly stated in the first two statements. For one thing, we do not know what happened to the 86,000 plus marriages performed. They all may be blissfully happy. Some may have left the state. Some may be seeing lawyers. We simply do not know. Furthermore, we do not know from where the 34,000 plus divorces came. Some may have come from the marriage figure quoted. Some may have come from marriages performed twenty-five years ago. Some may have been those of persons who moved in from a neighboring state to take advantage of easier divorce laws. To give an accurate representation of what your **authority** said, you need a very simple statement: "Over the last five years, the divorce rate has been 40 percent of the marriage rate."

In order to make the point stick, you may have to read further from your authority:

"This compares with similar statistics gathered in 1960 covering a period from 1955 to 1960, in which the divorce rate was 33⅓ percent of the marriage rate and information from the period 1935 to 1940 in which the divorce rate was only 20 percent of the marriage rate."

Your authority may not draw a conclusion. You might, if you want to, conclude that, "The divorce rate is increasing. More and more persons who marry today may expect to end up in the divorce court."

You may, if you want to, drive the point home by citing your authority. You have reduced the numbers you will present in order to make your point and to clarify your ideas.

In general, people do not listen well to numbers. When you are compelled to use numbers it is often wise to use some kind of visual reinforcement so that the audience can keep their minds on your message. Most listeners are easily confused by just three or four numbers, so it is relatively pointless to try to snow them under with numerical information. They will simply stop listening to you. Most speakers understand that statistics go hand in hand with examples. They will try to give some kind of dramatic example to illustrate the point that the numbers make.

Towards the end of World War II, a traveling exhibition attempted to show Americans the nature and extent of German war crimes. Statistical charts were on display. They showed that millions of persons had been tortured and killed. But the charts had little impact on the viewers. The numbers were too large to mean anything. People cannot comprehend quantities like a million, or even a thousand. The real impact came from a photograph of children's shoes stacked outside a gas chamber. The visual example was much more moving than all of the arrayed statistics. The charts took on meaning only in the light of the example in the picture. Statistics remain important to the experts; words about the statistics are what need to be given to an audience.

Exercise time

Get your hands on an almanac. Any current one will do. **New York Times** publishes one and so does **Information Please.** Write your congressman and get a copy of **Statistical Abstract of the United States.**

Now organize into teams. Each team works on the same topic and tries to support the same residual message. The only source will be the almanacs. Your job is to pull statistics out of those almanacs and give them an honest phrasing so that they will:

Support the residual message.

Remain faithful to the intent of the table from which you took them. Be sure to come up with one good example to go along with each statistical statement made. (Incidentally, if you use a standard almanac, you can rely on the source and you can cite it. About the only distortions you will get in an almanac are the result of typographical errors, which is more than can be said for some of our major publications.)

Here are your residual messages.

1. Support this message: The American family is threatened by divorce, zero population growth, and excess moving.
2. Support this message: The federal government is spending too much on military hardware to permit it to play a fair role in welfare.
3. Support this message: The rising cost of living is driving the American voter to the political left.
4. Support this message: There doesn't seem to be much of a positive result to show for educational compensation programs.
   On this one, somebody might bring in Christopher Jencks's book, **Inequality.** This book makes one dilly of a statistical case.

Your instructor may add more messages or you may devise your own. Remember, your job is to make the statistics palatable to the audience.

If you would like to start a debate, take some of the articles of William Shockley and some of the answers made to him by various scholars. Invite others to look at them along with the Christopher Jencks book we mentioned earlier. You can get a good, healthy debate going over whose statistics are trustworthy. When you think of it, there are many major decisions made on a basis of statistical reasoning, and there are a lot of ways in which to distort the numbers. Your library probably has a copy of Darrell Huff's, **How to Lie With Statistics.** From your own standpoint, you might need this book to help you understand how the number-users are conning you.

Your authors are mildly concerned about the whole business of statistics and their importance in our society today. Maybe there ought to be a required course in high school in which everyone learns how they are used and how to resist those that somehow don't fit. You might want to see what you can do about supporting that residual message.

Minor forms of support

Comparisons (Metaphors). Comparing or contrasting can help to clarify a complicated idea for your audience. Sometimes your ideas will seem alien or confusing to listeners. A strange or complex concept can be made familiar by comparing it to something that the audience already knows and pointing out the similarities and differences. A learning specialist, for example, wanted a school system to adopt a complicated proposal that involved special treatment for neurotic children. He made a simple comparison:

> It's the same as putting children on different reading levels and treating them accordingly. My system would create levels for emotional stability and give the children on the lower levels the treatment they might need to move up to a higher level.

Note that this is an elaboration of definition. The speaker is trying to offer a technical definition of his proposal by talking about its contents, and he finds that it is easiest to do this by comparing the method to something familiar. His audience might not be sophisticated enough to understand the psychiatric argument behind the proposal, but they can at least see how the proposal might work. By comparing an unfamiliar idea to a familiar one, the speaker made his point.

Another specialist wanted teachers to be more understanding in their dealings with younger children. In his explanation, he used a phrase, "meeting the needs of the child." A teacher replied, "Oh, you want me to put a psychiatrist's couch in my classroom?" This teacher had used a metaphor to respond. The specialist quickly contrasted the psychiatrist metaphor with his proposal. "No! There are some real differences between a classroom teacher and a psychiatrist. First . . ." He then proceeded to list the differences in such a way that there was little doubt in anyone's mind that his proposal had nothing to do with psychiatry. By making the contrast he made his point. He also capitalized on the fact that a metaphor does not deal with reality, so no matter how artful the metaphor looks, since it is not real, it can be exploded by referring to real things. Incidentally, the teacher that raised the objection was insulted and was very hostile. This didn't matter much to the speaker. He made his point with the other teachers. You can't win 'em all!

Comparisons are easily made, though often hard to defend. Most of the time, two examples, or illustrations, or even statistics can be shown side by side. Because they are close together, similarities and differences are easy to point out. But a speaker must be honest. Much can be left out when making comparisons and showing contrasts. A listener might back you into a corner by asking for an unrealistic comparison. "Which is better, soul music or classical music?" A question like that leaves you high and dry. What you need to do is show that soul music could be classical and therefore you have overlapping categories. This makes the questioner look foolish, however, so you may have to reconcile yourself to losing at least one member of your audience.

Keep in mind that you have a formal set of structures, analogy and contrast, which deal with comparisons. If your comparisons get too long and involved, you probably can't use them as forms of support, but rather you will need to revise your structure and use the required formats.

Literary forms. There are some artistic forms that can be used to enliven your speech, although they may not have much effect on your residual message. You will find them mostly used to support highlighting definitions. Though literary forms work beautifully in writing, in a speech they may sometimes sound awkward, affected, or phony. They are not substitutes for explanations or proofs. They are eye-catchers, seasoning. They provide pleasure stops between the more formal directions of the speech. Use them where you can, but don't be a show-off.

Some possible literary devices are:

1. Maxims and proverbs. "The early bird catches the worm," or "Don't give up the ship," may not pack the power to bowl over the audience, but they do have a talent for providing a neat little summary of some major point. Maxims and proverbs are easy for people to remember and they give the audience a chance to breathe, smile, and pull things together. Remember, "The only helping hand you will ever get is right at the end of your own shirt-sleeve."

2. Slogans. Russian speeches are made up of slogans, as are the orations of most radical organizations. Slogans, when used well, tend to inspire people and stick in their minds like catchy tunes. Political campaign organizations and advertising agencies turn out slogans on a mass production basis. "Ask the man who owns one." "I like Ike" packed enough wallop to play a major role in electing Dwight Eisenhower president in 1952. A generation of young people has been inspired by "It's the real thing." Anyone for a beverage? Let's choose up sides between the Uncola conspiracy and the Pepsi generation.

3. Rhetorical questions. These are unanswered questions, thrown dramatically into the air for the audience to fill in. They are intoned seriously by politicians, "Do you think we can escape a nuclear war?"

You've heard them in a thousand movie scenes when someone says to the hero, "Are you gonna stand by and let them get away with this?" The person who hears a rhetorical question fills in the answer in his head. When you use this technique, be sure that the audience will fill in the answer you want. "How long will we let the incumbent remain in power?" may evoke extreme impatience from a committed group of anti-incumbent partisans, but from a neutral audience, the question may well evoke the answer, "As long as possible."

Actually, rhetorical questions seem to work best in print. If the reader fights back, at least the writer can't hear him.

4. Wit and humor. Everyone enjoys a good joke. But nothing is worse than the agony of a man who knows he has told a bad one. There are thousands of books on the market that offer to the speaker gags packed with dynamite for every occasion. Beginning speakers buy them and forage through them looking for stories that might save their speeches. Jokes are like stylish clothes, however. What fits one person looks clumsy and strained on another.

Most people have no real skill at story telling. Their funniest jokes plop out of their mouths and break at their feet like fumbled eggs. A story, such as the following, tacked haphazardly into a speech has little chance of working: "Since we are talking about the corruption and decadence in the funeral business, let me tell you the story about the two Irishmen at the wake. Pat says to Mike . . . "

Genuine humor can spark up a speech. But a speaker should not count on his ability to tell a joke until he has tested it. Most of us have encountered the "funny" professors who build the jokes right into their notes:

> Physics professor: We all know Newton's third law: one fig per cookie. Ha! Ha!
>
> Chemistry professor: If H_2O is water, what is H_2O_4?
> Student: Washing and drinking.

After the first ten years, the jokes are not so funny.

Your best bet, if you are tempted to use humor, is to watch some of the professional stand-up comedians and note their style and timing. Often they can make some very direct points by the way they string their jokes together. There is usually a joke to illustrate every point, but only in the hands of someone who can tell it well. Don't strain to be comical. If a joke slaps you in the face and says, "I fit here," try it.

If something funny pops out of your mouth and the audience convulses with laughter at just the right time, then thank the ancient muses of humor for the inspiration and go on, hoping that it might happen again. Otherwise, leave the joke-telling to the pros.

5. Irony and sarcasm. Unlike W. C. Fields, most speakers are not adept at casting barbed statements during a pressing situation. "Anyone who hates small children and dogs can't be all bad."

The British seem to be better at it than we are. "He is a self-made man who daily worships his creator." American students were jolted by a British debater on a touring team, who said to his American partner, "You tell him! He can't understand an intelligent person."

Biting statements add zing to otherwise dull situations. But this kind of refreshment is not always desirable. People are often turned off and offended by sarcastic comments. Irony and sarcasm work best with sophisticated audiences. As a speaker, you can get away with it if the audience knows you and trusts you enough to understand that it is all in fun.

Try for a rebuttal:

> My colleague has covered the ground with his remarks. What he has covered it with, I do not know, but it should be a bumper crop next year.

6. Climactic repetition. The great orators of the past milked this method to its fullest. The name describes the process, and the best modern example we have is Martin Luther King's great speech in which he repeats over and over, "I have a dream." By continually repeating the message between examples, the speaker can build to a thundering climax. But of course, it does not work with something trivial:

> Freddy Deutcher and Pam Sobolski got salmonella.
> Our lunchroom must be improved.
> The hamburgers are 40 percent waste paper.
> Our lunchroom must be improved.
> We do not have a balanced diet.
> Our lunchroom must be improved.

is not quite it.

A recent speech by a local labor organizer gives a somewhat better idea of the approach:

> Each year the cost of living has crept a little higher.
> Inflation is the cause.

> Building a home is twice as expensive as a decade ago.
> Inflation is the culprit.
> We need to work 22 percent harder today to buy the same things we bought five years ago.
> Once again, inflation.
> We can no longer afford to be sick, even when we have medical insurance.
> Inflation is out of control.
> Our government knows how to raise taxes but can do nothing to help the working man put down his economic burden.
> Inflation must be halted.

Such a climactic repetition has an enormous power to hold attention. It cannot be used all the time, but used sparingly and only in very important places for very important topics, it can act as a valuable reinforcement to a residual message.

7. Metaphor and simile. Metaphor and simile (Remember them? You learned about them in eleventh-grade English, but you never knew why.) splash color through a speech. A metaphor compares (and finds similarities between) two apparently different things. We talk in metaphors all the time without realizing it: "The problem was nipped in the bud." "That pig!" "We're up tight." The automobile manufacturers seem to be having a romance with metaphors. People can be seen driving the streets in Mustangs, Pintos, Cobras, Jaguars, Larks, Thunderbirds, Roadrunners, Dusters, and Toronados. We even put "tigers" in our gas tanks. A simile does the same thing, but less directly, by employing the words "like" or "as": "He's as slimy as an eel." "He's as fast as lightning." "Freddie has hands like an octopus." Similes and metaphors attract attention, but they do not serve to replace proof or explanation.

A speaker should develop his metaphors carefully. A clumsy metaphor can be damaging. A local clergyman, for example, tried to compare the social and financial needs of the affluent family to the parts inside a hi-fi speaker, "The financial woofer and the social tweeter must be brought into balance." The audience snickered and the metaphor exploded. In another case, a rabbi compared the "struggles of the Jewish people" to "a salmon crawling upstream on its belly to spawn." Once again, the audience, contemplating the ludicrousness of the image, burst into laughter. In the metaphoric words of Shel Silverstein, nonpareil songwriter, the rabbi was "flushed from the bathroom of (their) hearts."

Sometimes a speaker gets carried away with his ability to create metaphors. His speech becomes the ceiling of the Sistine Chapel, and he hangs beneath it on a scaffold, a veritable Michaelangelo painting his masterpiece through the supports of his residual message. If you want to see yourself that way, OK with us, but spare the audience and save your own neck. Control your similes and metaphors. They should provide color and life and not interfere with your residual message.

One big, grand, super exercise

Now you are ready to put together a great speech. You can test yourself by setting up your main structure and then finding one support in each of these categories to fit into each box.

1. Definition
2. One example
3. One narration or citation
4. One citation of an authority
5. One good quotation
6. One statistical reference
7. Three miscellaneous supports

You probably will not need to use all of these supports in your speech, but you should be able to check each support against your audience analysis, so that you can remove what might not work and strengthen the kinds of supports you think the audience would best react to.

You'll need a lot of practice in learning how to set up your supports. Using the "because" test is one way in which to check connections. Having someone listen to you to see if your speech makes sense is another way.

Most beginning communicators (speakers or writers) somehow think things should fall into place correctly on the first try. This just plain "ain't so" and the quicker you get a critical eye for your own work, the quicker you will become a skilled speaker—if that's what you want to be. If you just want to get through the course, well, keep doing the exercises. Some of them are bound to rub off.

SEVEN

Audio-Visual supports

It's worth another chapter to deal with audio-visuals. This is the Howdy Doody generation. We were raised on Walt Disney and the Mickey Mouse Club. We patronized the movies and supported the move away from extravaganza and toward the kind of realism that characterizes today's flicks. Authorities say the reading scores for freshmen entering college are dropping drastically. We have no way in which to measure watching and listening skills, but we can assume that watching and listening are the order of the day. Marshall McLuhan says we are "cool," immersed, soaked in stimuli.

Most audiences are tuned in to audio and visual supports. In many circles it is rare for a speaker to appear without a load of equipment. The sales meeting, the anchor of merchandising, operates normally by having some sort of visual (slide or film) presentation followed by an illustrated pep talk from one of the managers. Professional film-makers and media companies prepare the audio-visual materials for these conferences.

Audio-visuals are not complicated; they are really nothing more than forms of support. Their purpose is to help get a residual message to the listener. They provide a form of repetition however, when well used, that cannot be equalled with an oral presentation alone. An ancient Chinese said, "One picture is worth more than ten thousand words." Maybe. We are not sure. What we know is that by blending words and pictures, it is possible to have a genuine impact on the audience. By mixing words and pictures ineptly, it is possible to bore your audience to tears. Consider:

> Now, here's a picture of me and Pat up by Lover's Rock.
>   (click, click)
> Now here's me trying to get a kiss from Pat.
>   (click, click)
> Now isn't that cute? Pat has ducked out of the way.

Find out if your audience needs visual aids.

And so has the audience. They have made for the nearest bar or the nearest subway depending on their aversion level.

The purpose of this chapter is to offer some suggestions about how you can use audio and visual supports in your speeches. We are not going to plague you with a set of rules, since there really are none. Every situation has its own needs, and every audience has its preferences. You, as speaker, have goals you need to accomplish. By blending your needs with the preferences of the audiences and using visuals legitimately as a form of support rather than as a tack-on, your chances of getting your residual message through are greatly expanded.

Finding out if you need visual aids. Despite the fact that schools have thousands of dollars of visual aid materials in their storerooms, and stationery stores sell poster board by the ton, it is **not** necessary to use visual aids in a speech. Audiences are accustomed to watching professional presentations. They have been weaned and teethed on television and slick movies. Your little slide show will not impress them. Consider how difficult it is to impress your own relatives with your little slide show. Thus, no one sets out to do a visual presentation unless he is a professional hired to do it for a specific purpose.

It may be sensible for you to use some visuals in your presentation. To find out, examine your residual message. If there is some concept that is exceptionally difficult to explain, and a diagram would help, draw the diagram. If you need to explain the operation of some kind of machinery, it may be helpful to have a mock-up or a model of the machinery. If you are talking about a geographical region and you think it would be a good idea to give the audience the flavor of that region, then two or three (not twenty or thirty) slides would be helpful. If you are talking about particular forms of music, you might need some audio support to help define and illustrate what you are talking about.

If your analysis of the audience indicates that you have had some experiences that are completely alien to them, some visuals might help bridge the gap. If you are talking about a small rural community to an audience of inner-city dwellers who have never been out of the city, a few slides of the region would make some of the differences clear in a way that words might not accomplish.

Visual materials can make powerful supports for some points and premises of a speech. The basic advantage of visuals is that, when used well, they capture and hold attention. On the other hand, when used poorly, they can distract from the main point of the speech and cause attention to wander.

An advantage of a visual aid is that it provides a vivid image. It stands out above lifeless words. Of course, the speaker is not the main focus of attention, but if the visual aid is properly used, the speaker remains associated with it. If a visual aid is used to support the residual message, the speaker will have little difficulty regaining attention. The experience of television shows that vision combined with words has the power to command more attention than words alone. The fact that television quickly surpassed radio as a popular entertainment medium bears this out. People like to see what they are being told. However, a speech is not a television program, and thus, the visuals cannot dominate the speech. The speaker, himself, is a visual aid, and the audience needs to be focused on his movements as well as his words. Thus, the use of visual aids confronts the speaker with a paradox, for if he needs visuals to clarify his point, he runs the risk of moving attention away from himself and his point and focusing it on the visuals. If the visuals cause just a little slippage away from the residual message, the speaker will have a very difficult time picking up the thread.

Visual aids have a potential for a number of uses in a speech. They are magnetic targets for audience interest and they help clarify material. They supply an image which the listener can incorporate into his thoughts, and which the speaker can use as a point of reference for his later remarks. Visual aids underline and emphasize evidence and make it easier for the listener to understand complicated ideas. But, most important of all, visuals can give life to many other forms of support. Statistics have greater impact when expressed visually. Examples can be underlined in drawings or photographs. Exposition, narration, and story-telling can be captured in drawings and film strips. And the main points of the residual message can be impressed on memory merely by writing them clearly on a blackboard.

Requirements for the use of visual aids. Visual aids must be easy to see. They are worthless if people have to stand on chairs, hunch up or rent binoculars in order to see them. When people have to struggle to watch what you are showing them, your residual message disintegrates like a soggy cracker.

Many beginning speakers (it's an old high school trick) like to bring in books and lard their speech with the phrase, "and here's what it looks like." Then they stand closer to the audience holding the book over their faces and do a slow turn clockwise, about twenty degrees right and left. Everyone in the audience hunches up, but the picture never stands still long enough for even the people in the front row to see it.

Another stunt is to take the book and say, "If you want to see what Russian wolfhounds look like, here's a picture in this book and I'll pass it around." The book starts down the rows and the speaker is now confronted with the problem of deciding whether he should start talking or wait until everyone has seen the picture. It is mildly embarrassing to be standing there without talking, so he usually starts right in on the next point. However, out in his audience the people who just had the book are trying to catch up with what he is saying, with little success, and the people who haven't had the book are waiting with anticipation, so they do not hear a word he says.

Conclusion: If the person in the last row, farthest corner, cannot see your visuals comfortably, forget them. Just keep talking.

Visuals should be tasteful. Your audience analysis will help you decide what might be in good taste with your particular group of listeners. Recently, a group of college students developed a multimedia show about their own lives to show to various audiences. It was noticed that older people in the audience, for the most part were distressed by the whole program. Investigation showed that the music used as background assaulted their ears. Some said it even caused them pain. And some of the psychedelic scenes, particularly those showing a bit of nudity were offensive, and even though there were very few of these kinds of scenes, just one was enough to turn off some viewers entirely. The students learned that they had pictures that they could use in one place and not in another, and they were very careful to moderate the sound when the show played to an older audience.

In general, audiences will be offended by excessively flashy colors, gross sloppiness, illegibility, and overly complicated material. In-group material will also be seen as offensive. At a parents meeting, the principal of one of the local schools was showing some slides to illustrate the new modular grouping program in the school. He slipped into the box some slides of two or three of the teachers in embarrassing positions. This drew laughter from the teachers, but it offended the parents because they were not in on the joke.

If you are a "no talent" kid, like the authors, you may have some problems with your visuals. If you are sloppy, an unskilled artist, with no sense of color, get a friend to do your visuals. If you try it yourself, you will probably do more damage than good.

Good taste also dictates that your visuals be in harmony with your own personality. Dayglo colors would probably not help a serious speech on budgeting problems in the country. Excessive sex and violence are always risky to portray; they are rarely necessary to make a point (unless you are talking about excessive sex and violence and

the audience has been warned about what to expect). Insulting cartoons, psychedelic prints, and loud music should be used with extreme
care.

Anything that does not fit the residual message should not be used.
That goes for visuals as well as your talk. The visuals should be subjected to the same tests as the verbal material used to support your
message. The speech should not be doctored to match the available
visual aids. Rather, the visual aids should be selected according to
how well they support the speaker's objectives. Like other supporting
devices, the visuals should be fitted into the structural diagram of the
speech. They must be inserted into the proper bins, and if they do not
fit, they should not be used. If they fit, but overshadow the rest of the
speech, they should not be used.

Visual aids can never be more than secondary in the speech. They
are not the reason you have come to speak, and you dare not let them
pull attention away from the residual message. The speaker's job is
to get attention on the residual message not on the visual aids.

Visual aids should be kept at the front and under the control of the
speaker. If what you have to show is too small to be seen, then it should
not be used at all. Passing information around is like a note being
passed in a study hall. People are anxious to see—more anxious than
they are to listen to your speech. Some speakers have tried the technique of handing each member of the audience a diagram or picture
so that he can follow the details as the speech proceeds. This too is
very distracting. An overhead or opaque projector can be used to
magnify and project images as small as a magazine article if need be.
If such equipment is not available, you are better off relying on words
as opposed to using visuals ineptly.

Words are important in any case. Visual aids are not designed to
stand alone. They need to be related to the speech. Even if the reason
for the visual is totally obvious, the speaker needs to say something
about it. Not, "This picture illustrates what I mean," but, "The diagram
on the screen shows the relationship between the components of. . . .
Note the foofram, here, as it connects with the gleeb. This is the inside
view of the khulyages." In no case should the visual substitute for
words.

Visuals should be easily handled by the speaker. A billboard sized
diagram or a one-hundred-pound example should not be used if the
speaker is required to move them. A speaker should not let himself get

tangled up in the operation of his visual aid, for it will break the continuity of the speech. Visuals must be set up in advance so they can be used easily. Otherwise, he and the visual aid may end up a twisted mass of man and machine, a ridiculous sight in the eyes of the listener, and the end of any chance of accomplishing the speaker's goal. The speaker should be familiar with the operation of any mechanical equipment he plans to use. He should test it to see if it works, before he commits himself to its use before an audience.

How to select your media. Once you have decided that a particular point would be better made if done visually, you need to select the precise form of visual support. It is not helpful to grab at whatever is around, or try a sloppy and hasty slap-together picture. For one thing, there is usually a blackboard, and if all else fails, that can be used. For another, even though a visual seems appropriate, unless it is well done, you are better off relying on verbal supports.

Basically, you can select from still pictures, moving pictures, objects, written words, and audio equipment. Each has particular advantages and uses.

Still pictures. They are relatively convenient and inexpensive and can be used to clarify complicated ideas, create a mood, or keep an image in front of the audience as a reminder.

Types of still picture presentations:

1. Large pictures or posters
2. Slides
3. Overhead transparencies or opaque projectors
4. Prepared maps and charts
5. Flannel boards
6. Blackboard writing

Using pictures is risky, since there are few pictures large enough to be seen clearly by even a moderate sized audience. Slides are usually very clear, but they must be used in darkness and depend on the operation of relatively complicated equipment. Overhead transparencies and opaque projectors are relatively simple to use but they depend both on darkness and the skill of the operator. Prepared maps and charts are usually quite expensive. Anyone familiar with the perennial falling map in the social studies classroom will avoid this risk. The blackboard is the most convenient medium of all, but it involves some special cautions and skills that we will deal with later.

Moving pictures. You may select from commercial or home-produced films or commercial or self-produced videotapes. The problem with the use of motion pictures is that the motion picture is usually a self-contained thought unit. A motion picture might be used in place of a speech, not within a speech. To use one- or two-minute filmed segments might be more bother than the worth of the segments, and at any event, the speaker loses control of his audience while the lights are out and needs to overcome the shock of relighting the room once the picture has been shown.

Moving pictures of any kind are very expensive. There may be times and places where a movie can carry your message better than a speech, and if this is the case, pay the price if you can and use the movie. Otherwise, mixing movies into a verbal medium may not be worth the expense and bother. And, incidentally, you may see yourself as a budding Ingmar Bergman and itch for the chance to show your home flicks to a large audience. Be careful. Most people are very critical about their films and they may see you as just another bore.

Objects. Objects are often employed very usefully to illustrate or clarify points in a speech. A person talking about karate or ballet could illustrate the moves with another person. The problem there is distraction. When the live person is sitting and waiting to be used, he draws attention away from the speaker. When used, he may overshadow the speaker, and after the demonstration, it may be hard to regain attention.

Models and mock-ups are also very useful. If you were speaking about the operation of the wristwatch, you could not use a wristwatch as a visual because it is clearly too small. But if you had enough money and time, you could have a mock-up model built, about one thousand times normal size, and you could use it to show the parts. The use of mock-ups is important in scientific lecturing. Some splendid ones are to be found in museums like the Chicago Museum of Science and Industry which has a human heart in mock-up so large that people can walk inside it. For the typical speaker, however, mock-ups are much too expensive.

Demonstrating with the real thing is useful if the thing is large enough to be seen. You can demonstrate the use of a tennis racket, and perhaps even a putter, but it might be hard to demonstrate the use of a micrometer or a microscope. Your decision here is based on what the audience can really see, and whether, if they see it, it will clarify your speech and help you achieve your residual message.

Written words. Probably the most convenient and inexpensive mode of augmenting your speech with visuals is to present the audience drawings of words and phrases to underline some statement you have made. Another possibility is to present the audience with a graphic outline of your speech and refer to it as you proceed from main heading to main heading.

There are many types of delivery systems that might be used. Commercially prepared flannel boards are available, for example. With a flannel board, you need to plan carefully what kinds of words and phrases you are going to use and you must prepare them in advance. You can also get an easel with a large pad (usually two feet by three feet) on which you can write with Magic Marker. Some speakers prefer the overhead projector because they can face the audience as they write words on a transparent sheet. The hazard with the overhead projector is that it must be used in darkness and consequently, you run the risk of losing the attention of the audience. The most common medium of all is the chalkboard. The chalkboard visual is so efficient that we shall devote a special section to it at the close of this chapter.

When using written words to augment the speech, you need to be careful not to confuse the audience by writing items that do not relate to the speech. Even with a medium like the chalkboard, your use must be carefully planned, for if the audience sees something that conflicts with what it hears you say, it will be distracted. Furthermore, you need to strive for legibility. The rule that the person in the back row must see easily holds with written visuals as with all other visuals. If your printing is excessively sloppy; if you have difficulty reaching high enough on the board, you had better make alternative plans.

Audio materials. Sometimes it is useful to present the audience with units of sound: the voice of a great speaker, the sound of the bird you are discussing, whatever. When considering this possibility, remember that **you** are your own best visual aid, and what takes attention from you jeopardizes your relationship with the audience. If you use audio portions, they must be very brief and very pointed. The longer the portion, the more likely it is that your audience will drift off. It has been discovered, for example, that tape recordings of lectures are the most ineffective method of presenting ideas and information. It works well for physicians, and other specialists, when distributed as cassettes to play in the car driving from office to hospital. But audio alone should be used only when there is no other alternative.

Get to know your visual aids before you use them.

Criteria for judging effectiveness of visual supports. There are some general guidelines that you may use to select the most effective materials if, and only if, you have decided that some kind of visual is needed to make your residual message stick with the audience. You should be able to tell yourself, and anyone else who is interested, why a visual support is the **best** way to reinforce your message. If you cannot make the argument that visual support is the best method, you are probably wasting your time using visuals. In any case, never use a visual just for the sake of using it or because you happen to have it.

Movies and multi-media productions are not visual supports—they are specialized units with which to deliver information and ideas. They can be used instead of, but not concurrently with, a speech. The mind set for listening to a speaker is vastly different from that appropriate to watching a movie or a media production. If your residual message would be better suited to a multi-media or movie form of transmission, then do it that way, throughout. **Don't try to blend the media.**

Your visuals must not be the tail that wags the dog. If your media presentation is so complicated that it interrupts the flow of the speech, you have defeated your purpose. Some novices will attempt to use visual equipment, the operation of which is unfamiliar to them. **Never use equipment with which you are not totally familiar.** You need to be particularly careful with videotape, for example. There is no piece of equipment that can cause more difficulty than the videotape recorder. You need to be your own trouble shooter. Audiences will not wait around while you thread tape and make adjustments on the machinery. All of this must be done in advance, and even then, there is no guarantee that the recorder is going to keep working throughout your speech. You might have the same problem with slide carousels, overhead or opaque projectors. If you need to use this kind of equipment, make sure you are thoroughly trained in how to work it and how to solve the problems that it most frequently presents.

Using equipment freezes your position on the platform. If your natural speaking style is to move about, you will need to take care with your timing so that you end up back at your equipment when it is necessary to change a slide or a frame. Furthermore, when using equipment you are confronted with two problems: (1) the need to make sure of the operation of your equipment; (2) the need to attend to the contents of your visual to make sure they are worked into your speech so that the audience is not confused. You need to be concerned about not getting in between the projector and the screen, about the problem of reading your notes in darkness, about the effect of darkness on your audience's attention, about how to handle the shock to the eyes when the lights come back on. All of this is in addition to the problem of explaining what the complicated graph you have on your slide has to do with your residual message. The use of any visual equipment presents you with logistical problems that must be solved before you get onto the platform.

The content of your visuals must be thoroughly clear to you before you use them. You need to know what is written on the slide. Some speakers have been known to pick up boxes of slides from a friend and then improvise a speech around them. This is unsafe. The content must be examined in advance and checked, perhaps with a friend, so that you have some confirmation that what you are using will be understood by the audience. Visuals should not introduce any information not already in the speech. They are there for support only. If you need visuals to introduce new ideas, you are better off showing a film in its entirety rather than to try to integrate two media.

If you have produced your own visuals, you might want to have expert criticism from an experienced person. Audiences will put up with a lot in a speech, but their visuals have to be near perfection. Sloppy visuals can injure an otherwise effective job of speaking. Thus, hand-drawn charts or homemade slides are often wastes of time for the speaker. Visuals are often added as an afterthought, drawn hastily and then plugged into weak spots in the speech. Poorly drawn visuals alienate the audience and do not help reinforce the residual message. If you do not have the time, energy, and talent to do a first-rate job, forget it.

Visuals should not be used to mislead. If you have read Darrel Huff, **How to Lie with Statistics,** you have seen how speakers can confuse an audience with distorted charts and graphs. For both ethical and practical purposes it is wise to avoid this kind of visual representation. In the first place, if you are detected, the presumption will be that you are either malicious or stupid. Neither helps your standing with the audience. In the second place, distortion that appears in conflict with what you say tends to confuse the audience. A confused audience is often a hostile one. Thus, honesty should be preserved in any visual representation.

Once you have decided on the particular visuals you are going to use, try to estimate the time you will need to handle them in the speech. If they consume a major portion of the time allotted to you, then you had better reconsider their use. The most effective visuals are simultaneous, that is, you show them while you continue talking. If you have to take time out to explain your visual presentation, it will appear to be a digression and tend to change the focus of your speech. It is for this reason that we suggest you give careful advance consideration to every visual you use to be sure that it fits your speech and does not become a speech in itself.

Visuals usually are expensive. Often you will be tempted to use visuals but will discover that the cost of renting equipment or buying the materials you need to prepare your visuals is prohibitive. If this is the case, don't fret. If your speech absolutely needs visual support and it is impossible to provide it, there should be several ways in which to adjust the structure to eliminate the portion that requires the visuals. Remember that the visuals are not the reason you are giving the speech. Any time they occupy a major part of your effort and energy, you are wasting time. The authors have seen many speakers who used brilliant visuals but gave a poor speech. They got "A" for visuals and "F" for speaking. The speaking is the most important component.

If you have decided to use complicated equipment: overheads, slides, and other devices, then you will need to plan the logistics. You will need to figure a way to get your equipment to the place where you will be speaking. You will need to check out the room in advance to make sure there are electrical outlets, extension cords where necessary, screens or white walls, and so forth. You will need to set up tables to accommodate the visuals and rearrange chairs where necessary so that the visuals can be seen. You will also need to get there early enough to set up all your equipment and **test it** to make sure it is in working order. Audiences will not wait while you fiddle around on their time. If you need help in operating the equipment, this must also be arranged in advance, and your helper must be briefed so that he will do his work in harmony with your directions. Careful planning is necessary wherever complicated equipment is to be used.

In any case, throughout your visual presentation, you will have to maintain contact with the audience. If you are using a brief film clip, the audience will need to be oriented to its purpose both before and after its use. If you are using any other visual form, you will need to keep talking while it is in front of the audience. The talk should consist of the information that your visual is supposed to support. Blocks of silence in a speech tend to distract the audience's attention. They begin to think that you forgot your lines. Furthermore, it is not smart to get in between the audience and your visual. Make sure that the audience can see you **and** the visual at all times. And if you are using projection equipment, make sure that you never get white light on the screen. This is a glaring distraction, and the audience will pay more attention to it than they will to you. **The best policy for any use of visuals is to practice in advance until everything is perfect.**

Remember to make sure that:

1. Your visuals fit the speech and do not become speeches in themselves.
2. Your visuals are appealing and not amateurish.
3. You know how to use the equipment.

4. You can pay the price.
5. You can use the material smoothly.

And pay attention to the following section.

Using the chalkboard

The simplest and most convenient form in which visuals can be presented is the chalkboard. While planning is important here, also, the chalkboard can be used "inspirationally." If an idea occurs to you during your speech that you think ought to be visually reinforced, you can write a word or a phrase on the board. You can erase it immediately, when it is not necessary. You can use the chalkboard to write a semi-permanent record of what you have said in the form of a reinforcing outline, or you can use the chalkboard to reinforce particular ideas and then clear the board when you are done.

When you are using the chalkboard, you become your own visual aid. If you use the board properly, audience attention stays focused on you throughout your presentation. As you move around the board and **keep talking while chalking,** your actions, the words on the board and what you say blend into a heavily reinforced message. Of course, if you use the board poorly, your audience will be as distracted as they would be with any inept use of visuals.

The chalkboard can do the most for you if you will follow some simple rules.

1. *Make sure your chalkboard is clean.* A smeared board shows up as a meaningless blob to the people in the back of the room. Everything the previous speaker left on the board has to come off. Most of you can recall coming into a classroom and being mystified by some words on the board that were left there by the previous instructor, so mystified that you paid no attention to the ongoing lecture. Incidentally, there are all kinds of chalkboards. Some of them are made of inferior slate, and they never get clean. If you are stuck with that kind of chalkboard, try some alternative idea—maybe an easel arrangement and a felt-tip pen. The rule that your visuals do you no good if the people cannot see them conveniently holds for the chalkboard as well as it does for any visual aid.

2. *Be sure that chalk and erasers are close at hand before you start to speak.* A frantic search can leave an embarrassing hole in a speech. And you can lose much rhythm by erasing the board with your hand. Have

plenty of chalk. If you drop a piece, pick up another. Janitorial motions on your part will pull the attention of the audience away from your message. Remember that chalk dust is blowy; it gets on your clothes and in your nose.

3. *Remove all obstructions to vision.* Make sure the board can be seen from all angles of the room. Some classrooms have chalkboards on all four walls. People who use them sometimes get their listeners spinning around like whirling dervishes until finally the audience exhausts its attention span and stops trying to listen altogether. Also, don't be like the photographer who blocks his lens with his hands. Make sure you don't block the vision by positioning yourself right in front of the board.

4. *Don't turn your back on the audience.* The life you save may be your own. Seriously, in some situations it is downright unsafe for a teacher or lecturer to turn away from the audience. Things are probably more civilized where you are, but some of you may have gone to high schools where the teacher who turned his back to write on the board took his life in his own hands. If you try to write with your back to the audience, your words will tumble harmlessly off the slate. Hardly anyone will hear them. Learn how to write on the chalkboard in profile. When you have written what you need to on the board, you can stand back and use a pointer to indicate the important points.

5. *Preplan your board work.* While the chalkboard can be an inspirational visual medium, you are safest if you know in advance what has to go onto the board. Anything that you can write in advance will help. Sometimes you may get the urge to write reminders on the board to reinforce or dramatize something you have said. If so, erase it immediately afterwards. Too many spontaneous phrases on the board make a garble, and your audience will drift away as they try to figure out the meaning of the mysterious words and phrases.

6. *Print rather than write.* Much handwriting reads no better than the crawlings of a worm dipped in paint. On the blackboard those scrawls can preoccupy a whole audience. Print! Print the message so large that the nearsighted person, with defective contacts, in the last row can see it.

7. *Keep talking while you're chalking.* If you have long and complicated diagrams to put on the board, you are better off placing them in advance, or preparing some other kind of visual. The main advantage of the chalkboard is the ease and speed with which it can be used. Don't sacrifice that feature. You ought to be able to write on the blackboard

quickly and keep talking while you do it. Thus, the audience will be drawn both to the spoken words **and** the written words. But when you turn your back and write silently, you will have to forgive your audience if they get distracted, doze off, or start murmuring to one another. And once they do this, you have lost them.

8. *Be strategic.* Choose carefully what you put on a blackboard and when you use it. If you find yourself in a poorly lit room with a portable green chalkboard that doesn't erase and is smudged from a whole generation of previous speakers, abandon your plan to use the board. To play it safe, make sure you know what visual equipment is going to be in the room in which you speak. Prepare in advance as much as you can.

Visual aids are most effective when they are simple and painless. It is easy to get hung up with visuals—to bore the audience with yards of charts and diagrams that scare away attention or intimidate with their very presence. It is good to be original in your use of visuals, but you needn't be a museum of modern art on tour. Members of the audience should understand your ideas because of your visuals. When they start bidding on your visuals to hang in their local galleries, look out. Anything puzzling, excessively ornate, or complicated should be avoided.

Some authorities suggest that any time a speaker feels uneasy on the platform, he should use a visual of some kind. The advice has its merits. There is a preparation challenge in combining a verbal and visual stimulus. This challenge focuses the speaker on the task at hand. It draws him away from his own problems and involves him in the effort of presentation. The visual aid gives the speaker something to hold onto when he speaks. It supports him personally as well as his residual message. Because of this complete focus on the speaking task, he has a greater chance of reaching his goals. For this reason alone, try to work some visuals into your speeches.

Now hold it

There ought to be a way to coordinate visuals with structures. In fact, it appears that the structures are visuals themselves. That means that a shrewd speaker can make a visual out of his main structure, and he can keep it in front of the audience as a constant reminder of his residual message. (In fact, in a classroom, the teacher-lecturer could put his structure on the board—if he knew how to do it—and the students could copy it and write notes in the appropriate boxes. What a study aid!)

Try to prepare **one** visual illustrating the residual message of each of the following proposed speeches:

1. The origins of the monetary crisis, using a time structure
2. America's finest vacation spots, using a space structure
3. Ways in which to beat the energy crisis, using a classification structure
4. The impeachment process and how it is similar to a normal felony trial, using a comparison structure
5. The differences between the Ford and Nixon administrations and their relations with the press, using a contrast structure
6. The influence of mass media on the American family, using a cause-effect structure
7. The advocacy of unconditional amnesty for Vietnam deserters, using an argument structure

Set up your visual aid so that the main heads in your structure add up to the residual message. See what supports might be most useful, given your main heads. How could they be supported with visuals? How could you use the visuals to illustrate minor points without interfering with your main visual?

A good idea is to check out the speaking facilities of your institution. Form a committee to test various rooms for visuality. Which would be suitable for film and slide projectors? Why? What is the state of the various chalkboards? How do you go about making sure your chalkboard is clean, in a given room? How large must pictures be for visibility at the rear of the various rooms? Does the overhead lighting interfere in any way with visuals (check out shadows, glare, and so forth)?

For your next round of speeches, try to get at least two visuals into your speeches. Have one illustrate the residual message and the other, a point that is too complicated to talk about.

EIGHT

Polishing up and finishing off

Preparing the introduction and conclusion

The purpose of the introduction and conclusion is twofold:

To focus attention on the residual message.
To grab the attention of the audience and hold it.

Like the blinders on a horse, they limit the field of vision and aim the audience in one direction. Introductions should grab the audience and tie attention to the speaker. The introduction declares:

I will be interesting with this important message.

and the speaker wants to make sure that no one has a remote control unit that can tune him out like the commercial on a TV set.

A straightforward approach usually works best. Somewhere in that introduction there must be a statement of what you intend to do, i.e., "Every one of you plays a role in conserving our natural resources."

The rest of the speech, if it has been carefully prepared, is a network of support for this idea. The speech continually stresses the importance of the residual message, and the conclusion should restate it one more time, as: "Thus we see that our natural resources are in danger, and it depends on you to save them from . . . " whatever it was that you wanted to save them from.

Appearance can be a factor in your speech.

Introductions and conclusions are vital parts of the speech. They are not awkward additions tacked on because of some textbook rule. There are no magic tricks, no secret formulas for success, to make your introductions and conclusions charm the audience. Careful preparation works much better.

All of us have heard public speakers or lecturers begin like this:

> Dear friends, it is so good to be with you here today speaking to you, and I hope you will find my remarks interesting. That reminds me of the story of the two men who were walking down the street and one said to the other, "Why does a chicken cross the road?" and the other replied, "That was no chicken, that was my wife." Well, ladies and gentlemen, I'm no chicken, but I hope that my speech will make you my wife, in a manner of speaking, because maybe we can have a wedding about the topic I am speaking on today. We need to get married on the idea that the prime interest rate needs to come down.

That kind of introduction is artificial and pointless. It tries too hard to be cute. If you have to depend on cuteness to catch the attention of your audience, then you probably have not prepared a sufficiently supported speech. If you have done a competent job, your topic, simply announced, should be sufficient to hold attention once you have caught it.

But you must do something in the introduction to attract attention in the first place, and a bad joke is not enough. The audience is a strange creature. It wanders into the room, mills around, sits, stands up, talks, stares, involves itself in weighty matters of business miles away from the meaning of the occasion. The audience will keep on with this kind of activity until the speaker invades it with some reason to pay attention to what is going on. The simplest method, of course, is to rap for order. The chairman rises to his feet and begins to introduce the speaker.

> Ladies and gentleman, the man I introduce to you here tonight really needs no introduction. All of us know him as one of the truly fine people in our neighborhood. His greatness of spirit has made him a willing worker for our cause (by this time, 50 percent of the audience is yawning). He is a good husband and father, one of nature's noblemen. In fact, the last part of his name is what he gives his wife every night. Ladies and gentleman, Waldo Hotchkiss . . . And heeeres Waldo . . . ! (Polite applause from Waldo's relatives. Tillie is still fumbling in her purse. Max asks Sam if he is going to the bar after the speech. Elliott and Sherman are having an argument about the Green Bay Packers. Ad infinitum.)

And poor Hotchkiss rises to his feet. He has to overcome apathy, and he does this by invading the audience's indifference with a reason to listen. President Lyndon Johnson used to accomplish this with, "Mah fellow Americans." But everyone has a good reason to listen to the president of the United States. The rest of us need to have the natural courtesy of taking the audience into our confidence and treating it as if a friendship were about to begin. Be simple and direct:

> Thank you for coming. Tonight we are going to take a look at an issue that might spell death for our grandchildren. I have just come back from a six-month tour of our western states and, ladies and gentlemen, I am afraid. I am afraid that this great country of ours is wasted—that the resources that made us great are so close to depletion that we are near the point of no return. My topic tonight is: All of us are responsible for saving our natural resources. All of us!

The next step, after requesting the audience's attention and telling why the topic is important, is to partition the speech. This is done simply by running over the main heads of the structure:

Our natural resources have been pillaged by manufacturers, wasted by farmers, and ignored by citizens. Waste and neglect, lack of interest, and lack of knowledge have brought us to this crisis. Let us begin by looking at the state of affairs as it affects minerals, arable land, and usable water.

This technique is a highly effective way of getting and holding attention. The steps are simple:

1. **Ask for attention.**
2. **State your topic.**
3. **Tell the audience why it is important to them.**
4. **Give them the main headings of your speech so that they will have an overview of what you are doing.**

And then get on with it. Your partition can be a reference point throughout the speech. As we pointed out in the section on visual aids, it doesn't hurt to put your main headings on the blackboard and point to them as you give each support, so that the audience can **see** as well as hear where it fits.

Some speakers try to surprise their audiences. They hold back their residual message until they have given the supports, hoping to build suspense. There are dangers in this technique, however. The audience is usually not sure of what is coming. And when it comes, they may not be able to relate to the speech because they heard it so long ago. Aristotle's advice, many hundreds of years ago, was first to state the message and then demonstrate it. This advice holds good today. A speech is not a novel, and the techniques of dramatic suspense that serve creative writers so well do not seem to work in public speaking.

Only when the audience is clearly hostile to the speaker's ideas does it make sense to hold back the message. Even then, the listeners are likely to rebel against it, no matter how overwhelming the proof may seem. But by holding back the message, you restrain some of the possible hostility. On the other hand, the audience may feel duped when you make your point. Thus, in the long run, a straightforward message is the most reliable for handling the problem of getting and holding attention.

The introduction must work for you, or you are "dead in the water." It must grab the audience's attention and show them why the message is important to them. It must spell out the message in plain words and give the main headings of what is to follow. On occasion, the introduction must take into account some special reason for the gathering. And, if there is a master of ceremonies, he should be cautioned to take it easy in his introduction of the speaker. Some emcees like to hear themselves talk and give a fifteen-minute introduction to a ten-minute speech. If you happen to be working on an occasion where there is a master of ceremonies, caution him in advance to take it easy when introducing you. A flowery introduction by the emcee makes your job harder. The audience may expect more than you can deliver.

Try it out

Take some of the topics you developed for yourself in earlier exercises and prepare introductions for them. Keep in mind that you must:

1. Ask for attention.
2. State your topic.
3. Show the audience why the topic is important to **them.**
4. Give the main headings of your presentation.
(Sometimes take into account the occasion.)

Prepare your introductions for the following addresses:

1. To your classmates
2. To the faculty of your school
3. To a group of persons hyper-hostile to whatever you are talking about
4. To a group of union members
5. To a civic service club (Kiwanis or other)
6. On the occasion of the founding of a PTA chapter
7. At a Fourth of July Republican or Democrat picnic
8. As a youth sermon at your church during Christmas vacation

Have you wondered yet why you wait until your whole speech is prepared before you prepare the introduction? Doesn't it seem more logical to prepare the introduction first, and then prepare the speech?

Did someone say, you can't introduce the speech until you know what you are introducing? Correct! It is so important to be precise and careful with the introduction, that you don't dare prepare it until just before the speech is to be given. If you wait until the very end, you can take advantage of topical information, current events, even events in the speaking room. And, there are even some authorities who advise you to write out your introduction and use notes for the rest of the speech. This is not bad advice. A written introduction makes sure you can check out your points in advance and get a running start into the speech.

Conclusions are really introductions done one more time. To finish a speech, you must do something more than just run down as does an unwound clock. Old-time professional speakers tell the story of the preacher who had the perfect formula for success at speaking. (See page 177.) Your conclusion, according to this formula, is the last chance to make your point. You can't redeliver the speech, but you can run quickly over the main points, stress once again what this means to the listener, summed up, perhaps, in the form of a succinct story tying the loose ends together. The conclusion does not add anything new to the speech—there is no point in adding new material. The conclusion provides a smooth exit from the platform, leaving the audience with your message to take home, neatly tied up in a verbal package that they understand and believe.

A conclusion must be faithful to the content of the speech. If your original goal was to give information to the audience, don't tack on an unexpected call for action. If you were talking about how American Indians live on the reservation, the concluding statement, "Consider the plight of the poor Indian and give money," will do nothing more than annoy the audience. If this was your point in the first place, you should have been giving a persuasive speech.

In short, the conclusion must do the following:

1. **Tie up the main points and stress the most important support.**
2. **Restate what this means to the audience.**

And that's it.

The last lines of the conclusion should clearly announce that the speech is over. Some speakers like to build to false conclusions throughout their speech. They hit crescendos, and the audience waits for them to sit down. This toying with the attention of the audience can change real interest to downright hostility. The audience feels the end coming. They feel the steering wheel in their hand, the first mouthful of beer sloshing down; and then the speaker goes on. It can't be possible! He has more to say. Audiences do not like this. It puts them on edge, and their ears turn away. The conclusion of the speech is the only place to ride home an emotional climax, and it must be in harmony with the rest of the speech. If you were talking about rock formations in Sicily, for example, it would be ridiculous to conclude:

> And thus, ladies and gentlemen, we see the absolutely critical nature of Sicilian rocks, and we understand that the fate of men and nations hangs on . . .

Although you might conclude:

> Sicilian rock formations are different from most in the Mediterranean area. Their volcanic nature makes them both interesting to the geologist and frustrating to the farmer. They account for the way life is lived on the island and why it is different from the mainland.

That's enough.

Both introduction and conclusion are prepared **after** the first of the speech is completely blocked out and supported. The conclusion, like the introduction, may be written out, so that you, as a speaker, can have a formal place at which to quit. It is more sensible, however, to extemporize introductions and conclusions from main headings so that you can take topical events into account. But be sure that the main headings get in, and nothing else, because a new point in the conclusion can seriously distract the audience and do a great deal of damage to your residual message.

There are some forms of support that seem to go well with introductions and conclusions. They support the message and they catch attention. But it's not good to use a lot of them at one time. Choose the ones that will be best received by your audience and still support your message.

1. A crisp, but direct, delivery of a message with no apologies, is one way to capture an audience. Some speakers are good at wringing a laugh from their audience, but for those who are not naturally inclined to be effective at humor, a crisp, businesslike approach is most effective. Get into the speech quickly and keep moving. So long as you are delivering lines in logical and understandable order, your audience will stay with you and not go to sleep. On the other hand, try to resist sounding like a talking machine gun.

2. A history, or summing up, of events that gives background to your message can involve the audience. It explains how we got to where we are and provides a field in which the audience can understand your subsequent remarks. On the other hand, this cannot be-

come a tail that wags the dog. Some speakers get so eloquent with the summing up in introduction or conclusion that the rest of the speech is sacrificed. If your residual message is historical, the whole speech can be a narration. If you are using narration as an introduction, about a minute's worth in a ten-minute speech is sufficient.

3. If you are going to use words or ideas that are new and strange to the audience, you may explain those terms at the beginning of the speech. You shouldn't use too many terms, however. Three or four are about enough. If you try to explain too many terms, you will sound like a dictionary and bore your audience to tears. If you find you have a great many technical terms and ideas to explain, you had better reconsider your entire speech and use a simpler segment for this particular audience.

4. The partition is very important and should be used in virtually every speech. Any technique that helps the audience follow along is very useful to you. Either voice the main heads, or voice and also print them on a blackboard, or write them on a poster board and display them. Particularly with an informative speech, this kind of partitioning helps the audience remember both the main headings of the residual message **and** the supporting details.

5. Mention something you have in common with the audience. They probably have a great deal in common with you. Try to find some idea or experience you can share. If you are speaking to credit union personnel, it doesn't hurt to mention that you have a few shares invested in a credit union. If you are speaking to members of the same political party, it helps if you can say, "fellow Republicans." Be careful, however, not to go out on a limb. You might alienate your audience if you tell a group of construction workers that you understand their problems because you "worked on a construction job one summer," or if you tell a group from a ghetto, "While I was in college I roomed near a ghetto for almost six months." Even if you mean to be honest, you will look the fool if you declare something to be a common ground which is not common at all.

6. You may show that you are aware of some local points of interest in which your listeners take pride. "The drive here took me through your splendid mountains and forests" or "It's a pleasure to be speaking in the town that gave us our respected governor." The local interest could even be a sore point experienced by all who pass through. "If they ever remove those railroad tracks from the middle of town,

what will us speakers give as an excuse for being late?" But be careful
not to overdo the thing. The idea is to show in a few words that you
are sensitive to their uniqueness. You don't have to act like an immi-
grant to do it.

7. Ok, you have this funny story that you can't resist telling. Please,
before you tell it, check it out to make sure it fits your residual
message. You might also check it out to make sure it is in good taste,
that it doesn't insult members of the audience, that it doesn't take
too long to tell, and that it is truly funny. Try to remember that you
are not Bill Cosby or Don Rickles. They tell jokes; you give
speeches.

8. You can snag attention for a few moments with some shocking
facts, the inside story of some news item or a humorous incident.
Again, you must make sure that what you do fits your residual message and doesn't detract from it.

9. If you can find a story that captures in short form the entire
residual message, this is your most effective opening or conclusion.
The brief illustration will help the audience recall all of the ideas in
the speech because it ties things together for them.

The speech, as a whole, should work like the structure of a symphony. The residual message is the main theme, the basic melody.
All through the symphony it will be played in different moods and in
different ways. As in music, the introduction and conclusion have a
purpose vital to the success of the whole. The introduction must
spark the original interest, and the conclusion must bring everything
together into a glorious coda. Each different manner of presenting
the message should have its own small introduction and conclusion,
the transitions from point to point. Each internal conclusion will help
wake up flagging interest and will reinforce the main theme.

The conclusion of each point should indicate logically the start of
the next, as though each conclusion were the introduction to another
speech. The final conclusion should tie everything together and be
another demonstration of the central unity of the speech. It should be
a tribute to the planning of the speaker and a revelation to the mind
of the audience. The speaker is like a composer building a symphony
in words and ideas. The composition is a test of his skill at organizing, preparing, planning. The real work is done before the speaker
reaches the platform. Take a run at doing some conclusions for the

speeches you plan, just as you did for introductions on page 236. But then, hold it. Before we start talking about how to deliver the speech, we need to tie everything together.

1. Pick an occasion. (Let's make it a meeting of the state legislature considering the problem of aid to higher education. You are going to give testimony. Testimony? Yes, a ten minute speech.)

2. Pick a topic. (What would you like to say to your friendly legislator?)

   Our college is a private college. We need help.

   There is a lot of waste at this state institution.

   This community college can't make it on local taxes alone.

   You'd better get some coordination between the offerings at the different institutions in this state.

   With the recession and all, students can't afford to go to college anymore.

   The problem is, you legislators don't seem to understand some of the things that students do.

   (Or, what else? Get a topic that you think the legislature needs to hear.)

3. Now take a look at yourself. What do you know? How strongly do you feel? Where can you get information?

4. Let's pin down the old residual message. Tightly! Write it down in big letters so you'll remember it.

5. Find out something about the legislature in your state. You can start by reading the front page of the local paper. Ask a politician. Go to the library. What kind of people are on the education committee of your legislature? Get a team working on this. Who knows, you may need the information some day.

6. Sit down in a quiet place and make some note cards on what you already know about the topic.

7. Then go wherever you have to in order to get more information.

8. Pick your structure. It will most likely be a problem-solution type, unless you are just giving the legislature some information and not asking for anything. Set up the structure and the main headings.

9. Now you may start messing around with your information and getting it located in the proper box on your structural diagram.

10. Add an introduction and a conclusion. You may have heard that

there is a standard introductory statement for testimony before a legislature. How can you find out for sure?

11. You are at the point where you are almost ready to pack your brief case and head for the state capital. And we are at the point where the next section makes sense.

Set up working notes

We are about ready to approach the actual task of delivering the speech. The president of the United States reads his speech from a manuscript because he dares not make a misstatement. In fact, his speeches are not speeches at all but declarations of public policy. He does not have to worry about interacting with an audience for every word he says will be both published and pondered. He takes no questions unless he solicits them and is prepared for them, and even then, they come in a formal setting surrounded by formal rules.

The typical speech, the kind you will give, is normally not read from a manuscript, and unlike when in junior high school, you don't need to memorize it. The problem with a manuscript speech is the difference between a spoken and a written style. Sentences that look good on paper often do not sound right when read. To the audience, they seem stiff and impersonal. Memorizing also presents a problem in addition to the awkwardness of the style. What if you forget, and have to stand in front of the audience with a silent grin, searching the top of your mind for the right words. An audience can tell when you are reciting rather than speaking. Deliveries that are memorized or manuscript-read seem clumsy compared to the freshness of an extemporaneous speech.

To extemporize is to choose your words at the moment of delivery. This does not mean you are unprepared. In fact, every suggestion in this book should be taken as preparation for an extemporized speech. You have already learned how to structure ideas and gather forms of support for a residual message. Thus, you are prepared.

At the time of delivery, you need to put the speech into language that will appeal to the audience, using a style that can be understood. In writing, it is possible to use very complicated sentences, because the reader has the option of going back over what he does not understand. At the time of reading, the writer is an absentee. The words carry the message.

This is not so in oral communication. Besides the words, the speaker can impress the audience with his alertness through facial expression and bodily movement. The speaker can support himself through the use of his personality. In speaking, you need to depend on the relationship you can build with the audience. Therefore, you need to be free to react to them and with them. Your style must be open so that you can bend with the mood of the audience at any given moment.

The most effective way to support yourself through an extemporaneous speech is to refer to a set of working notes. Your notes can be as complicated as you like. You will need to experiment to find what is best for you. Some speakers need only one or two cards on which they jot down key words. Others prefer complicated outlines or flowcharts on full-size pieces of paper. There are certain basics that have to be included in your notes:

1. State the residual message at the top of the first card and at the bottom of the last card. In this way you will have a constant reminder to keep the message at the front of your thoughts and to be able to join it to all parts of the speech. You may even want to write the residual message on the cards for each of your subpoints so that when you make transitions you can show how every subpoint relates to the residual message.

2. Each submessage (the heading for each box in your structure) should be written on a separate card along with some effort to relate the card to the main residual message. On each of these subcards you can note the supports you will need to use in order to make the point.

3. Write down any material that must be repeated without mistakes. Formal quotations should be copied as they were originally spoken or written. Complicated statistics should be placed on note cards. If you plan to draw a diagram on the blackboard, don't rely on memory. Draw it on a card so you can copy it accurately. References should be made in your notes as to where visual materials fit.

4. It is smart to write on cards the first three sentences and the last three sentences of your speech. This will enable you to get started and to close without apprehension.

Figure 8.1 presents a working set of notes for the speech structured in Figure 5.36 on page 163.

Residual message: College area schools have shown steady growth and improvement

Introduction. As parents you need to know about the schools your children attend. As taxpayers you need information to vote. I will discuss.
1. How rural features influenced the schools.
2. Problems created by growth of industry.
3. How consolidation operated.
4. What problems we face in the future. To show how we have grown and improved.

Schools grew from rural-dominated institutions

1. Sparse population resulted in small schools.
   14/sq. mi.   Benner Run.   Butler diary.
2. Poor transport = little contact between schools.
   Show map.   Pictures of roads.
3. Poor teacher training = weak program.
   State requirements.   Typical course: Weaverville.
4. Little academic demand = low community support.
   $23/pupil maximum. Farm needs.   Editorial objection.

Schools grew and improved from these beginnings.

Industrialization caused problems that stimulated growth

1. Better educated population demanded better schools.
   Growth of university citizens movement.
2. Available jobs motivated student learning.
   Support technical jobs at university.   More college-bound.
3. Financial stability increased duplication in spending.
   1950–$3800 family income.   Township systems.
4. Improved transportation made overall solution possible.
   Show road map of area compared to earlier Smith consolidation plan.

Industrialization made it necessary for system to improve and expand.

Figure 8.1 Working Notes for Speech Structured in Figure 5.36.

1950 consolidation met needs of that time.

1. Better schools possible by reduced duplication.
2. Larger schools improved student motivation.
3. Consolidation eliminated overlapped spending.
4. Consolidation led to improved planning.

Recent growth and improvement have been in harmony with 1950 plan.
We still have schools to meet the needs of a semi-rural community.

New improvements will be necessary because we are taking on urban features.

1. We are getting a wider variety of students, races, incomes, ability levels.
2. Social changes are demanding programs like alternate school, work study.
3. System needs better integration into state programs. College compatible. Meet needs of industry.

Continued growth and improvement means taking recent changes into account.

Conclusion:
We have seen how our local schools have grown from their rural beginnings into a very complicated system now able to adapt to new needs.

Let us stay in touch so that we can continue to keep you informed.

The notes in figure 8.1 are just an example. Another possibility would be to form an ordinary outline, the kind that you used to prepare for your junior high school theme writing. We have not advocated outlining in this book because it is our contention that once you have prepared a structure, an outline would be redundant. Still, some speakers prefer to speak from outlines. They simply take their structure and work it into outline form, as follows.

Outline of speech from format of Figure 5.36

I. **Introduction:**
Welcome audience.
Important to you because you are parents and taxpayers.
I will show:
  1. Rural origins of Schools.
  2. Problems caused by industrialization.
  3. Effects of consolidation.
  4. New problems we face.

Area schools have shown steady growth and improvement
A. Rural Origins.   To 1920.
  1. Sparse population.   Small schools.
      a. Population figures.   Refer to visual aid.
      b. Profile of Benner Run.
      c. Butler diary.
  2. Transportation poor.   Limited contact between schools.
      a. Map of local area. Show it.
      b. Rail lines. Public transport limited.
      c. Show pictures of local roads.
  3. Teacher training poor.   Weak program.
      a. State requirements. Read copy from 1911.
      b. Background of typical teacher.
  4. Minimal demand for academic product.   No place to send graduates.
      a. Most people farmers.
      b. Farms needed students during planting and harvest.
B. Growth of industry and university led to demands for better schools.
  1. Better-educated population demanded better-quality program.
      a. University growth from 1920 to 1950.
      b. Political pressures on community around university.
  2. Brain industries plus university brought demand for better trained students.

        a. Examples of new jobs. Cystallography, technicians, etc.

        b. Students motivated to finish school.

    3. Financial stability allowed more money for schools.

        a. Local districts duplicated one another.

        b. Give examples of comparative systems. Stormstown vs. Lemont.

    4. Improved transportation and communication permitted more contact.

        a. Show recent map of area.

        b. Examples of consolidation plans proposed. (Smith Plan)

C. Consolidation solved some of the basic problems.

    1. Provided more efficient plant and expanded curriculum.

        a. Show comparative space and pupil figures. Before and after.

    2. Provided more opportunity for student contact.

    3. Eliminated overlap in spending.

    4. Permitted improved planning.

D. Changes are still necessary because we are becoming more urban.

    1. Diversity in students. Ethnic, economic, ability.

    2. Demands for alternative programs, vocational training.

    3. School units are becoming excessively large.

II. **Conclusion**

A. Area schools have grown and improved steadily.

    1. They have moved from rural to urban.

    2. They provide great opportunity for the future.

B. But there will be problems in the future. More changes are needed.

C. Let's keep in touch so that you will have all the information you'll need.

The outline you use in your working notes need not be as detailed as a formal outline. Presented is an outline by Charlie Gatski, which served as his notes also. This speech was given in fun for a class period and should not be taken seriously.

Outline of Charlie Gatski's "Superman" speech

Residual Message: **Superman will never marry Lois Lane.**

I. Superman cannot afford to have a woman interfering with his crime-fighting.

    A. He could not be tied down to social engagements.

    B. He could not devote proper time to family life.

     C. He couldn't allow emotional appeals from Lois to influence his direction in crime-fighting.

     D. His family would be a target for criminals.

II. Superman must protect his identity at all costs.

     A. It would be nearly impossible for Superman to keep his identity a secret from his own wife.

     B. He could not take the risk of his family's bragging about their husband-father, thereby exposing him.

III. Superman would be concerned about his wife's psychological stability.

     A. Lois may not be able to handle living with two different persons: Clark Kent and Superman.

     B. Lois may not want to accept the fact that her husband is perfect and will never die.

     C. Superman's attractiveness appeals to all women, and Lois may become jealous.

IV. Finally, Superman's family must remain protected.

     A. Lois would certainly want to meet Superman's family, thus exposing his sister and parents to possible threats.

     B. Even Superman's foster parents' identities must be kept secret.

V. Superman would not want to be the first of his kind to marry.

     A. Let Robin, Batman, or somebody else go first.

Some speakers prefer to use a flow diagram. A flow diagram maps out the order of points as they will be made in the presentation. To plan the order, you lay your information cards on a table to meet the structural demands of the speech. The order appears on the table before you. During the speech, you will be moving from message to submessage, back and forth, making connections between them as you go. By laying out the cards and mapping your moves with arrows, you are assured a logical structure.

A good example of such a flow diagram is found in the Eugene Erickson layout in Figure 5.30, pages 156, 157. Just by following the arrows in the diagram and giving the main headings, you are assured of a set of logical statements. What is missing, of course, is the supporting material which Erickson could fill in. The "Grevitz" speech laid out in Figures 5.38 and 5.39, pages 166 and 167, is another example. If you satisfactorily work the problem, you can give the speech just by following the arrows.

Flow diagrams are made redundant by returning consistently to the main headings so that there is a constant summing up of how the parts of the speech connect. If you have trouble making transitions from point to point, you might find it helpful to use a flow diagram, for there is no way to avoid transitions with this kind of diagram. Just talk your way through the two examples and you will see what is meant.

Return to page 242.

You should be able to set up notes for your speech now. Try each style: the reminder cards, the outline, and the flow diagram. You will be able to decide which helps you the most. From here on you will have to make a great number of choices in selecting those with which you feel comfortable. Some speakers achieve enough expertise to work without any notes at all. You might have that as a goal, but you should at least try the different forms of notes.

Practicing and rehearsing

An extemporaneous speech does not have to be rehearsed as does a Broadway play. Too much rehearsal can stiffen you to the point where you will be unable to roll with the needs of your audience. The best way in which to prepare for the delivery is to get some response to the organization and logic of your speech. Use someone you respect, like a close friend, a fellow worker, or someone who speaks frequently as part of his or her job.

If you care to be daring, gather a few friends and have an "idea-bouncing" session. In such a session, you would lay bare to your friends the ideas and reasoning in your speech. They would respond with the stiffest arguments, objections, and questions they could think of. By defending yourself against their attacks, you could strengthen your speech and get yourself ready for the audience. You can bet that no one in the audience would be as hard on you as those friends.

Idea-bouncing is risky and potentially can hurt your feelings, but if you have a thick skin and you know how to take criticism it can be your most useful form of practice or rehearsal. Whatever you do, don't practice in front of mirrors or by yourself. You will deliver your speech to an audience, and your practice should be done in front of an audience. Outside reactions can help you in a very special way by getting you to see how normal and ordinary individuals might respond and by enabling you to revise your structure and support to accommodate to their responses.

Knowing your material well is also practice. By preparing carefully, structuring, inserting supports, and preparing your delivery notes, you view and re-view your material. Sometimes, with this kind of preparation, all you will need to do is run over your notes a few times silently before going onto the platform.

Time out. Why not set up a group practice-session for your testimony before the legislature? See what kind of skin you have as you and your classmates do a little "idea-bouncing" in order to strengthen your preparation.

Delivering the speech

There have been enough textbooks written on how to deliver a speech. There are also sufficient exercises in voice, diction, projection, and animation to make you qualified at least for summer stock. "Speak from the diaphragm," "speak in natural tones," "enunciate carefully," are among a multitude of advice you might receive. If you have some concerns about your voice, you ought to see a specialist and work through the necessary exercises.

Most of us however should not, and do not, have concerns with how we sound. We are quite able to adapt our voices to different situations. We can talk quietly on a bus and loudly in a crowd. We can be heard at the back of the room, regardless of the size of the room. Of course, there are some places where the room is so large that mechanical amplification might be necessary. When you check out the situation, you can discover whether or not you will need a public address system in order to be heard.

Audiences no longer expect to be addressed in the style of Demosthenes. In classical Greece, and even in the early days of the United States, speaking was synonymous with oratory. Believe it or not, audiences looked upon it as recreation. Now people look to the speaker to provide them with information and ideas. And they expect to hear it in a relatively normal tone of voice, adapted, of course, to the situation in which the speech is given.

The safest policy is for you to assume that your delivery is all right. Concentrate on communicating the message in your speech. The message is the only reason you have for making a speech. If you had a voice like Alexander Scourby, they might hire you to read important TV commercials or to introduce the opera, but even if you had that rich and rolling a voice, you couldn't hold an audience unless you had something worth saying. You are not there to impress the audience with your dramatic talent; you are there to communicate the content of your speech.

One reason beginning speakers get hung up on delivery is that their critics have a hard time explaining what went wrong. Some critics can only see a speech as a collection of sounds and gestures. We shall talk about criticism next, and you will get some idea of what is worth listening to after your speech is done. Meanwhile, just get up and talk in your normal tone of voice.

We don't have an exercise here. Just continue reading until you find out something about criticism and then we will have an exercise —the last one, maybe.

Seeking an evaluation

If you are reading this book because you are taking a course in speech, you have probably been criticized already. If you are reading this book because you want to learn how to give a speech (and the two are not necessarily exclusive), you will need to learn how to get criticism. Criticism is easy to come by; everyone is a critic. A critic, according to some, is a person who can tell you what is wrong with what you are doing, even though he can't do it at all.

However, to obtain real success at speaking, you are going to have to find a way to evaluate how well you did. By evaluate, we do not necessarily mean: A, B, C, D, F. We mean: To what extent did you accomplish your speaking goal? Did your residual message stick? Why, or why not? If you did something right, we think you ought to know it, so that you can do it again. If you did something wrong, you ought to know that also, in order to avoid doing it. If you have some problems that you can't do anything about, you ought to know this so you can work around them.

It is hard to get the information you really need in order to improve. Some critics will babble about your voice, even though there is nothing you can do about what nature gave you. Some critics will tell you that you would have done better if you had been taller. A lot

of help that is! Some critics will give you the "enlightened generali-
ties" of the college classroom:

> I think you were a little weak in documentation in point two and you
> could have used a bit more stress on the third subpoint of your third
> point in support of the old r-m. In fact, there needed to be a more sincere
> quality expressed, a kind of, well, message that you were with us, you
> know?

Answer: No, I don't know. That kind of criticism is about as helpful as
a case of warts.

The point is, there is very little objectivity possible in speech criticism. The critics can't help but inject themselves into their evaluations
in one manner or another. The only way in which to judge a speech
is to view it as an interaction between the speaker and his audience
in which the message is at stake. Remember, at the beginning of this
book we talked about speaking as a process and a relationship. It is
through the process that the relationship is established and strength-
ened, and it is the relationship that gives form and limit to the
process. The critic cannot comment from eternal truths. Anything he
says has to be limited by the conditions under which the speech was
given, the particular audience, the particular message, and the
particular performance of the speaker. No two audiences are alike;
messages change each time they are delivered, and the speaker is a
different person with each experience. How, then, can we apply
principles of effective speaking so that they make sense in criticism.

In the first place, there are some crucial questions that can be
raised in any case. For example:

1. Was the topic worth speaking on? Was it appropriate for this audience,
   this occasion, this speaker?
2. Was the speech coherently organized? Did people understand it?
3. Were the points adequately supported?
4. Could the audience hear the speech?

Note that all of these things are very mundane. They are the kinds of
things that a speaker can do something about. This is the first
principle of speech criticism.

It doesn't make sense to criticize anything except aspects that the
speaker can do something about.

A speaker can pick a topic, organize it, support it, and say it. He
might not be able to make a personality change, or develop a stage

delivery, or suddenly discover the wit of the Marx brothers, but he can accomplish the basic operations in speech preparation. This represents the first level in effective criticism and should guide the critic to talk only about things that can be changed by the speaker.

Another basic problem is to make sure that criticism notes what was well done as well as what was ineffective. A speaker doesn't need to be complimented because he is handsome and his eyes have a merry twinkle. He should know that he supported a particular point well because the audience responded positively to it. He can then remember what he did and repeat his performance the next time he has to speak to a similar audience. Futhermore, commenting on what was well done makes the negative more palatable. We tend not to want to hear how rotten we were, but we are all interested in improving a good performance.

The final point about criticism is that when a flaw is pointed out, a remedy ought to be available. It is not sufficient to say, "Your organization was faulty." As a critic, you should be able to point out precisely what was wrong and make a recommendation for improvement. That gives us three main points:

1. **Criticize only what can be improved.**
2. **Comment on what was done well before pointing out defects.**
3. **When you point out a defect, be able to point to a remedy.**

As a speaker, you will get a great deal of criticism, from your classmates and from others. Take it with a grain of salt. If it fits the requirements above, then you can take it seriously because you will be able to do something about it. Keep your own critical faculty sharp. When you set goals for your speech, make sure you take the time to examine the audience response to see how well you did. You can do a great deal to monitor your own performance. And you can do a great deal to improve it by hanging on to those steps presented in Figure 3.2, page 57.

Wrap-up exercise

By this time, you should know how to prepare a speech. What you need is experience. You can get some in the classroom, but by and large, classroom speaking really gets to be more of the same. The conditions under which you speak in the classroom are never going to be duplicated outside of the classroom. Even if you "luck out" and become a college professor, the lectures you will give are not the same as classroom speeches.

The question is, how and where can you get experience as a speaker under real conditions? You might make it a classroom project to find some speech opportunities: maybe a campus speaker's bureau; perhaps a public-speaking contest; or work with campus organizations, political parties, religious groups. How about setting up a number of Sunday sermons? Or, after completing your speech class, offer yourself as a model to a beginning class to listen to and question.

What you must know is that your improvement as a speaker will come only when you begin to speak in public and take the responsibility to make your voice heard. That is what this book is all about. If you have profited at all from it, you will want to practice and you will find a way to do it.

So? Go do it!

Index